I hope you find this... helpful. Since you are a friend of Bills, I would enjoy meeting you.

MIND, MONEY & MARKETS

A Guide for Every Investor, Trader, and Business Person

Dave Harder (signature)

___

Dave Harder & Janice Dorn, M.D., Ph.D.

RBC Wealth Management
Dominion Securities

PRIVATE
INVESTMENT
MANAGEMENT

Professional wealth management since 1901

Dave Harder, FCSI
Vice President & Portfolio Manager

RBC Dominion Securities Inc.
Suite 301 - 2001 McCallum Road
Abbotsford, BC V2S 3N5

Tel: 604-870-7126
Fax: 604-870-7171
1 866 928-4745

dave.harder@rbc.com
www.davidharder.ca

Copyright

Cover design by Janelle Penner, Wellington Art Group.
Art Director, James Wiens. Artist, Curaga/Bigstock.com

Table of Contents

Acknowledgements

The authors thank the following for their help in this project: Danielle Boegli, Marilyn Burkley, John DiCecco, Dan Dunlop, Mike Elliott, Jim Flom, MaryAnn Tjart Jantzen, Catherine Jeansonne, Perry Martin CFA, Ceilidh Marlow, Neil Matlins, James McKeough CMT, Robert Sluymer, Jennifer T. Smith, and Dave Tupper. Special thanks to Peter and Katherine Harder for their extensive input and editing.

Janice Dorn and Dave Harder

To my husband Tom, and my sister and best friend, Diane: Thank you for supporting me, loving me and believing in me. I am eternally grateful to you.

Janice Dorn

I thank my wonderful wife Marianne for her patience as I worked on this project over the last three years.

I am also grateful that the firm I work for granted me permission to write this book. It is a privilege to work for a company that values independent thinking and differing opinions.

Dave Harder

Preface

From time to time, media reports announce a major failure of a company due to trading disasters or investments that went horribly wrong. Bankruptcy is a calamity that is suffered in private. To the best of our knowledge, greeting card companies do not produce cards to send to people who declare bankruptcy.

It is easy to gloss over news like this and forget that real people who were wealthy and influential may have lost everything. Their families might have been accustomed to a family estate in the U.S., a luxury apartment in New York, a ski chalet in Whistler, a villa in Tuscany, a beachfront home in Hawaii, a yacht in Florida, a share in a private jet, children's education at Harvard, and a deluxe retirement home for parents. More importantly, personal financial loss, loss of a business, a tarnished reputation, and the possible loss of money earmarked for friends and family members can produce emotions that negatively impact family and friends.

We do not know anything about the personal life of the individuals involved in the corporate failure mentioned below. However, it undoubtedly had a profound impact on many people involved with the company, especially the CEO. When you read the paragraphs below, remember that these are real people.

In 2008, the oil trading firm SemGroup LP was the twelfth-largest private company in the United States. Under the direction of the co-founder and CEO, Thomas Kivisto, SemGroup used a specific strategy employing a wide variety of investments that produced a profit if crude oil prices fell and created losses if oil prices rose. In a *Forbes* article published on July 28, 2008, Christopher Helman wrote, "One Tulsa businessman, well connected to SemGroup executives, says he is 'not shocked' at SemGroup's failure, having first heard of the company's oil-trading troubles six months ago, when oil had scarcely breached $100 a barrel. Even then, the company's traders were stubborn, having convinced themselves that the soaring oil price was irrational and was sure to reverse itself."

Instead of unwinding their positions as losses mounted and the trend continued to move against them, SemGroup officials held firmly to the conviction that their strategy was correct. Corporate officials kept borrowing from credit facilities to maintain their positions until prices turned down. In doing so, SemGroup officials made the fatal error of adding money to losing positions. By May 2008, net liabilities on SemGroup's derivatives increased from $873 million to almost $3 billion when crude oil prices reached $140 a barrel. After prices remained high for a month and rose to $141.65 on July 10, 2008, SemGroup had exhausted its credit facilities. It was forced to realize losses of $2.7 billion and declared bankruptcy on July 22, 2008—the second-largest bankruptcy of a nonfinancial firm that year. According to media reports, CEO Tom Kivisto also lost $290 million (allegedly borrowed from SemGroup) in his personal trading company. Ironically, oil prices rose as high as $147 on July 11, 2008, one day after SemGroup was forced to sell out, and then fell to a low of $32.40 only five months later.

What's the lesson here? It appears as though the very experienced and successful senior officials at SemGroup formed the opinion that oil prices should decline, even though they were rising. Although oil prices were actually overvalued, as economist John Maynard Keynes would say, oil markets remained irrational longer than SemGroup could stay solvent. The traders were right in their analysis that oil prices were overvalued, but they were absolutely wrong in their timing.

Shorting an up-trending asset, as SemGroup did, is like trying to stop a blast from a shotgun with your hand. SemGroup invested against the trend and paid a very high price. SemGroup would have made a fortune had it been able to hold its position until oil declined below $35 in December 2008.

Contrary to popular belief, the object of investing is not to buy low and sell high, or to sell short at a high and buy to cover when prices are low, like SemGroup tried to do. The object of investing is to buy when prices have already started an uptrend and to sell when they have started a downtrend. NYSE (New York Stock Exchange) trader Bernard Baruch said, "Don't try to buy at the bottom or sell at the top. It can't be done—except by liars." He became a millionaire in 1900, by the time he was thirty.

The story of SemGroup is a recent real-life example that highlights the disastrous consequences that can emerge in the wake of decisions to invest against the trend. This error has been repeated throughout the ages by both corporate and individual investors. History shows that individuals at the highest levels of prestige, reputation, education, power, and wealth are just as vulnerable as anyone else, if not more so. The first mistake is to believe that "it will never happen to me."

We hear of the high-profile financial losses, but there are countless other cases of smaller trading and investment disasters and failed real estate ventures that cause just as much personal anguish. After 2006, many lost their life savings or their homes by making wrong decisions. Like everyone else, the authors are not immune from bad decision making, as we have made many mistakes over the years as well. We want to share what we and other seasoned investors have learned from our mistakes so that readers may not have to repeat them.

"The arrogance of the present is to forget the intelligence of the past."
Documentary filmmaker Ken Burns

Introduction

During the great sea expeditions in the 1500s, explorers kept journals outlining dangerous waters, shorelines, and other navigational data. These books were called *routiers* by the French, rutters (not to be confused with the rudders used to steer ships) by the English, and later became known as waggoners. Rutters enabled captains to learn from the experiences and setbacks of previous journeys so they could travel with less risk to distant areas.

With the advent of the Internet, there is more information than ever available to investors and traders. However, the fact that so many individual investors and sophisticated professional money managers suffered greatly during the collapse of technology stocks after 2000 and the Financial Crisis in 2008-2009 shows that more information does not necessarily produce better results.

There are significant differences between data, information, opinions, knowledge, and wisdom. Data, information, and opinions are everywhere in this age of instantaneous global communication and social media. This constant barrage often produces overload and loss of focus by distracting investors from what really matters.

During times of fear and uncertainty, investors desperately seek information and opinions. This insatiable thirst is often used by the media, which know one thing for sure: if it bleeds, it leads. Fear sells. Add a focus on "experts" with extreme forecasts, and you have people confronted with a morass of opinion/information overload that serves no purpose other than to produce a state of confusion. Information overload can lead to a number of unpleasant psychological states, including stress, anxiety, and depression.

A generous measure of knowledge and wisdom is essential when one is investing or trading. However, critical knowledge about how markets really function and how human nature interferes with making wise investment decisions seems to be ignored. History shows (we will give specific examples later on) that even Nobel Prize winners in economics, managers of multibillion-dollar investment funds, and CEOs of some of the world's largest financial firms often seem to be sailing without a rudder. Many were shipwrecked in 2008 and 2009. Even the U.S. Federal Reserve, with its army of researchers, was caught off guard by the Financial Crisis. The web of financial products is so complex that few in government or business have a grasp of the real state of financial affairs. As a result, the majority of the investing public is sleepwalking into the future.

The purpose of this book is to provide a compilation of knowledge and wisdom gleaned from the authors' combined five decades of analysis and real market experience. We will show individual investors, traders, and professional money managers what to focus on in order to make wise decisions and reduce stress. It is our hope that readers will reach a greater level of understanding about markets in order to minimize financial losses and maximize financial gains. We also believe that better conclusions can be reached by analyzing meaningful information, instead of accepting everything that passes our eyes or ears. This enables investors to be more efficient with their time and energy. Nuggets of wisdom learned from the authors' combined fifty years of studying markets should enable all types of investors and traders to avoid many mistakes and to attain greater success.

Janice Dorn, M.D., Ph.D., received a Ph.D. in Anatomy (Neuroanatomy) from the Albert Einstein College of Medicine in New York. She is also an M.D. psychiatrist certified by the American Board of Psychiatry and Neurology and the American Board of Addiction Medicine. Dr. Dorn understands how our brains and emotions affect us when making investment decisions. She also has eighteen years of experience in short-term trading of futures and has coached and mentored hundreds of traders. Janice has written over 1,000 articles about the financial markets and published the book *Personal Responsibility: The Power of You*. Her work has been profiled on numerous financial websites, including CNBC, Investor's Business Daily, Minyanville, and Financial Sense.

Dave Harder, FCSI, is a Vice President and Portfolio Manager who has more than thirty years of experience with one of Canada's most respected corporations, which is also one of the most respected financial corporations in the world. Throughout his career, Dave has analyzed the markets using a variety of indicators, both fundamental and technical. He is an expert in market history and technical analysis, having produced over 300 weekly investment reports for individual and institutional investors. *The Globe and Mail, Investors Intelligence, Phases and Cycles Inc.,* CNBC, and other leaders in the investment industry have published his work.

This book chronicles the authors' experiences in trading, investing, traveling, and other aspects of their personal lives in order to share important lessons applicable to the financial markets. Most of these lessons seem to be all but ignored by the media and other experts. Even institutes of higher learning do not appear to acknowledge how markets really function. In a speech to Harvard Law School in 1995, Charlie Munger (Warren Buffett's partner at Berkshire Hathaway) said he graduated from Harvard Law School with a "terrible ignorance" of how markets function.

Dee Hock, founder and former CEO of the Visa credit card organization, said, "We are now at a point in time when the ability to receive, utilize, store, transform, and transmit data, the lowest cognitive form, has expanded literally beyond comprehension. Understanding and wisdom are largely forgotten as we struggle under an avalanche of data and information." The authors affirm the reality of this modern-age trait. This book is our response to present-day challenges and confusion. It attempts to provide wisdom, knowledge, and understanding for everyone, from the general public to professional portfolio managers, businesspeople, and government officials.

The first section of the book details the challenges faced when investors deal with markets, which behave in ways totally opposite to our natural instincts. The chapters that follow provide simple, yet profound ways to invest and trade in markets in a disciplined, unemotional, and profitable manner.

Many individuals and families have suffered great financial and emotional hardships in recent years as a result of the Financial Crisis and the collapse of U.S. real estate values. Because of the intimate relationship between body and brain, such hardships often manifest as mental or physical illnesses of varying severity. It is our sincere desire that the knowledge and wisdom provided in the following pages will help our readers to avoid serious financial setbacks in the future. We also hope they will provide a sound basis for making prudent investing and trading decisions that will grow and preserve the mental, physical, and financial resources of our readers.

We hope you will be enlightened and enriched and will look at markets and investing with fresh eyes.

Shall we begin our journey together?

Dave Harder, FCSI

Janice Dorn, M.D., Ph.D.

1. We Are Risk Takers by Design

Figure 1.1: Whether or not the ad above actually ran in the newspaper is up for debate, but its statements about the hazardous nature of the journey reflect the real characteristics of a mission led by Sir Ernest Shackleton, the British explorer who led three expeditions to the Antarctic.

In the early 1900s, Antarctic explorer Sir Ernest Shackleton placed grim-sounding but realistic ads to recruit a crew for his expedition. One would think that the description of "hazardous journey, small wages, bitter cold, long months of complete darkness, constant danger, safe return doubtful, honor and recognition in case of success" would not receive a positive response. However, some 5,000 men applied to join him! The twenty-seven men chosen for the 1914-1917 expedition included ship captains, sailors, a surgeon, a biologist, a physicist, a geologist, a photographer, a carpenter, a chaplain, an artist, a meteorologist, a navigator, a dog handler, and more. The men who responded to Shackleton's recruitment ads knew the risks and took them anyway. Despite their diverse backgrounds, these men had two qualities in common: lust and passion for risk and adventure.

Throughout history, men and women have had to face hardship, loss, fear, and uncertainty. God has given us the ability to handle struggles and take risks in order to survive and raise our families in the face of an uncertain future. For thousands of years, the main focus of humankind was to provide for our primary needs of food, shelter, and clothing. However, in recent years, especially in the developed world, many individuals have confidence that they will be able to provide the basic needs of life. As a result, much of the energy humans formerly devoted to hunting and gathering is now redirected to a wide variety of other pursuits.

Taking risks is a part of life. Hungry people will do almost anything for food. Taking risks and doing whatever we can to feed and provide for our families is laudable and necessary. Taking risks to die for one's country to preserve freedom is one thing; taking risks for fame with Ernest Shackleton is quite another. Taking all manner of risks with the sole goal of accumulating money is not only questionable, but often ends badly.

When it comes to investing, it can be prudent to take some risk. For example, studies have shown that investing in a diversified group of businesses or stocks yields a much more attractive return over the long run than investing in bonds (guaranteed investment certificates), term deposits, or money market funds. However, investing or trading in commodity futures or using borrowed money to invest in stocks and real estate (with the exception of borrowing to purchase your own home) adds additional risk and a completely different dimension to both emotional stress and potential outcomes. We are all forced to take some risks—accepting a job, deciding to have children, buying a house, managing precious financial resources, or trusting someone to help us with many complicated and critical aspects of life, including investing.

Figure 1.2: Monte Carlo, Monaco. Photo by Dave Harder

Boats were designed to handle the open ocean, not sit in a protected harbor like the one in Monte Carlo (Figure 1.2). By the same token, human beings are well suited to manage adversity and take some risks. There is no life or progress without movement.

Ernest Shackleton was very clear about the risks he was asking people to take. People who start a business, participate in a triathlon, or enroll in a university usually know what is involved in achieving their goals. However, when it comes to investing, people often do not devote enough time and energy to understand the risks they are assuming.

On August 9, 2010, two brothers in their twenties and one of their wives decided to go for a canoeing trip on Harrison Lake (Figure 1.3), more than 100 kilometers east of Vancouver, B.C. At a local Canadian Tire store (a popular retail chain that sells automotive products and outdoor gear) they purchased a canoe, paddles, life jackets, and fishing rods. When they arrived at the lake in the early afternoon, the waters were calm and the scenery was so inviting that they left shore for a two-mile trip across the water to a large island called Echo Island to do some fishing. Even though they lived near the lake, they did not realize that often, in late afternoon, the water becomes very rough when a strong thermal wind blows along the long body of water.

Figure 1.3: Harrison Lake, in Harrison Hot Springs, B.C., can be very inviting when waters are calm, but afternoon winds can change without warning, causing dangerous conditions. Photo by Dave Harder

One of the brothers was supposed to be at work at 5:30 p.m., so when the group had not returned by 9:30 p.m., the brothers' mother called 911. As a result, the local RCMP (Royal Canadian Mounted Police) requested the assistance of the Kent Harrison Search and Rescue team (KHSAR–Dave is a member) to look for the missing canoeists. Having spent a lot of time on Lake Harrison in his windsurfer Seadoo, Dave knows all too well how fast the waves can come in! Dave's hunch that they went out in calm conditions and got surprised by the rough water proved to be correct. As the team members searched by boat, they noticed coolers and bottles in the water. Then Dave picked up a brand-new paddle with a price sticker from Canadian Tire. That was a worrisome sign, since the water was quite cold, and there are very few level spots on Echo Island to climb out of the water. As the boats searched along the edge of the island, their lights illuminated a man and a woman running down to the water toward a person lying on the rocks just above the water level. All it took was one look to realize that the man lying by the water was dead. The surviving brother and his wife were taken to shore while Dave and some other team members stayed with the body to wait for the RCMP and coroner to arrive. Sitting there on the rocks with his teammates in the dark of night, Dave pondered the serious consequences of not taking time to adequately prepare before plunging into an adventure or activity with which we have little experience. (This incident was profiled in the TV series *Callout: Search and Rescue*, Season 2, Episode 5.) In life, the impact of innocent errors can be irreversible. Fortunately, when it comes to investing, we often have chances to recover from decisions made with a lack of experience.

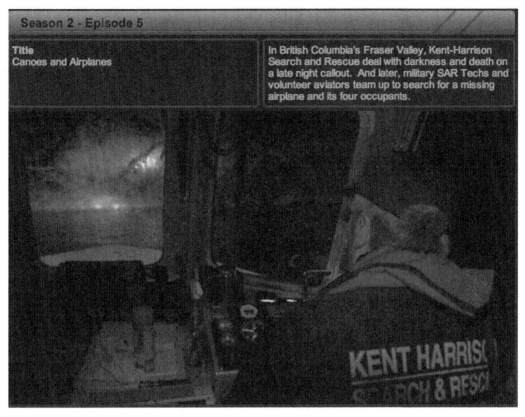

Season 2 - Episode 5

Title
Canoes and Airplanes

In British Columbia's Fraser Valley, Kent-Harrison Search and Rescue deal with darkness and death on a late night callout. And later, military SAR Techs and volunteer aviators team up to search for a missing airplane and its four occupants.

KENT HARRIS
SEARCH & RESC

Figure 1.4: The KHSAR team President, Marvin Anderson, piloting one of the Search and Rescue boats toward the spot on Echo Island where the canoeists were found. Picture courtesy of *Callout: Search and Rescue*

Inexperience, lack of knowledge, natural emotions, overconfidence, and pride can cause investors and businesspeople to make mistakes with severe consequences that impact their families, retirements, relationships, health, and careers. A slowing economy and bear market will amplify the impact of inexperience or errors in judgment. On the other hand, a strong economy and a long-term bull market can be very forgiving. In such an environment, we can do something risky and suffer no ill effects at all. It is often said that everyone is a genius in a bull market. Dave had such an experience on April 1, 1998, when he climbed to the top of a volcano. He recalls it this way: There are three majestic volcanoes just south of British Columbia in Washington State: Mt. Baker, Mt. Rainier, and Mt. St. Helens. Mount St. Helens erupted on May 18, 1980, but the other two volcanoes are dormant. (Even though I lived 500 kilometers or 300 miles north of Mt. St. Helens, I remember being in my bedroom on the morning of the eruption, hearing a loud boom and seeing my window curtains billow.) On April 1, 1998, some friends and I took our snowmobiles to the south end of Mt. Baker and drove them straight up the mountain to the crater. Mt. Baker is 3,286 meters—or 10,781 feet—high, so the top of the mountain is always covered in snow. (In fact, the Mt. Baker ski area holds the world record for the most snow in one season: 29 meters, or 95 feet, during 1998-1999.) Over the years, very high snow levels have created large, deep crevasses on the mountain. Spring is a relatively safe time on Mt. Baker, since there is enough warmth to melt some snow during the day so that it can form a strong top layer when it freezes at night. The hill was so steep that we had to stand on our snowmobiles and lean over the handlebars to keep them from going over backwards. We made it safely to the crater's edge where we could hear hissing and smell sulphur rising from eight or so plumes of steam. Previously, I had tried to hike up Mt. Baker from the bottom on the north side, but I turned back due to bad weather. Since I was 85% of the way up and the skies were totally clear, I was not going to let this opportunity to reach the peak pass me by. At the least, I should have had snowshoes, ice axes, and a rope for safety purposes, but my friend Randy Regier and I decided to take the risk and hike the rest of the way to the top of the mountain. The view from the top was magnificent, and the area on top of the crater was as big and flat as a football field. We made it up and down without incident. Afterward, the locals said we were crazy to do what we did, but we survived. In this case, ignorance was bliss. Perhaps good conditions bailed us out. Sometimes life and markets treat us that way. Sometimes they don't.

Figure 1.5: Dave standing at the south side of the Mt. Baker crater. Photo by Perry Martin, CFA

We all have to take risks, but they must be managed in a disciplined manner, especially when one is responsible for the safety of others. Dave is a trained volunteer and Swiftwater Rescue Technician with a local Search and Rescue (SAR) team 100 kilometers (60 miles) east of Vancouver, British Columbia, Canada.

No matter who they are.

KHSAR, as a registered non-profit society, delivers a professional-quality search and rescue service to the community

Figure 1.6: The home page of the KHSAR website (www.khsar.com) with paramedic team member Nick Morley (left) and Dave (right) carrying a stretcher up a steep bank during an actual rescue.

This area includes rivers, lakes, and treacherous mountain terrain. Unfortunately, a few times a year, "weekend warriors" drive their vehicles or ATVs off the road down steep embankments or cliffs. Dave's team is then called to rescue them. Descending a steep embankment or the face of a cliff at night and in the rain is not a safe thing to do. However, SAR has team members certified to set up rope systems using approved equipment. They always use two separate rope systems with different anchor points, manned by two experienced members, so that in the very unlikely event that one rope system fails, there is another secure rope system to rely on. Each rope system is designed to handle ten times the required weight and stress. By over-preparing this way, an inherently dangerous activity can become very safe.

Individual or professional investors must also have a similar process or system to reduce risk. Most people now know there is always the potential for a serious decline in any investment. The economy and stock markets never experience steady growth for too long (three years or so) without scary setbacks. In addition, the longer the period of growth, the worse the slowdown or market decline. There have been many serious market declines in the past, and this pattern will continue in the future. In our experience, most investors say they are investing for the long term. However, when stock prices are in a free fall and most pundits are calling for even further declines, most investors are tempted to change their stance. Some do. In our combined fifty years of experience, we have seen quite a number of investors and portfolio managers end up selling right near the lows, when pessimism is rampant. After a low forms, stock prices often recover with a vengeance. Even so, those who sold are still fearful. They will only feel comfortable when the outlook is much brighter. By that time, most of the recovery in stock prices is over.

On the other hand, some investors will wait for a long period of steady gains and an almost unanimous consensus that the future is bright before investing their hard-earned savings. It usually does not take very long before there are major losses and bewilderment over what went so very wrong. Professional money managers are not immune to this tendency either. Governments often seem to get involved in business sectors just at the wrong time.

Therefore, even if you think you are a long-term investor, you must have a system you can rely on to reduce (not eliminate) and manage risk. The experiences of the 2008-2009 Financial Crisis show that many individual and professional money managers did not have in place a discipline that works when the going really gets tough and we experience what is supposed to be a once-in-a-generation event. After the Financial Crisis, Dr. Henry Kaufman, president of the consulting firm Henry Kaufman & Company Inc., and a former economist at the Federal Reserve Bank of New York, told the *Wall Street Journal*, "Consequently, the magnitude of the current crisis calls into question whether, even after markets stabilize, sophisticated risk modeling can ever regain its former status."

Value investing did not work in 2008, when stocks became more attractive as prices declined. Investors who purchased stocks after the steep fall in September 2008 experienced huge losses as prices kept falling much more than expected. When was the time to buy?

Mathematical models also failed. According to many investment models, the odds of a financial crisis like 2008 occurring were so miniscule (once in 10,000 years!) that they were still maintaining that stock prices were "value buys" in the early stages of the stock market free fall. Professional investors who followed this discipline, which was (and still is) all the rage, also experienced agony, stress, and losses as the decline continued. The losses up to the 2009 lows ended up being much more severe than most of the models forecast.

While it is unwise to use a discipline that does not work at market extremes, it is critical to use a risk management system that works all the time—especially at extremes! Risk management systems based on momentum always work. Later chapters of this book will give you specific guidelines and examples of a momentum-based discipline that works in any kind of market environment. Before we get to this, however, we believe it is important for you to understand how markets really work.

2. The Process for Making Investment Decisions Is Unique

Most of us, when we want to buy an electronic device, a car, or a pair of jeans, usually follow a simple process to reach a decision. We ask our friends, relatives, or coworkers for advice. Some of us conduct research using the Internet, newspapers, or publications like *Consumer Reports* to check for quality and reliability. In the case of clothing, cell phones, or vehicles, we might also use the popularity of a product as a guide.

Similarly, if someone has a medical concern, a mechanical problem with a vehicle, or wants to remodel a house, it seems only natural to consult several well-respected experts in their field for an opinion. If five doctors, mechanics, or engineers come up with the same way to resolve a problem, it is usually best to follow their advice. However, because of the way markets function, if five investment experts all make the same recommendation, it most likely will turn out to be the wrong advice. Famed money manager Howard Marks said, "The bottom line here is simple, and I'm thoroughly convinced of it: common sense isn't common. The crowd is invariably wrong at the extremes. In the investing world, everything that's intuitively obvious is questionable and everything that's important is counterintuitive."

Dave recalls the following: In the formative years of my career as an investment advisor in the early 1980s, I thought I would use the same process for choosing investments that I did for selecting an automobile or a pair of snow skis. Every year, surveys showed the most respected analysts in each investment sector. I believed that by following their stock recommendations I would be making wise choices, and my clients' portfolios would perform well. For several years, this strategy worked well, and then the 1987 stock market crash blindsided investors with a two-month 40% decline—20% of which occurred on a single day, October 19, 1987.

That was a day I will never forget. My mind was numb. I remember going out for lunch with my colleagues after the markets closed. The owner of the restaurant came to us and said, "I guess stockbrokers have to eat too." My friend and colleague Dan Dunlop said he felt like he had just driven a bus with his clients off a cliff. I could relate. Since this event was similar to the 1929 stock market crash, many thought we were going to head into a 1930s-style depression. There was no Internet at that time, so I tried to watch every television program I could that evening. I remember watching the *PBS Nightly Business Report* with host Paul Kangas.

One of his guests—a money manager in his fifties—when asked by Kangas what he thought of the day's decline, responded, "A few more days like this and we will all be on the beach." I love being near the water, so I thought that was one of the best responses I had ever heard. Of course, there were no more days like that, and the economy continued to hum along, even though stock prices would stay in a frustrating trading range until 1993.

For more than a year after the crash, every time the telephone rang, my body temperature would rise and my heart rate would increase. I also lost ten pounds very quickly. My wife and I had bought a newer house in February 1987, and the youngest of my three daughters was born on August 12, 1987. I wondered if I would be able to support our family so that my wife could stay at home to raise our children. During the 1973-1975 bear market, some of my colleagues had driven taxicabs at night to support their families. I was preparing to take over the janitorial contract for the office during the 1982 bear market, but markets soared soon after. Many professionals left the investment business in the years after 1987 because it was so challenging and unrewarding. Those who did missed out on the period from 1993-2000— one of the greatest stock market rallies of all time.

Prior to the 1987 crash, I had followed the best-rated economists and market strategists. It turned out that they were just as surprised as I was. At that point, I realized that there were factors impacting stock prices that neither I nor the experts I relied on seemed to notice. This was an "aha!" moment.

It was like the difference between driving a car and flying an airplane. I thought investing was like driving a car. When you drive a vehicle, you can go left, right, fast, or slow. An airplane moves right or left like a car, but it also banks left or right and goes up and down. An airplane can go fast or slow, but if a plane flies too slowly, it can stall or fall down flat.

In the early 1990s I took flying lessons so that I could fly the Lazair ultra-light aircraft. At first, it was so challenging to handle the plane with all these variables that I would eat breakfast before my one-hour flying lesson, and then eat another breakfast afterwards to recover from the experience. It would take me the same sort of effort, over many years, to understand how to manage investing in markets.

Buying a product at a store is like driving a car. Investing in an asset is more like flying an airplane. People who know how to drive a vehicle do not jump into an airplane and try to fly it without adequate preparation and training. Yet, many investors continue to invest or trade without understanding how markets actually operate.

THE ANALOGY OF THE RAFT

Investing and trading can be compared to sitting on the beach at a lake looking at a raft anchored some distance from shore. As it gets hot at the beach, some people swim to the raft and enjoy sitting on it, away from the crowd, dipping their feet in the cool water. Seeing these people enjoying themselves, others on the beach are prompted to swim out to the raft. However, as more and more people get on the raft, it gets crowded. Consequently, the people who first swam to the raft, and have enjoyed a relaxing experience, begin to leave because the experience is not as pleasurable as it was before the others arrived. As more swimmers arrive and climb onto the raft, it starts to sink. What was a pleasant experience now becomes unpleasant and possibly dangerous. As a result, many get off the raft and swim back to the comfortable beach. When this happens, the raft floats above the water again and dries off. Eventually, new sunbathers who just arrived at the beach are enticed to swim to the raft, thereby starting the process all over again.

Investors are like swimmers at the beach. For example, let us assume that gold prices have been rising for a while. Investors who purchased gold when it was near the low are very happy with their decision. As the price rises, more analysts will recommend gold as an attractive investment. An asset's price typically rises when analysts become more positive and raise their price targets. The increase in the value of gold, together with the positive view of more analysts, attracts a greater number of buyers to gold. As the price continues to advance to new highs, almost every expert you hear on the news believes gold prices are going to move higher and higher. At this point, nearly everyone who wants to buy gold has bought it. Once this happens, it cannot go up any more. No matter how positive the situation is, there are simply no more buyers. This is what happened to technology stocks in 2000 and U.S. real estate in 2006.

A more recent example happened with Apple shares when their price soared to $700 in September 2012 before the iPad mini and iPhone 5 were unveiled. Just when it seemed that Apple was going to become even stronger, its share price dropped 25% to $525 over the next two months and more than 40%, to $400, eight months later. This decline happened even though most analysts remained positive on Apple shares.

Prices usually fall at least three times as fast as they advance, since humans respond much faster to fear of loss than to the desire to make money. This is another way of saying that fear is a stronger emotion than greed. Responding quickly to fear serves us well in dangerous situations. However, it is a personality trait that can impair the making of prudent and rational investment decisions.

Let's go back to the gold story. As soon as the price falls, other investors who still have profits jump in quickly to sell before it drops any more. Those who invested early sell what they want to sell at a profit. In the meantime, those who purchased gold just before the decline began cannot understand how they could be so wrong.

After the price of gold has fallen, some experts will forecast lower prices for the yellow metal. This will encourage some investors to sell, which moves the price lower still. As the value continues to fall, more investors sell and more experts in the media lower their price targets and recommend selling. Eventually, when almost every expert suggests that gold is a poor investment, everyone who is tempted to sell will sell. At that point, no matter how negative the environment, the price cannot go down anymore. When the selling is exhausted, and the price of gold is "lower than a snake's belly in a wagon rut," price rises again.

Investors who sold near the low are flabbergasted that prices could rise when the outlook seemed so dire. However, the outlook was not the key factor. The key factor was that every investor who wanted to sell had sold. This is what happened when North American stock prices started to rise when trading resumed after markets were closed following the September 11, 2001, terrorist attacks. This same scenario repeated itself at the Financial Crisis bear market low in March 2009 and the market low sparked by the U.S. debt ceiling crisis and European debt crisis on October 4, 2011.

A recent example occurred in November 2012 with BlackBerry Inc. shares (symbol: BBRY on the U.S. Exchanges and BB on the Canadian S&P/TSX Exchange. TSX is the abbreviation for Toronto Stock Exchange). The share price for BBRY had been falling precipitously (more than 90% since 2008) as iPhones became more popular, causing BBRY to lose market share. Even though many investors and experts thought BBRY shares were going to turn around because they were a good value over the years, prices kept falling.

The share price finally stabilized over the summer of 2012 and even started to rise a little in October 2012. As the media focused on the decline in Apple shares, the value of BlackBerry shares was approaching its 200-day moving average for the first time in eighteen months. This was a significant change. As a result, Dave contacted a few clients who had been interested in buying shares and informed them that he thought it might finally be a good buy for the first time in eighteen months. When asked if the fundamentals had improved, Dave said that BlackBerry (or Research In Motion, as it was called at the time) planned to unveil a new smartphone in early 2013, but other than that little had changed. That was November 9, 2012, when the share price closed at $8.72 on the S&P/TSX. A week later, analysts in the U.S. and Canada raised their price targets on BlackBerry, and by November 23, 2012, the stock was trading at $11.66, some 33% higher than it was only two weeks before. During the first few months of 2013, BlackBerry traded in the $15 range. However, by June 28, 2013, moving average indicators turned negative, providing a sell signal at a price of $10.46.

We tend to think we are the only people who feel a certain emotion or hold a particular opinion. This could not be further from the truth. Dave relates the following story: Many years ago, a friend of mine was an election officer. He asked my wife Marianne and me to help out at a polling station for a mayoral election. When it was time to begin counting ballots, we received the first batch of just over one hundred ballots. For my own interest, I kept track of the percentages of votes and was intrigued to discover that the percentages of the votes barely budged as time went on, no matter how many votes we counted. It was proof that we, as human beings, tend to think and react to circumstances in a similar way.

When we make investment decisions, we must be mindful of how our opinion compares to popular opinion, especially at market extremes. This is critical to investing, because the best results often occur when one goes against what everyone else is doing or recognizes a trend before most others do.

The same concept impacts the advice of analysts and experts. When there is broad consensus among the experts and investors follow this advice, investors will "push" the markets to do the opposite of what the experts project. The analysts and experts may be correct in their assessment, but neither the analysts nor the investors have factored in the impact of how prices would react if everyone did what the experts recommended.

All open markets for stocks, real estate, commodities, bonds, and currencies (these are called centralized markets as opposed to markets for automobiles, houses, etc., that are called decentralized markets) operate in a similar manner. Most investors and experts seem to concentrate on news and published information (annual reports, conference calls, research comments,

message boards, newsletters, and, increasingly, social media) pertaining to these investments. However, they are missing the most important piece of the puzzle, as they did with Apple Inc. and BlackBerry shares. One must understand how crowd behavior affects the demand for an asset, because it can have a significant impact on the price. For this reason, being aware of crowd behavior can be just as critical as being up to date on all of the latest news releases.

What is the lesson here? It's simple but not easy: when you are making an investment decision, remember the analogy of the raft on a lake.

Figure 2.1: The Grand Canal in Venice. Over a thousand people were in a mad rush to get a ferry ride from St. Mark's Square after the canal was closed to boat traffic due to the America's Cup World Series Race in May 2012. This picture demonstrates a good analogy for investing. In the text, we compare the captain and crew of the ferry with the CEO of a company and his employees. Photo by Dave Harder

The captain and crew of the ferry in Figure 2.1 have been trained and have passed certain standards to ensure they can transport passengers safely. The boat has also passed regular checks to ensure that it has the proper safety equipment on board and will be seaworthy. There is a maximum capacity of passengers the ferry can safely hold. When the number of passengers reaches that limit, no more passengers are permitted to board. In the photograph of the Grand Canal in Venice, you can see that the captain on the bridge makes sure the crew helps passengers to board, keeps track of the count, and guides them around the boat so it does not list. While the captain cannot stop other boats from crashing into his vessel, he is in total control of his boat and has complete confidence that he can take his passengers to their destination without incident. The passengers also have confidence that they will have a safe and uneventful journey, since they know there are standards in place to protect them.

A company that trades on a stock exchange also has a person in charge, the CEO. Like the crew on the boat, a company has directors, officers, and employees who must be qualified to do their jobs and follow the rules and regulations of the land. They have control over how much of a product or service they can supply, even though they cannot control how much will be purchased or used.

While the captain of a ferry can limit the number of passengers that board his vessel to ensure it does not get overloaded, the CEO and company officials have no control over the number of investors that can "jump" on or off the shares of a company that trades on a stock exchange. Investors and analysts pay close attention to every word a senior executive has to say about his or her company. This important information can impact the price of the company's shares. However, company officials have no idea or control of the popularity or unpopularity of the company's shares. The level of buyers' demand for shares and share supply from sellers is completely out of the control of the CEO or company officials. While it is good to get all the fundamental information for a company from the best sources, it is only part of the equation. Yet, that is what most people concentrate on because it is the way we are used to gathering information. Economist Mark Skousen wrote, "Why is it that some of the most successful people in business and life can be utter failures in the stock market?" The reason successful people fail at investing and trading is because they do not realize that markets function differently from almost everything else they are involved with.

It is very obvious when a ferry is overloaded or next to empty. It is not as easy to spot an investment where too many people have invested their money and driven the price much higher than its fair value. Therefore, it takes a little more effort to discover where the level of involvement in the latest investment fad has peaked, as the Apple Inc. one did in 2012, or where the selling after a long downtrend has reached a nadir, like BlackBerry shares in 2012.

Abe Lincoln said, "If I had eight hours to chop down a tree, I would spend six hours sharpening my axe." It seems as if most investors spend so much of their time analyzing every tidbit of corporate and economic data that they forget to "sharpen their axe." One of the ways they do this is by ignoring investor sentiment or the overbought and oversold condition of the market. In *Stock Market Profit Without Forecasting: A Research Report on Investment by Formula*, Edgar S. Genstein wrote, "The absolute price of a stock is unimportant. It is the direction of price movement that is important."

Lining up around the block (or camping overnight in front of a store) to get the latest version of a new cell phone or running shoe can be exhilarating. Some people enjoy buying the new model of the most popular vehicle as soon as it appears in the showrooms. Wearing the latest fashions makes us feel attractive and included. It is a natural desire for us to conform to what others are doing. Making decisions based on popular consensus works out well for many things. Very few are disappointed with their choice following this normal decision-making process, as long as they have the cash to pay for it.

Consequently, it would only make sense that a logical decision-making process that works well in most cases would also produce good results for making financial or investment decisions. This is the first serious mistake that most people make when purchasing investments, real estate, commodities, or currencies. Professionals, who are considered intelligent, such as doctors, dentists, lawyers, and teachers, are often the first to fall into this trap.

Steve Irwin, known around the world as "The Crocodile Hunter," survived numerous encounters with very powerful crocodiles because, over many years, he developed the skill for dealing with them. Perhaps his confidence in dealing with such a dangerous creature caused him to be a little more daring than he should have been with other dangerous animals. In 2006, he died when stung by a poisonous stingray while shooting a TV show on the Great Barrier Reef, leaving a wife and two young children to mourn his passing. Likewise, many people suffer when they assume that skill and expertise in one area of their life can automatically be transferred to investing.

A famous investment bubble occurred in Britain during the 1700s. The British South Sea Company borrowed ten million pounds to purchase the rights to trade in all southern seas. This seemed like one of the best monopolies on earth. According to Investopedia, South Sea shares were so popular that they traded as high as 1,000 pounds (a figure not adjusted for inflation) before they became worthless in 1720. After losing much of his money when the South Sea Bubble burst, English physicist, mathematician, and astronomer Isaac Newton stated, "I can calculate the motions of heavenly bodies, but not the madness of people." Isaac Newton was an extremely intelligent man who conducted thorough research. Unfortunately, he thought he could apply the same reasoning and thought processes he used to discover scientific truths in making investment decisions. He understood science and physics, but not markets. They are not the same. Markets are dictated by human behavior, for which there are no formulas or equations. As a result of making and losing several fortunes, Jesse Livermore said, "There is nothing like losing all you have in the world for teaching you what not to do."

We have all been told that the aim is to buy low and sell high. However, due to the dynamics of crowd behavior, many tend to do the opposite. A market is like an evil temptress, trying to lure the most people to buy when everyone else is buying at the highest price. When reality strikes, investors discover they have been caught in what seems like a devious trap to separate them from their hard-earned money. Then, when prices are low and the outlook is hopeless, the temptation to unload investments that seemed so promising just months earlier is almost impossible to resist. Those who succumb to the herd mentality must sell to finally seek some relief from their stress and anxiety. However, just as the masses lock in their losses and feel a burden lifted off their shoulders, prices skyrocket for months. It is at that point, when investors have gone through the wash and rinse cycle of the markets, that people as bright as Isaac Newton wonder how they could be so horribly wrong.

This phenomenon is not unique to stock markets. Currency, commodity, and bond markets also provide investors with the same "thrill." U.S. real estate investors went through this turmoil from 2003 to 2008. It also happened in the 1630s when people in Holland bid up the price of tulip bulbs to the point that the value of a mere three bulbs was equal to that of a house! Then prices dropped by 99%, ending the Tulip Bubble.

Wheat farmers in the Canadian prairies and the U.S. Midwest are also subject to boom-and-bust cycles. When grain farmers make excellent profits, more wheat is planted. However, once a crop is harvested, all that extra wheat floods the market and lowers prices. As farmers fail to realize a reasonable return for their efforts, they plow up their wheat fields and plant different crops. This reduces the wheat supply, which in turn causes the price to go back up. Then the cycle repeats itself all over again. A few years ago, more farmers in the Fraser Valley in B.C. planted cedar shrubs because the prices were so high. However, by the time the shrubs grew to the point that they could be marketed, the excess shrubs created a glut, so the prices fell. In 2012, more farmers planted blueberries because they had become quite popular with health-conscious consumers and the prices were attractive. What will happen to blueberry prices once all of these new plants start producing?

Markets operate in exactly the same way for everything, from precious metals to pork bellies. Most investing and trading courses place little emphasis on how human behavior impacts markets. After all, markets are supposed to act in a rational way. That is what we have been taught. Therefore, the only way most people learn how markets really function is through experience. We do not learn much when we make nice profits. Usually it does not take very long before we learn our first lessons as a result of gut-wrenching losses. Even though investors may have thorough experience with how markets operate, they do not always understand why markets function as they do.

In his book *The Age of Turbulence*, former Federal Reserve Chairman Alan Greenspan said, "Perhaps someday investors will be able to gauge when markets veer from the rational and turn irrational. But I doubt it.

Inbred human propensities to swing from euphoria to fear and back again seem permanent; generations of experience do not appear to have tempered those propensities."

Momentum-based indicators do not enable an investor to gauge if markets are acting in a rational manner. They do, however, provide a disciplined method for determining when a market trend has changed. By indicating that human market behavior has changed from buying to selling, or vice versa, momentum-based indicators are some of the most reliable tools for investors to focus on. We have learned this lesson the hard way and are still learning.

Momentum indicators do not predict the future, but they accurately tell us if money is actually flowing in or out of an asset. Paying attention to these indicators is more reliable than following our own views or what experts think money should be doing. A hard-earned lesson of trading and investing is to listen to what the markets are doing, rather than to act on what we think they should be doing.

Assets priced by markets are totally different from items with a "price tag." If people line up around the block to buy the most popular children's toy, retro sneaker, or video game, it does not impact the price of the product or the outcome of the purchase. On the other hand, if people line up around the block to buy gold bullion, a condominium, or a new stock issue, it can have a dramatic impact on the price of the asset and the outcome of the purchase. Usually, when an asset is very popular, the price is overvalued and a very negative outcome follows. This is simply a function of how markets operate.

While we were in the process of writing this book, people in North American cities lined up to buy the new iPad on March 16, 2012, the first day it was released. The next day, March 17, 2012, the Canadian CTV network reported that hundreds of people had lined up to buy condo units that were to be constructed at the Marine Gateway complex in Vancouver, B.C. Over 11,000 people registered to buy. All 415 units were sold in a matter of hours with construction to be completed more than one year later.

Those who purchased the new iPad or condo will likely be happy with the product they acquired. All iPad purchasers in the U.S. paid the same price for the unit. They knew the unit would become outdated and depreciate as new models were released, but also that the product would still be useful for years. To be a part of its release was likely a memorable, exciting event for many purchasers.

However, some of the "fortunate" few able to buy a condo in Vancouver likely made a 10% down payment and borrowed the rest of the money. In 2012, real estate prices in Vancouver were some of the least affordable in the world. The fact that so many were interested in buying the condos suggests that the purchasers likely paid a high price for them. These condo owners could be devastated financially and psychologically if market prices for their units decline more than the value of the down payment.

People may think the justifications for lining up to buy iPads and condos are similar. They are not! The actual experience may have been the same, but the long-term ramifications for the purchasers could be drastically different. Lining up to compete with others to buy assets at sky-high prices is dangerous. Time will tell if the condo purchasers in Vancouver were fortunate to buy one of the 415 units. The lessons of history suggest that these purchasers could be in for a nasty surprise for which they may not be prepared. By the end of November 2012, Vancouver home prices were reported to be down 5.9% for the year, while sales were down more than 25%. This means it may now be more difficult for an owner to sell one of these condos at the purchase price.

The investment community was buzzing with excitement when the initial public offering for Facebook (FB on the U.S. exchanges) shares took place in May 2012. Facebook is very popular and has revolutionized how people interact. Consequently, there was great demand for the shares, which drove up their original issue price. Investors who focused too much on the popularity of Facebook were likely delighted to be able to get some shares at the new issue price of US$38. However, the price fell immediately after the shares started trading. By September 2012, the share price had declined almost 50% to US$18, and disgruntled shareholders had filed fifty lawsuits.

While people will line up for a new product or a "50% off" sale on Black Friday, apparently investments are the only thing that people will line up to buy when there is a "50% up" sale.

Markets act in a way totally opposite to our natural instincts. It makes sense that the price of assets that trade in open markets rises when the outlook is overwhelmingly positive and falls when there is almost universal agreement that the future is bleak. However, market prices are determined by supply and demand, not just the outlook for the future. Thus, when the outlook is very positive, and almost everyone who wants to buy has bought, the price cannot move any higher no matter how positive the future appears.

During all the European problems in the spring of 2012, even a high school student could have read the news and presented many sound reasons why the value of the euro should plummet. However, the level of short selling (selling an investment you do not own, so that you can profit by buying it back at a lower price) for the euro was at an all-time high, indicating that many investors had already sold the euro short. Sure enough, much to the surprise of many, the price of the euro rose sharply in the summer of 2012.

Most people know the basic economic principle that the price of a product is affected by supply and demand. The price of a stock is not only dependent on demand and supply for its products and/or services, but on the demand and supply of the stock itself. However, it seems that many investors and experts spend most of their time focusing on the supply and demand for the company's products and/or services. In doing so, they ignore this most critical factor. When a critical factor for decision making is ignored, it only makes sense that the outcome can be different from what is expected.

While they sell for many reasons, investors buy for only one reason: to make money. Once the popularity of an investment has peaked along with the buying, prices usually decline. If prices have risen too high, values do not just decline; they can fall violently, as though they have just hit an air pocket. Conversely, after prices have been declining for a while and the outlook deteriorates, more and more investors sell out of their investment positions. Markets do not usually bottom and turn up when the outlook becomes rosy again. They bottom when almost all of the investors who want to sell have sold. At this point, prices cannot go down anymore, no matter how bleak the outlook. Therefore, asset prices usually rise when the selling dries up and pessimism peaks, not when the outlook for the future improves. This was the case at the bottom of the 2009 bear market, with the euro in the summer of 2012, and with BlackBerry in November 2012.

3. Are Markets Logical?

"The world is both chaotic and orderly."
Dee Hock, founder of Visa International

Markets are controlled by the actions of people. Therefore, the real question is, do people act in a logical manner? We like to think we do, especially in this enlightened age. However, in 2012 millions of Americans lined up in stores to spend $1.5 billion with only a one-in-176-million chance of winning a $640 million lottery. The United States is not the only place in the world where this happens. It seems as if the human mind could still use some enhancement.

In 1993, I (Dave) volunteered with the Prison Visitation program for M2/W2 Association–Restorative Christian Ministries. (M2/W2 stands for man to man and woman to woman.) I did this because God has granted me His gift of grace and I wanted to pass it on to others. The purpose of M2/W2 is not to reduce the time inmates have to serve, but to offer them friendship and a chance to connect with someone who can support them if they want to have a successful reintegration into society upon release. We may not be able to change the world, but we can at least try to make a difference one person at a time.

M2/W2 connected me with a man named Paul. When I met him in the visitation area of the medium-security prison, he told me that I was the first visitor he had had in fifteen years. He was a mild-mannered man in his fifties from a good family background, who was serving a life sentence. (A life sentence in Canada is 25 years.) After I had visited him every two weeks for three years, he told me that he had picked up a teenage girl who was hitch-hiking and killed her. Needless to say, this revelation was thought-provoking, since my wife and I have three wonderful, precious daughters. I continued to visit Paul and to attend M2/W2 dinners and functions. During these occasions, Paul would introduce me to his fellow inmates. While Paul accepted responsibility for his actions, I was surprised at the number of inmates who claimed they were in jail because they were wrongly convicted. It is possible that some may be imprisoned for a crime they did not commit, but likely not as many as claim to be innocent.

This experience demonstrated to me that we, as human beings, have the ability to rationalize almost anything. We like to think we make logical decisions most of the time. Even if we are perceptive enough to realize that we do not always make rational decisions, we still tend to believe that those in important positions have the ability to ignore all influences and make pure, rational judgments. However, history shows that this is harder to do than we imagine. (To complete my story, after we shared a friendship for ten years, Paul passed away in prison in 2003, shortly before he was to be released.)

Volunteering with M2/W2 was a good experience, but after ten years, I decided to focus more on Search and Rescue. All Search and Rescue members have a backpack in their vehicles at all times that holds the gear necessary for them to complete any task and survive one night out in the field, wherever that may be. In a similar way, all Air Crash Investigators on the "go team" with the U.S. National Safety Transportation Board have a suitcase with them so they can travel to an aircraft accident as soon as possible. The goal of the investigators is to collect all the factual information relating to an incident and produce a report of the findings. Even though these specialists are trained professionals, they are instructed not to listen to any news reports of the incident as they travel to the accident scene. This protects them from having any preconceived notions about what may have happened. This policy helps them to focus on the pertinent facts they discover, not on reports that may or may not be accurate.

Legendary money manager Warren Buffett deliberately works out of Omaha, Nebraska. Sir John Templeton worked out of the Bahamas to reduce the influence of the mainstream thinking in financial centers such as New York City and London. The well-respected investment expert James Stack, president of InvesTech Research and Stack Financial Management, works more than 2,000 miles away from Wall Street, in Whitefish, Montana. These examples show how important it is for us to avoid being influenced to the point where we end up arriving at a wrong or illogical conclusion.

While some experts live close to a global financial center, sometimes they remove themselves from the trading screens to gain a more objective perspective. I recall Jim Cramer advising those watching his *Mad Money* television program to go outside and take a walk as brutal declines caused widespread fear during the 2008 Financial Crisis.

Sometimes, individual and institutional investors should just ignore economic releases, even though they may seem important. A much-esteemed friend and colleague emphasized this in his March 8, 2013, comments about the Employment Situation Report and the nonfarm payroll component:

> As we have warned for the past two and one half decades on a very, very consistent basis, the historical tendency to material revisions in this monthly data forces us to have little, if anything, to do with it. Indeed were it up to us we'd not even acknowledge this report until a day or two after its release for the revisions are so large and are so constant that the report rings utterly hollow to us. However, everyone else hangs upon this report and so then we've no choice but to wait for its release.

> We know this: that those who "missed" the number when it was released a month ago, will likely have their estimate proven right today when last month's number is revised, as it shall be. We know this: that today's number will be revised materially when it is released next month. And we know this: that he or she who "hits" the number for a supposed bulls-eye today shall

be proven wrong when the revisions are reported next month. And finally we know this above all: when the annual revisions are reported in retrospect, all who had forecast this monthly figure will be proven wholly wrong. What nonsense is this? Puck, in Shakespeare's *A Midsummer Night's Dream* was right: "What fools these mortals be."

All of that said we offer up our condolences to anyone anywhere who has made, or shall make, a trade predicated upon consensus guestimates, the guestimates put forth by anyone else, or our own guesses. We shall be around when the report is made public, but it is our intention to head straight to the gym once the report is made public, giving the market a full two hours to digest the surprises that are always incumbent in the report before acting. It is only reasonable.

This illogical process is repeated over and over again. Therefore, if you wonder how the person who manages your money can be out for a run during what seems to be an important day in the market, he or she may be smarter than you think.

A development in the investment community during the 1970s is another example of how irrational investment professionals can be, even though we think they always act in a logical manner. The 1970s were the period when the Efficient Market Hypothesis (EMH) came to dominate investment thinking and strategizing. The EMH proposed that market prices accurately reflect all the information available to investors. According to this theory, the market price of an investment always represents true value. This assumption is like concluding that medical doctors will never be overweight and that nurses will never smoke tobacco because they have access to all the research showing how detrimental these situations are to health. If we always acted rationally, women with a closet full of the latest fashions would not continue to shop for more clothes. If we all made wise decisions, a man would not risk destroying his family, reputation, and career by having an affair.

The EMH also ignored all the historical evidence of irrational markets presented in Charles Mackay's well-known book *Memoirs of Extraordinary Popular Delusions and the Madness of Crowds,* written in 1852.

I recall watching Louis Rukeyser's *Wall Street Week* in the late 1970s, one of the few television programs at the time geared to investors. By using data from Investors Intelligence (a New York research firm which provides the ratio of optimistic to pessimistic newsletter writers), Rukeyser illustrated that equity markets often bottomed when pessimism peaked and reached a high when optimism peaked. To me, this was proof that markets were often influenced more by investors' emotions than by rational thinking. Nevertheless, EMH seemed to gain credibility after the 1970s. For the most part, North American equity markets were orderly during the 1980s and 1990s, except for the utterly chaotic 1987 crash. The "chaos" of the 1970s and 1987 returned after 2000.

After many years at Berkshire Hathaway, Charlie Munger stated that he observed "...patterned irrationality, which was so extreme." This comment supports the contention that markets are not only irrational; at times they are extremely irrational.

Minyanville, an Internet-based financial media company, stated that the EMH "created the illusion that there is an explanation for everything." Investors believed that the more information they absorbed, the smarter they would be. Therefore, for investors to listen to as many market experts as possible to determine the profitable course of action seemed like a good thing to do. If the markets moved differently from what was anticipated, an investor assumed that he or she must have overlooked some important information. Yet, even with the advent of the Internet providing more investment information than had ever been available before, the bear markets which followed the years 2000 and 2007 still devastated most individual and institutional portfolios. Clearly, the volume of information and collective wisdom failed to be of much value.

The irrational behavior of investors in early 2009 pushed stock prices so low that only a month or two later they seemed ridiculous. In contrast, investors seemed to possess an insatiable desire to buy soaring Internet start-ups with limited prospects for earnings as share prices soared in early 2000. There is simply no logical explanation for how markets sometimes collapse after a long decline or skyrocket after a long advance. As Warren Buffett wisely said, "Nothing sedates rationality like large doses of effortless money."

While education and accumulation of knowledge are very helpful in many professions, they are not always useful in starting a business or investing. Few successful business owners or money managers have a Ph.D. In many respects, investing is similar to flying—it is experience that counts. Yet, many investment strategies and risk management systems have been and still are based on the flawed EMH.

Brian Milner of the *Toronto Globe and Mail* writes, in his July 4, 2009, article, "Sun Finally Sets on Notion That Markets are Rational":

> Nothing in the hypothesis can explain speculative bubbles and busts, bizarre stock valuations and the inconvenient truth that some shrewd investors can indeed do better than the market. No wonder Yale Professor Robert Shiller once labeled it "one of the most remarkable errors in the history of economic thought." And that was back in 1984.
>
> Yet starting in the 1970s, the theory paved the way for a slew of modern investing and risk-management methods. It also provided the intellectual underpinning for the exuberantly embraced deregulation that enabled Wall Street investment banks to eventually blow themselves up in an orgy of excess.
>
> Among other innovations, we can thank the more practically minded EMH adherents for giving us option-pricing models, risk-weighted portfolios and index funds (if it's impossible to beat the market, why try?). These are also the math whizzes who conjured up the wonderful world of derivatives, securitized mortgages, and the like, which were supposed to spread and reduce risk. Instead, they spread contagion and reduced their investors to tears.

"All of these finance guys assumed that the market performance of whatever period that they were able to measure would be a good representation of what the future would be like," says Mr. Fox, whose lucid book, *The Myth of the Rational Market: A History of Risk, Reward and Delusion on Wall Street*, has attracted far more interest than your average tome on economic thought, thanks to its fortuitous timing.

And what the theoreticians were primarily measuring was the relatively long period of market stability stretching from the end of the Second World War to the 1970s.

"It's this general human trait, and it seems to have been picked up by the finance professors and a lot of the quantitative types on Wall Street. It's this naive willingness to assume that the past is a pretty good guide to the future," Mr. Fox said in an interview.

It has long been apparent to anyone actually involved in the markets that they are far from always right, that they can be thoroughly irrational and that they can diverge from economic reality for long stretches.

"One of the more interesting features of financial markets is that even if something is sort of a correct observation, once enough people come around to believe it, it stops working," Mr. Fox says. "Every good idea on Wall Street eventually becomes a bad idea. That's just the way markets work."

Yet the failure of the EMH hasn't stopped the deep thinkers from trying to come up with another all-encompassing theory to explain what the heck is going on.

The increasingly influential financial behaviourists would have us believe they have all the answers. But Mr. Fox doesn't buy that either.

"Clearly, the prices on the market are more volatile, less reliable, less rational than is envisioned in any of the rational market theories. But it's not like there are these great answers out of psychology that explain how everything works," he says.

The fact is there is no economics version of string theory that neatly ties together all the pieces of the complex financial markets puzzle. And that's because the whole thing is still as much art as science.

We have to remember that the Efficient Market Hypothesis became widely accepted in the 1960s. That was a time when cars had "wings," the U.S. army was experimenting with personal jet packs, America was planning to put a man on the moon, and the supersonic Concorde was on the drawing boards. It was a time of optimism when society believed that science could solve every problem, and that drugs could soon cure every illness. The most recent investment bubble had occurred more than thirty years earlier, in 1929. Widespread optimism and confidence in science gave rise to the concept that experts could finally create an explanation for what makes markets move. The EMH emerged from this mindset.

The optimism for what science could do in the future collapsed in the 1970s. Birth defects caused by thalidomide were just one example, showing that "wonder" drugs can have harmful side effects. In the 1970s we also discovered that human interference in nature caused more harm than good, giving rise to the environmental movement. We realized that mankind is not so smart after all. Fifty years later we are still driving cars on the road instead of flying them, and Concorde airplanes are displayed in flight museums. Even though many new concepts that were accepted in the 1960s were debunked a decade later, confidence in the EMH somehow lasted much longer. What enabled this to happen in the supposedly rational investment industry?

People in the investment business tend to be driven, optimistic, and focused on the future. Consequently, the investment community seems to be eager to embrace new concepts without evaluating how they would have performed during previous crises. Confidence in themselves and the future tends to compel prominent money managers to accept explanations for the unexplainable and to trust models for things that cannot be modeled. While the EMH has finally been relegated to the trash heap, confidence in economic theories still persists. The 2008 Financial Crisis exposed the flaws in many of these theories. Now that the EMH has been debunked, one wonders how long it will take for society to finally realize that economics is not a science. The sooner this realization happens, the better.

Since unpredictable human behavior drives markets, investing is indeed more of an art than a science. One can try to analyze volumes of information to sort out why the markets are acting as they are, or why they should move in a certain direction in the future. We believe it is more prudent and much more efficient to focus on technical tools to determine where the money is flowing and to wait for the explanation to be revealed later. Momentum-based indicators or moving averages do just that. While models based on valuations and mathematics work most of the time, they can falter during times of crisis. Momentum-based technical tools that follow the trend always work. We will discuss these tools later in the book.

Often, relying on market prices is not efficient at all. Nevertheless, many still believe that making a rational decision based on the study of economic and financial data is the key to investment success. The study of economic and financial data can be helpful, but only if interpreted against the backdrop of how market forces of supply and demand are impacting current prices.

In a way, investment trends are also like fashions. After a fashion trend has been in place for a while (often a very short time), designers create new looks for the runways in Milan, Paris, and New York and then see what sticks. When some famous trendsetters such as Sarah Jessica Parker, Lady Gaga, or Kate Middleton (the Duchess of Cambridge), like what they see, they start wearing these fashions. Soon the latest designs appear in high-end stores; next, they appear in the mainstream retailers. Finally the fashions reach the Walmarts of the world. By the time Walmart and Target stores are stocked with the most recent designs, the style is near the end of its popularity. When this clothing is on sale at Walmart, one knows the trend is over and that the trendsetters have already moved on to something else.

We like to conform. When so many people are doing something, we like to be doing the same, since this gives us a feeling of security. As social beings, we depend on each other for information when we are uncertain about something. Part of being a good member of the crowd is to go along with what the crowd is doing. Most people derive a lot of security from conforming to what others are doing, saying, or wearing.

For example, in 1981 Princess Diana saw a wedding dress from an Italian designer in a magazine. She liked it and had it made for herself. Once she endorsed the style, many brides followed her lead, until some clever designers changed the trend, and the fashion choice of another celebrity was suddenly in fashion. Heidi Klum, host of the popular reality show *Project Runway*, starts every program by saying, "In fashion, one day you're in, and the next day, you're out."

Present styles that are all the rage suddenly appear dated and dowdy, while the new fashion, often seemingly so unattractive years earlier, now looks fabulous and chic. It is often the same with investments, except that the stakes and risks are so much higher.

If we see smoke in the air, and everyone is running away from it, it makes sense to run away, too, and ask questions later. Our natural way of thinking works well for many things we encounter. Our human nature helps to protect us and keep us safe. However, this way of thinking can backfire when it is used in a market environment.

In 1971, psychologists Amos Tversky and Daniel Kahneman published the results of a study they conducted about human thinking. David Orrell summarized their findings about herd behavior in his book *Economyths: Ten Ways Economics Gets It Wrong*. He writes, "One might think that a group of people would make better decisions, and in some ways they do." But, as Kahneman explains,

> …when everybody in a group is susceptible to similar biases, groups are inferior to individuals, because groups tend to be more extreme. In many situations you have a risk-taking phenomenon called the risky shift. That is, groups tend to take on more risk than individuals. Groups also tend to be more

optimistic, suppress doubts, and exhibit *groupthink*. In larger informal groups such as markets, this can translate into herd behavior, in which investors all rush into the market, or out of it, at the same time.

I remember 1980 when people were lining up around the block in Vancouver to buy gold at US$650 an ounce. In December 1980, my future father-in-law took my girlfriend, her sister, and me to see Wayne Gretzky's first hockey game in Vancouver against the Vancouver Canucks. Observing the long line for the men's washroom between periods, the man standing behind me remarked, "You'd think that they're selling gold bars in here."

Gold was indeed very popular in 1980, but the luster of gold turned rusty when commodity prices collapsed in 1981. Gold prices finally bottomed nineteen years later at US$250 an ounce. The bubble in technology stocks ended in 2000, and stocks endured a bear market in 2001 and 2002. By 2003, the technology stocks that were so popular in 2000 were like a dirty word. (In 2011, the NASDAQ was still only trading close to half of what it was at the 2000 peak.)

Herd behavior feels just as comfortable in investing as it does in fashion. The only difference is that in investing the consequences for following herd behavior are so much worse. The consequence of following herd behavior for fashion is that we often end up throwing out an expensive, perfectly good item of clothing since we do not want to be seen in something that is not in style anymore. Those who enjoy shopping are then rewarded with the pleasurable experience of buying new clothes.

The result of following herd behavior with our investments is that we can lose our life savings, homes, families, and careers. Our human nature works against us when we are investing. This is why James O'Shaughnessy wrote,

> "Successful investors do not comply with human nature; they deny it."

In 2000, the church I attended needed more drummers. I had played the violin when I was small and a trumpet in the high school band, but I had always wanted to play the drums. Even though I was forty-five years old at the time, I enrolled in weekly drum lessons. At first it seemed impossible to play a beat on the snare drum with the left hand and another beat on a cymbal with the right hand, while playing a separate beat with the right foot on the bass drum. However, it is amazing what the human body can accomplish with practice and determination. Like learning to play the drums, attaining the ability to accept how markets really function requires learning how to react to what is happening in a way that does not come naturally.

After the bubble in technology stocks burst in 2000, stock investors had a bad taste in their mouths. Consequently, they turned away from stocks in 2003 and started buying real estate. For Americans, this seemed like a good idea, since residential real estate prices had been fairly healthy and stable for a long time. More and more investors followed that trend and real estate prices increased. Since prices were rising steadily, buying real estate also seemed like a good strategy for individuals who were not investors. Financial firms recognized the opportunity to lend to existing homeowners and developed products that enabled individuals to use the increased value of their home as equity for a loan. Executives at financial firms believed that there was not much risk of a decline in real estate prices, because there had never been a major price decline in real estate across the entire country before. Real estate was and is a good investment, but not at a time when everyone is investing in it. After the real estate bubble peaked in 2006, many who speculated in U.S. real estate lost everything. That is an extremely high price to pay for following the crowd, yet it happens over and over again. History repeats itself. It is important to learn from the lessons of history in order to avoid the pitfalls of herd behavior. This book is written expressly for the purpose of helping readers do just that.

4. Humans Are Prone to Move in Herds

"Men, it has been well said, think in herds; it will be seen that they go mad in herds, while they only recover their senses slowly, one by one."
Charles Mackay, *Memoirs of Extraordinary Popular Delusions and the Madness of Crowds*

Of the many lessons I (Janice) have learned about life and trading, perhaps the largest numbers have been found in and around airports. Over a period of eight years in the 1970s, I traveled the world doing clinical research and had the opportunity to visit or live in many countries outside of the U.S.

One late night, a colleague and I arrived jet-lagged and hungry at London's Heathrow Airport. Because of rain and storms, many flights were delayed, and passengers were irritable and impatient. It was yet another rainy night in London town, and taxis were difficult to find. All we wanted to do was get a taxi to our hotel rooms and get some sleep so we could be rested for a meeting the next day. The line for taxicabs was a long snake of over forty people who were shuffling in the cold rain and seemingly not moving forward at all. My colleague remembered that some terminals at Heathrow were within walking distance of each other, so we decided to avoid the long line and walk to the next terminal. Within twenty minutes we were in a taxi and on the way to the hotel. As we drove by the line at the other terminal, we noticed that people were continuing to "queue up" and the line was getting longer.

What were these people thinking? That is not the question. The question is, "How were these people thinking?" There were no cabs, a long line, and people were continuing to join the line. They were doing what is called herding. They were following the person in front of them, assuming that person knew what was going on. They believed that the person in front of them somehow knew that it was only going to be a short time until a taxi arrived. They went along to get along and ended up frustrated and cold in a very long line with little relief in sight.

When everyone is thinking the same thing, no one is really thinking. When everyone is looking in the same direction, no one is really looking. This is one way that market tops and bottoms are formed. Buyers are buying because everyone else is buying, until there is no one left to buy. Sellers are selling until there is no one left to sell to.

In markets, usually when you see massive buying or selling and people piling into trades, it is time to step back, get some perspective, and let the move play out before jumping in or out one way or the other. As we know, trades can get very crowded and almost too tempting to resist. You don't have to walk to the next terminal at the airport. You might want to simply shut down your trading platform and get away for a while, take a walk or a run or go to the gym to clear your mind. Don't allow yourself to be tempted by what looks too good to resist. Come back rested, with fresh eyes and a relaxed brain, and then make the decision whether or not to act. By doing so, you can often save yourself precious emotional and financial resources by not buying near the top or selling near the bottom.

Let's take a closer look at the herding impulse. Facebook, Twitter, and other social media have become pervasive and powerful forces in today's society. An interesting trend is that some employers and psychologists believe that people who aren't on social networking sites are "suspicious." The German magazine *Der Tagesspiegel* went so far as to point out that accused theater shooter James Holmes and Norwegian mass murderer Anders Behring Breivik share common ground in their lack of Facebook profiles. A related article by Kashmir Hill in *Forbes Magazine*, August 2012, entitled "Beware, Tech Abandoners. People Without Facebook Accounts Are Suspicious," reports that human resources departments across the country are becoming more wary of young job candidates who don't use the site.

Kashmir Hill writes,

> The term "Crackberry" seems silly today—and not just because consumers OD'ed on Blackberry and moved on to iDealers. The term arose in an earlier "aughts" time when Blackberry dominated the smartphone market and lawyers and execs were nearly the only ones who had them, due to their need to be able to respond to email immediately. Things have changed. Now we all need to be able to respond to email immediately. And to tweet. And to instantly share our photos on Facebook. We're all addicted to technology now, and not just to the Blackberry. We're "addicted" to our iPhones, and Facebook, and Twitter, and Android, and Pinterest, and iPads, and Words with Friends, and fill-in-the-blank-with-your-digital-dope-of-choice.

> The sudden and dramatic advent of social-media-enabling technologies into our lives seems to be causing some mid-digital-life crises. Not only has Silicon Valley developed a guilty conscience about addicting us to screens, we the users are starting to question how technology is changing us: making us fat, making us unhealthy, making us depressed, making us lonely, making us narcissistic, and making us waste time worrying about whether it's making us fat, unhealthy, depressed, narcissistic and/or lonely. That's leading some users to consider abandoning the whole enterprise.

James Montier, a pioneer of behavioral finance and behavioral investing at global investment management firm Grantham, Mayo, van Otterloo and Co., postulates that man is an animal that communicates, stampedes, and herds, saying, "This gives rise to Homo Ovinus—a species who are concerned purely with where they stand relative to the rest of the crowd. (For those who aren't up in time to listen to *Farming Today,* Ovine is the proper name for sheep.)"

At the most simplistic level, herding describes the tendency of a species to seek safety in numbers. Human beings are social animals. Numerous scientific studies measuring the effect of loneliness suggest it is an important public health concern. For example, there is evidence that the risk of developing and dying from heart disease decreases with strong social connections. It appears that loneliness or ostracism triggers the release of inflammatory chemicals in the body that lead to a variety of illnesses including arthritis, heart attack, stroke, diabetes, Alzheimer's disease, and other serious conditions that can result in depression, disability, and death. The pain of social isolation can be as intense as true physical pain. In light of these findings, we can postulate that herding has implications for human survival.

Circular milling is when ants follow each other around and around in circles until they become exhausted and die. First described in blind army ants, it is also called an ant death spiral. A circle of army ants, each one following the ant in front, becomes locked into a circular mill. They continue to circle each other until they all die. (If you think that's madness, you only have to look at the long history of market bubbles.) Sometimes, a few ants escape the death spiral. In 1921, famed explorer and naturalist William Beebe, in his book entitled *Edge of the Jungle,* described a circular mill of ants (Ecitons) he witnessed in Guyana. It measured 1,200 feet in circumference and had a two-and-a-half-hour circuit time per ant. Beebe writes,

> All afternoon, the insane circle revolved; at midnight the hosts were still moving, the second morning many had weakened and dropped their burdens, and the general pace had very appreciably slackened. But still the blind grip of instinct held them. On and on they must go! Always before in their nomadic life there had been a goal—a sanctuary of hollow tree, snug heart of bamboos—surely this terrible grind must end somehow. Through sun and cloud, day and night, hour after hour, there was found no Eciton with individual initiative enough to turn aside an ant's breath from the circle which had

been traversed perhaps 15 times. The masters of the jungle had become their own mental prey.

The mill persisted for two days, "with ever increasing numbers of dead bodies littering the route as exhaustion took its toll, but eventually a few workers straggled from the trail thus breaking the cycle, and the raid marched off into the forest." The cause of this behavior is the way that ant societies navigate on the ground. Since army ants are blind, they follow the trail pheromones (secreted or excreted chemicals that trigger social responses) laid down by other ants. Ants that are not blind follow pheromones, visual cues, or both. Normally, the system works well. A scout ant goes out and finds something. Other ants go back to get more by following the scent trail or each other. However, if a loop gets created, the ants will keep marching around and around, sometimes circling until they die. A similar formation of army ants *(Eciton praedator)* was described by Schneirla near the Panama Canal. The mill is shown in Figure 4.1. Schneirla concluded that the ants died of "desiccation" after traveling in a circle for more than twenty-four hours.

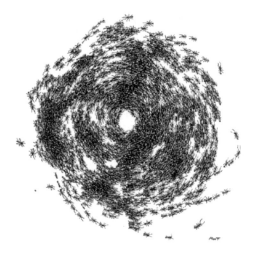

Figure 4.1: Circular Ant Mill. Source: T.C. Schneirla

In behavioral finance, herding is a collective and contagious confluence of and influence on ideas and actions related to trading and investing. In financial markets, herding occurs when either positive or negative feedback prevails. Imbalances between positive and negative feedback result in market inefficiencies. Numerous studies show that there may be a critical threshold beyond which either positive or negative feedback dominates and begins to feed on itself, resulting in either a bubble or a crash.

In the copious multidisciplinary literature on herding, the socionomic perspective is particularly compelling. Socionomic research posits that people herd when they are uncertain and that this herding impulse drives social behavior. This is another way of saying that there is safety in numbers. In a context of uncertainty, the herding impulse drives social behavior. There are clear evolutionary advantages to this, such as fleeing from predators or huddling together to stay safe from the elements. However, in the financial markets, such behavior can be disastrous and lead to large losses. Socionomics also hypothesizes that herding is unconscious and nonrational. This theory is given credence by brain structure where the primitive areas of the brain (limbic, phylogenetically old) subserve unconscious needs, and, in conditions of uncertainty, take precedence over the cortical (phylogenetically new) brain functions.

The human brain (Figures 4.2 and 4.3) is the most powerful, complex, and sophisticated information-processing system in the known universe, and is estimated to be one hundred thousand years old. Weighing about three pounds, it sits quietly inside of a closed, dark space (the skull), and knows nothing except what it is told by electrochemical impulses streaming into it. The brain contains some 86 billion nerve cells called neurons that branch out to form over one quadrillion connections called synapses. There are more synapses in the human brain than there are stars in the known universe. Memory and learning occur when the neurons and synapses reorganize and strengthen themselves through repeated usage.

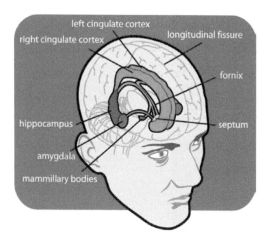

Figure 4.2: Major structures of the limbic system. Limbic structures such as the amygdala and hippocampus (purple color) lie deep within the neocortex (beige color). In the process of development of the brain, the neocortical (new) areas grew up and folded over the limbic (old) areas. Produced by Janice Dorn

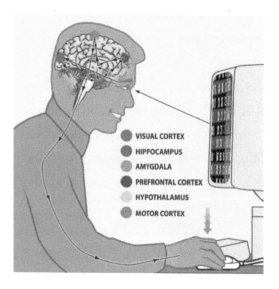

Figure 4.3: Brain areas that coordinate with each other in making decisions. The "old" brain is represented by the amygdala (orange), hippocampus (blue), and hypothalamus (yellow). The "new" brain is shown as the motor and prefrontal cortices (green and purple). Produced by Janice Dorn

In terms of functional decision making, the neocortical (new brain) areas are reasoned, slow, deliberate, and cognitive, i.e., they think (cogitate). The limbic (old brain) areas are fast, less than rational, appetitive, and not self-aware, i.e., they feel (affect). There is a constant battle going on between old brain and new brain that may lead to agreement or conflict. Such states are called consonance (agreement that may be cognitive or affective) and dissonance (conflict that may be cognitive or affective). Cognitive refers to thinking and affective refers to feeling.

According to socionomics, "...not all synchronized group action is herding behavior. While some academics look at the phenomena of people going to the mall when there's a sale, for example, as herd behavior, our perspective is that these people are simply rationally maximizing the utility of their resources. Socionomists only recognize herding when the behavior is nonrational and performed in the context of uncertainty."

We can make a distinction between herding and related but not identical concepts such as "groupthink" and mob behavior. We also distinguish between activity in non-centralized markets (buying a home or a car) and in centralized markets (financial markets). In his groundbreaking book *The Wisdom of Crowds,* James Surowiecki talks about the dangers of "groupthink." That's what happens when people become too collaborative and reliant on the status quo. Surowiecki points out that one reason the American invasion of Cuba's Bay of Pigs was such a disaster was because the people involved in planning the operation were the same people who were asked to determine if it would work.

A cautionary tale about herding in the markets comes from Warren Buffett's retelling of a story from Benjamin Graham, who was one of Buffett's mentors. I thank noted behavioral economist and psychiatrist Dr. Richard Peterson, founder of MarketPsych, LLC, (www.marketpsych.com) for sharing this story: A clever old oil prospector named Clem died and tried to get into heaven. In order to do so, he had to get past St. Peter at the Pearly Gates. Once St. Peter found out that Clem was an oil prospector, he denied him entrance to heaven, pointing to a large group of oil prospectors waiting patiently to get in. There was just not enough room in heaven to accommodate all the prospectors. Clever Clem, never one to miss an opportunity, asked St. Peter if he could say four words to the other prospectors. Not seeing any harm in it, St. Peter agreed. At that point, Clem yelled out to the other prospectors, "Oil discovered in hell!" Immediately, the group of prospectors ran out, looking to get to where the oil was. Yes, they were looking to get to hell in order to be near the oil. Seeing that the group of waiting prospectors had all but disappeared, St. Peter told Clem it was now clear for him to enter heaven because there was plenty of room. Clem thought about it for a minute, looked at St. Peter and said, "You know, I think I am going to go ahead with the others. There just might be some truth to that rumor after all!"

> "When everybody starts looking smart and not realizing that a lot
> of it was luck, I get really scared."
> Raphael Yavneh

Decisions about trading and investing bear many similarities to decisions made outside of the markets. Most people make decisions in the context of numerous societal factors, not in isolation. In this regard, they are functioning less as individuals and more as a social collective. This is nowhere more evident than in the multimillion-dollar marketing industry that targets our brains almost every waking minute of each day. The marketing industry has become increasingly sophisticated by putting human beings into brain scanning machines and recording their brain activity in response to marketing messages. The emerging field of neuroscience marketing will grow more powerful in the years ahead, and we are likely to find ourselves desiring and purchasing items for no logical reason. Neuromarketers are building models of persuasion that incorporate a variety of conscious and nonconscious factors that can influence the mind of the consumer. Mass psychology and the artificial creation of "absolutely have to have it" can be seen everywhere; these messages are often so subtle and pervasive that you don't even recognize them. Readers would be wise to prepare for the onslaught of highly sophisticated neuromarketing techniques targeted to keep us from knowing why we are making purchases. In the realm of trading and investing decisions, the importance of knowing what or how others are thinking is critical for success. Put another way, the social dynamic of herding is evident every day in the markets and its importance cannot be ignored. In market situations, behavior is motivated by certain assumptions and perceptions of what other traders and investors are doing. Social psychology, based on the perceptions of the decisions of other traders, becomes the basis for the actions of the individual trader. In this herding process, traders attempt to anticipate and mimic the actions of other traders. Decisions imitate decisions, setting off a chain reaction where more and more individuals are making the same decision simply because others are doing it. One need look no further than the momentum that builds in certain stocks during the trading day. This is not far removed from the situation of the circular ant mill. Momentum grows as increasing numbers of traders pile into the same position, much like the blind ants that moved in the same circle for several days before several deviated and broke away from the mill, while the rest suffocated or died from exhaustion.

There are numerous scientific studies that demonstrate the power of the need to conform to the group consensus, particularly in simple and clear-cut situations that involve decision making. One of the most profound thinkers in this area is Jamshed Bharucha, President of The Cooper Union for the Advancement of Science and Art. Dr. Bharucha was asked by www.edge.org in 2009, "What will change everything?" He responded that an understanding of how brains synchronize—or fail to do so—will be a game-changing scientific development. Dr. Bharucha writes on www.edge.org that this understanding "...will not emerge from a single idea, but rather from a complex puzzle of scientific advances woven together. What is game-changing is that only recently have researchers begun to frame questions about brain function not in terms of individual brains but rather in terms of how individual brains are embedded in larger social and environmental systems that drive their evolution and development. The new way of framing brain and cognitive science—together with unforeseen technological developments—promises transformational integrations of current and future knowledge about how brains interact."

In financial markets, the tasks of decision-making are made more difficult because of the instant availability of highly diversified, contradictory, and ambiguous information. What happens in situations where traders or investors are bombarded with large amounts of conflicting and confusing information, commentary from the financial media, the beliefs and thoughts of numerous "authorities," and the constant drumbeat of "breaking news"? They become uncertain and confused. In other words, the cortical (new, thinking, logical) areas of the brain are put into a situation of information overload. The new brain simply cannot process all of this information in the time needed to make critical trading decisions. This is particularly true with novice or inexperienced traders who find themselves tossed from stem to stern as they attempt to make sense of the informational barrage. In these situations, the new brain gives up and the old brain fires into action. The limbic brain (amygdala and surrounding connections) is the default mechanism, the low road, the quick and easy way that the brain makes decisions in the context of way too much information.

In the environment of overload, the brain searches frantically for some rule, some meaning, something that makes sense, finding it in the form of what are called "heuristics," or mental shortcuts. These are formed quickly in the old brain. The old brain waits for the new brain to give up thinking and reasoning and run on emotion. It just "feels" that this is the thing to do, and it doesn't look back. The old brain defaults to the easy way, and says, "Just do it now and think about it later." The old brain tricks the trader into thinking that the "big money" must know more than he does, so he just gets into the position because he sees it moving and absolutely must get in for the ride. Big money knows this behavior all too well, as it lures the old brains of the less-capitalized, small money traders to "get in now" so that it can exploit and take monies from them. Sometimes the small money trader is nimble, gets lucky, and catches part of the move. In the majority of cases, the trader gets trapped and fooled as he or she tries to buy breakouts or sell breakdowns that fail almost immediately.

Another explanation for herding in the financial markets has to do with the emotions of anticipated regret and fear. It is easier to be a loser in a group of losers than to be a loser in a group of winners. It is easier to experience fear and regret when others feel the same way. Misery loves company. Herding may be a reasonable option for traders and investors who are concerned about their reputations. By failing with others, they put themselves in a position to share the blame and do not have to deal with being ostracized by the group for individual success in the face of group failure. In the words of John Maynard Keynes, "Worldly wisdom teaches that it is better for reputations to fail conventionally than to succeed unconventionally." The next time you find yourself following the herd, you may be well advised to stop and ask if you are following the ant in front of you, and why you are doing it.

> "Zig when others zag. Sell hope, buy despair, and take the other side of emotional disconnects (in the context of defined risk).
> If you can't find the sheep in the herd, chances are that you're it."
> Todd Harrison, founder of www.minyanville.com

5. Is Expert Economic, Investment, and Market Advice Reliable?

Figure 5.1: Even wealthy people who own the best exotic vehicles make mistakes. When making forecasts, experts from very well-respected institutions have made more than their fair share of mistakes as well. That is because predicting the future has always been challenging. (The faces have been altered for privacy reasons.) Photo by Dave Harder

In most cases, the advice of experts in their field can be reliable and helpful. We, however, cannot extend that conclusion to economic, financial, and market experts. There are five main reasons for this.

The first reason: expert opinion is not reliable because an expert is still human and subject to making mistakes. One of the most tragic and horrific rescues my Search and Rescue team had to deal with occurred on April 28, 2012. On that day, a young man had arranged a hang gliding ride to mark a special occasion for his 27-year-old girlfriend from Vancouver. He had arranged a tandem ride with a certified, experienced instructor. The hang gliding ride took place at a popular hang gliding site in our team's territory on Mt. Woodside in Harrison Mills, B.C.

Figure 5.2: Paragliding and hang gliding at Harrison Mills, B.C. Photo by Dave Harder

The pilot had purchased a new video camera to record the flight experience and was excited about setting it up for the first time. He had also brought his young daughter along to watch him prepare and take off. When the hang glider was set up, the pilot and passenger ran to the edge of a cliff on top of the mountain and became airborne. As soon as the passenger's feet left the ground, it became obvious that she was not properly secured to the hang glider, even though she was wearing a harness. As she and the pilot desperately tried to hang on to each other, witnesses saw her plunge 300 meters to her death in the forest below. The Royal Canadian Mounted Police (RCMP) asked the Kent Harrison Search and Rescue Team to find her. The possibility that she was still alive could not be ruled out with all the trees and foliage in the area. However, the terrain was steep and the bush was dense, so searching was difficult. Late in the day, a running shoe was located which matched the shoes the pilot was wearing on videos taken from the mountain peak before take-off. It turned out that the pilot's running shoes had come off as the victim was losing her grip. Just before the search had to be suspended due to darkness, her body was found after a concentrated search around the area where the shoe was found. It was very obvious that her harness was not attached. Even though team members are trained volunteers with years of experience, we are still human. This incident was so disturbing that the team requested a Critical Incident Stress Debriefing.

This wonderful young woman and her boyfriend had relied on an expert to have a special experience. The pilot was well qualified, but he became distracted with his new video camera and forgot to do the most basic, important task—secure her body harness to the frame of the hang glider. A safety check was not done either. The tragic incident became international news when the pilot was arrested for withholding evidence two days after the accident, because he had swallowed the memory chip that was in his video camera. When the memory chip was finally "released" days later, it was blank. The pilot was convicted on charges of criminal negligence causing death.

Figure 5.3: Picture courtesy of Kevin A. MacDonald, KAM Productions

Figure 5.3 is a picture of Chilliwack Search and Rescue member Josef Seyward escorting the hang glider pilot into a helicopter shortly after the horrific accident. He was asked to help searchers determine the area of dense forest where the passenger might have fallen to the ground. Chilliwack Search and Rescue and Kent Harrison Search and Rescue are the second- and third-most-active Search and Rescue teams in the province of British Columbia. The two teams often work together when more resources are required for major incidents. The B.C. Lower Mainland corridor is the busiest Search and Rescue corridor in North America. B.C. handles more Search and Rescue calls than the rest of Canada combined.

This example is a stark reminder that all experts in every field are human beings and can make mistakes. This is the first reason why expert advice is not reliable. It is also a reason why you should always ask the person in charge to show you that you are fastened securely any time you or a loved one are engaging in a risky activity. (To protect the privacy of individuals involved and the commitment to confidentiality for our team, only information that was made available in media reports is included.)

The second reason: most economic, financial, and market experts are trained to analyze data from the past. Corporate financial information is released every three months. A lot can change in an economy, a company, and a company's share price within three months. Markets tend to take into account what investors expect will happen six to twelve months into the future. That is why anything that changes expectations can cause volatility to increase, even though fundamentals may not have changed at all. It is natural for us to believe that existing conditions will continue. Therefore, in many cases, experts often base their forecast on the premise that a current trend will just carry on. However, while trends may continue for a long time, they do not last forever.

My friend and colleague James McKeough is a CMT (Chartered Market Technician) who works for Montreal-based Pavilion Global Markets. He very wisely deduced,

"Market behavior is human behavior."

It is difficult, if not impossible, to determine in advance when human behavior will change. Consequently, it is almost impossible to know when a trend will end by focusing entirely on financial data, which in many cases was compiled months before. Famous Internet analyst Henry Blodget started his investment training in 1994 when he was twenty-eight years old. All he experienced for the next six years was rising markets. He ended up investing $700,000 in technology stocks just before the dot-com bubble burst in 2000 and lost most of it shortly thereafter. At the age of thirty-four, this influential analyst had his first real-life encounter with a bear market after the historic technology rally ended. His training and education at Prudential Securities and Oppenheimer & Co. turned out to be of little value. I am sure he studied bear markets and cycles, but learning about market events is not like experiencing them. It is like comparing the obituary of the father of an acquaintance in the newspaper with the obituary of your own father. There is a world of difference in the intense emotions one goes through and the impact it has on one's life.

Henry Blodget may have known about the past, but he did not realize how powerful and devastating a major trend change can be. Extrapolating current trends into the future is easy to do. Anticipating a trend change is the critical thing to do, yet it is rarely done. For this reason, expert advice may let us down when it is needed most. Driving based on what we see in the rearview mirror causes accidents.

The third reason: it is almost impossible to forecast surprises, and surprises almost always result in a negative outcome. The Cuban Missile Crisis in 1962; the sharp rise in Middle East oil prices during the early 1970s; 20% interest rates in 1981; the 1987 stock market crash; the Clinton impeachment; the Russian default crisis during the summer of 1998; the September 11, 2001, terrorist attacks; and the 2008 Financial Crisis came as a total surprise to almost every individual, corporate leader, government official, economist, and investment expert. Since most surprises are negative, they often result in high anxiety and market mayhem. How helpful can any forecast be if it cannot predict inevitable surprises? Research reports now contain pages of disclaimer in fine print, pointing out the risks in trying to predict the future. However, it is our human nature to place more trust in experts than we should. No one can predict surprises, so experts cannot be reliable all of the time.

The fourth reason: economists are presented as scientists. In the late 19th century, some intellectuals thought they could develop mathematical formulas for the economy and make it a science, just like physics or engineering. However, economics is the study of how individuals act with their money. Therefore, it is really more like psychology. One cannot create a formula for how people will react to economic situations, political actions, and negative surprises, or how they will vote in an election. Physicist Richard Feynman, one of the most respected scientists of modern times, commented, "I have a great suspicion that they don't know that this stuff is wrong and they are intimidating people."

For example, the International Monetary Fund (IMF) originally forecast good economic growth for 2008. Then global economic growth slowed sharply when the Financial Crisis struck in September 2008. In early 2009 the IMF stated that the recession was going to be deeper and last longer than previously forecast. They were wrong on both counts. In 2009 the U.S. National Bureau of Economic Statistics announced that the U.S. started a recession a year after it began, and heralded that it was over a year after it ended. Of what value is that? The record of economic and market forecasts by even the most respected organizations and think tanks, such as the International Monetary Fund and the World Bank, is questionable.

In July 2004, Henry Blodget wrote a series of articles for *Slate*, called "The Wall Street Self-Defense Manual." He wrote, "Predicting future market performance is not an exact science, and those who pretend it is do so at their peril." Many analysts, economists, the IMF, the ECB, government agencies, and well-regarded economic think tanks make forecasts with authority. Media outlets create headlines out of these forecasts to perpetuate the myth that they have predictive value; yet, most of this information is questionable.

Spencer Jakab, the writer for the Ahead of the Tape column in the *Wall Street Journal*, pointed this out in a March 19, 2013, article entitled, "Fed's Crystal Ball Could Use Some Shining." There are many experts at the U.S.

Federal Open Market Committee who have the responsibility of making economic forecasts which Federal Reserve officials rely on to make important interest rate decisions. Spencer Jakab states,

> Fed forecasters have erred on the optimistic side on economic growth the past few years, while being too pessimistic on jobs. In early 2011, they saw growth of nearly 4% for 2012 and more than 4% for 2013. That was based on the average of their "central tendency" range that eliminates outlying predictions. The latest reads were 1.75% and 2.65%. But in November 2011, they guessed unemployment would be eight-tenths of a percentage point higher than it turned out to be a year later.

He summarizes his article with the comment,

> That these 19 economic policy makers can't forecast their way out of a paper bag is slightly worrisome. Scarier is how quick some of them have been to suggest new targets—with the ink barely drying on existing ones. Now some of them say the 6.5% unemployment target may be flexible and the end of bond-buying may not necessarily mean selling the Fed's vast holdings of debt.
>
> In the delicate question of how and when to end massive bond purchases, the Fed's message has been: "Trust us, we're experts." That should inspire limited confidence.

In 2011, Dan Gardner wrote a book entitled *Future Babble: Why Expert Predictions Are Next to Worthless and You Can Do Better*, which uses landmark research to show that expert predictions are not reliable. The saying, "Researchers have discovered that people will believe anything that you tell them researchers have discovered," teaches us a truth of human nature. Therefore, it is unlikely that anything will change. The major problem with expert forecasts is that people always have, and likely always will, automatically put more trust in them than is warranted. This tendency is a fault of our human nature.

After I became an investment professional, it did not take me long to realize that economists and analysts raise the forecast after there is evidence of improvement, and reduce their estimates after it is clear that conditions are deteriorating. In a 2012 interview with Bloomberg, David Kotok, CEO of Cumberland Advisors, said, "The only thing we know for certain when forecasting interest rates is that we are wrong." This is what Charlie Munger said about economics at a speech about human misjudgment at Harvard Law School in 1995:

> And I came here because of behavioral economics. How could economics not be behavioral? If it isn't behavioral, what the hell is it? And I think it's fairly clear that all reality has to respect all other reality. If you come to inconsistencies, they have to be resolved, and so if there's anything valid in psychology, economics has to recognize it and vice versa. So I think the people that are working on this fringe between economics and psychology are absolutely right to be there, and I think there's been plenty wrong over the years.

Much more progress needs to be made, since it seems little has changed in economics since that 1995 speech. The Financial Crisis is proof of that.

To be fair, there are some economists who provide very good advice because they have a good understanding of how economies and markets function. They also realize their limitations. U.S. economist Ed Hyman, Chairman of ISI Group, stands out amongst all other U.S. economists. U.S. institutional investors have ranked him as the number one economist for more than thirty consecutive years. He has not developed sophisticated formulas or complicated models. He is an excellent economist because he uses very current, pertinent information. For example, his firm calls car dealerships to get their sales figures every week. This gives ISI Group an immediate insight into consumer confidence and economic activity, instead of waiting for statistics to be released in quarterly reports many weeks or months later. ISI Group is not affiliated with any investment firms, so it has a business model which relies entirely on subscription revenue. This is why Mr. Hyman rarely appears in the media.

Investors need to discern whom to listen to. Cas (James Castrission) and Jonesy (Justin Jones) chronicled their 3,300-kilometer paddle across the Tasman Sea from Australia to New Zealand in a film called *Crossing the Ditch*. In 2011, they set out to be the first people to ski unsupported from the edge of Antarctica to the South Pole and back. All of the other five teams that had tried it had failed. The 2012 *Banff Mountain Film Festival Magazine* reported that the two heard from many different people as they were planning their journey. When they thought of all the people they talked to, Jones said, "Generally they fell into two categories. People who have no clue what they were talking about—and these people were ignored. Or people who are experts in their respective fields or had more experience than us—these were the people that we listened to." Investors also need to discern whom they listen to for advice. Listening to experts in the field and to those who have more experience than us is not good enough when it comes to investment advice. Investors should focus only on experts who have a good track record and ignore most of the others.

British philosopher Bertrand Russell (1872-1970), is known for his work in mathematical logic and analytic philosophy. He wrote, "The whole problem with this world is that fools and fanatics are always so certain of themselves, but wiser men so full of doubts." Be aware that the mainstream media tends to highlight the fools and fanatics with the most outrageous predictions.

Many investors base much of their strategy on how the U.S. or local economy is doing. Mark Skousen is a former CIA economist with a Ph.D. in economics. He wrote, "Wall Street and Main Street are like a rocky marriage with frequent separations, but never a divorce." Economic information can be helpful. However, this respected economist learned that the economic data do not always impact the markets in the way we envision.

While there are some good economists, economic principles, in general, have many flaws. In his book *Economyths: Ten Ways Economics Gets It Wrong*, mathematician David Orrell maintains that the theory behind economics is "less science than an ideology." He says, "Superficially, they have the look and feel of real science, but they are counterfeit coin." According to David Orrell, the ten misconceptions of economics are:

1. The economy can be described by economic laws.
2. The economy is made up of independent individuals.
3. The economy is stable.
4. Economic risk can be easily managed using statistics.
5. The economy is rational and efficient.
6. The economy is gender neutral.
7. The economy is fair.
8. Economic growth can continue forever.
9. Economic growth will make us happy.
10. Economic growth is always good.

Readers may not agree that all of these statements are myths. Nevertheless, history shows that much of what we have accepted as truth does not corroborate what happens in the real world. The conflict in economic "science" was highlighted on October 14, 2013, when the Nobel Memorial Prize in Economic Science was awarded to two leading economic experts with opposing views of how rational markets are. Nobel Prize winner Eugene F. Fama developed the theory that markets accurately reflect all the information that is available. He shared the prize with Robert J. Shiller who collected information proving markets were irrational and inefficient. In spite of all the evidence, investors and the public are still interested in forecasts from experts because we are naturally inclined to use the same processes for making investment decisions that we use for making other choices in life.

When economist and Nobel Laureate Kenneth Arrow was a weather officer in the U.S. Army Air Corps from 1942-1946, a commanding general told him his weather forecasts were useless. Shortly thereafter, a military officer informed Captain Arrow that the same commanding general had requested a current weather forecast. When Captain Arrow questioned the military staffer about this, he replied, "The commanding general is well aware that the forecasts are no good. However, he needs them for planning purposes." No matter what the track record is, we are drawn to forecasts about the future from educated and knowledgeable people. It is our natural instinct.

The media know this and oblige by offering us many long-term predictions about the economy, markets, politics, and weather from reputable organizations. It can be good to listen to what experts are saying, but we must be vigilant to not let it shape our thinking. This is especially true during periods of very strong or weak market activity. At times of extreme highs or lows, it is more important to ascertain the level of investor optimism or optimism in the media than to try to understand what is happening in the economy. That is when it is most important to understand how mass psychology is influencing markets.

When investment news about stocks, gold, oil, or real estate dominates the headlines or becomes the feature story, it is a sign that an investment trend has become so prevalent that it is close to an end. Remember, when everyone who wants to act has acted on the opinion of experts, markets naturally respond by moving in the opposite direction. Very little else works that way, but markets do.

Previous comments mentioned that economists are not scientists. But, even if they were, scientists are not always right either. In 1895, physicist Lord William Kelvin, president of the Royal Society, said, "Heavier-than-air flying machines are impossible." The Wright brothers proved him wrong just eight years later. When I took lifeguard training in the early 1970s, we were taught to perform CPR with five chest compressions for each breath. In 2010, when I was recertifying a First Aid course for my position as a Search and Rescue volunteer, I was taught to do thirty compressions and only two breaths—a radical change! Medical experts used to maintain that the human brain could not survive for more than four minutes without oxygen. They have had to completely rethink their position after free divers, such as Peter Colat from Switzerland, have held their breath for an almost incomprehensible time of nineteen minutes and twenty-one seconds. Experts were forced to change their views in accordance with what non-experts were demonstrating. What used to be accepted as scientific fact turned out not to be a fact at all. Nobel-Prize-winning Austrian zoologist and founder of modern ethology (the study of animal behavior), Konrad Lorenz, wrote, "Truth in science can be defined as the working hypothesis best suited to open the way to the next better one."

As we get older, we tend to experience more and more shocking reversals of what we were taught was sacrosanct. It is very comfortable for us to just accept everything we hear, especially when regarding a topic about which we know very little. It may not be important for us to think critically about everything. However, when it comes to making important decisions about buying a home, starting a business, or making an investment, critical thinking can make a significant difference. Just talk to someone who lost their home in the U.S. after real estate prices collapsed in 2008!

Bernard Baruch was a very successful financier and stock investor in the early 1900s. He stated, "The difference between a rich investor and a poor investor is the quality and timeliness of his information." Perhaps that was true many years ago, but it does not seem to be as important now. The book *How Markets Fail: The Logic of Economic Calamities*, by John Cassidy, makes the case that relying on fundamental information and rational behavior to govern financial markets is illusionary. He shows that despite all the information and expertise in the financial sector, economists and analysts who scrutinize this data to forecast market movements have failed miserably. Consequently, the rationale that many investment decisions are based on is faulty. Economists and analysts explain what they believe the markets should be doing, and they have been wrong many times.

Numerous studies and a recent book by mathematician David Orrell, entitled *The Future of Everything: The Science of Prediction*, explain why predictions are so unreliable. The facts verify that the accuracy of economic predictions is no better than random chance. When it comes to predictions for interest rates, they are only 49% accurate. I learned this from my own experience a long time ago. To drive the point home, consider putting a Harvard-educated economist beside a teenager working at a fast food restaurant and asking them both if they think the economy will improve or get worse. Whose opinion would you listen to? Although it may be hard for us to accept, the teenager has just as much chance of being right as the economist. On November 27, 2012, CXO Advisory Group LLC of Manassas, Virginia, released the results of a study where they tracked the accuracy of sixty market gurus over two years. They were rated on how accurate they were in calling the direction of the U.S. stock market. Their findings show that the average accuracy rate was 48%. Bond manager Bill Gross of PIMCO, who oversees $1.8 trillion, was accurate 46% of the time. Jim Cramer of CNBC's *Mad Money* had a 47% accuracy rate.

Our first reaction is to wonder if these stock market experts are negligent, careless, and poorly informed. However, that is not the case. PIMCO manager Bill Gross oversees almost $2 trillion. He has not earned this level of confidence from investors by being poorly informed. So what does this study tell us? It shows us three things.

First, stock markets were extremely volatile during 2011 and 2012. Second, it is always challenging to predict how any market will behave in the future. In fact, it is almost impossible to predict the future of anything. Third, it means that while we can learn helpful lessons about investing from market experts, we must rely on other factors to make well-informed decisions. It is simply unrealistic for the public to expect that any human being can predict the future, no matter how smart they are, how much money they manage, or how much information they have access to. The best baseball players still strike out six out of ten times at bat. The rating of success in any vocation has to be based on the difficulty of the task. Predicting the future is an extremely challenging vocation!

Television newscasts and newspapers often provide abundant exposure to the forecasts of prominent economic experts. However, the facts show that listening to announcements from economic think tanks or prominent organizations such as the International Monetary Fund is really of little value. Sherry Cooper, formerly an economist at BMO Capital Markets, said that a new economist thinks he knows what is going to happen in the future, while an experienced economist knows that he doesn't know what the economy is going to do in the future. Legendary mutual fund manager Peter Lynch said, "If you have spent more than 13 minutes analyzing economic and market forecasts, you have wasted 10 minutes." Keep this in mind the next time a newscast has a thirteen-minute segment on a high-profile economic forecast.

The same goes for what we read in the news. Former U.S. Vice President and Congressman Adlai E. Stevenson (1835-1914) quipped, "Newspaper editors are men who separate the wheat from the chaff, and then print the chaff." Sadly, this is still true in many cases. Larry Swedroe was chairman of Prudential Home Mortgage and held senior positions at Citicorp. Presently he is Director of Research for BAM Advisor Services, LLC. He has fourteen Simple Rules of Investing. His rule number ten is, "…the forecasts of market strategists and analysts have no value, except for entertainment." It is important to notice that Larry Swedroe is referring only to forecasts of future values. Market strategists and analysts can still provide valuable insights about markets, the economy, sector comparisons, and individual companies.

In 2011, weather forecasters in Canada predicted a colder winter than usual. Instead, it was the warmest on record. Studies have shown that weather forecasts can be reliable for the next two days, and that is about all. Yet, we continue to hear newscasters and people around us warning that it is going to be a cold winter or a hot summer. It is fascinating to observe how interested we are in hearing about long-term economic and weather forecasts, when the facts show that this information is not reliable at all. If human beings acted rationally we would not do this. We do not act rationally because our emotions and instincts impact almost everything we do, from buying a pair of shoes to buying our first home.

Individual analysts usually have to use the data from the economic forecast of the company they work for when forming their opinions and projections for the companies or sectors for which they are responsible. How accurate can a research analyst's report be if it is based on information that has less than a 50% chance of being reliable?

A number of factors contribute to this low level of reliability: 1) We are fallible as human beings. 2) Most economic, financial, and market experts are trained to analyze data from the past. 3) It is almost impossible to forecast surprises. 4) Economists are presented as scientists, so their forecasts are expected to be as accurate as the laws of physics; however, one could achieve the same accuracy of expert advice by simply flipping a coin. 5)

Expert advice is not very reliable because the opinions of experts can work against themselves. Let us provide an example.

If you were going to go on a short flight on an airplane, you would choose your flight and arrive at the airport. If you saw a brand new, good-quality airplane and were introduced to the pilot who had thousands of hours of experience, and if the weather was good, you would likely feel very confident about getting on the plane. However, if the plane's carrying capacity was twenty passengers, would you get on the plane if thirty people carrying their baggage were standing in line to get on? The plane is still reliable, the pilot still has all of his skill, and the weather has not changed. But if all the people standing in line board the plane, it will be unsafe to fly! It is the same with any investment which is priced in a free market. The only difference is that it is not nearly as easy to see if too many investors have "boarded the plane." Very few experts take into account how many investors have come onboard as a result of all the recommendations from other experts. This significant factor affects the supply and demand of an investment, which then impacts the price. If this effect is ignored, a major piece of the investment puzzle is missing.

If we cannot rely on fundamental information and the advice of experienced and knowledgeable market experts to guide us, what can we count on? The next chapter will provide the answer to this question.

6. Following the Trend Is the Cardinal Rule of Investing

This section offers what the authors believe are the best solutions to the ever-present dilemma of dealing with and profiting from markets.

Consider the following scenario: You have some flying experience and have purchased a $100,000 plane kit from Chilliwack's own Murphy Aviation (Dave Harder lives in Chilliwack, B.C. Canada. Chilliwack is an aboriginal word that means "junction or meeting of two rivers.") After the purchase, you spend many hours building the plane in your shop and, finally, after two years of labor, finish it. Now comes the day that you have been waiting for—to fly this beautiful airplane in the Fraser Valley, just east of Vancouver, B.C.

Figure 6.1: The windsock at the Chilliwack Municipal Airport, Chilliwack, B.C. Photo by Dave Harder

As you may know, an airplane gets its lift by having air pass over and under the wing. Let's assume your plane requires an air speed of 50 mph to take off. If there is a 25 mph wind coming from the east, and the plane takes off with the wind, the plane would have to travel at a ground speed of 75 mph in order to lift off. Conversely, if the plane takes off into the wind, it only has to move at a ground speed of 25 mph to lift off.

Planes are designed to be flown, not to be handled on the ground. The slower the plane can go on the runway, the easier it is to take off or land. In addition, winds are often gusty, so the speed of the wind can fluctuate. Therefore, if you are taking off or landing with the wind, and the wind speed suddenly increases, it is much easier to hit an air pocket and crash than if you always take off or land into the wind. Consequently, it is safer to take off and land into the wind rather than with the wind.

Since wind direction is so important, you check the Canadian weather and wind forecast for the Fraser Valley on the day of your inaugural flight. This area is close to the U.S. border, so you also check the U.S. forecast for the area close to the border in order to see if it matches the Canadian forecast. To make sure nothing is overlooked, you check Doppler radar, heat maps, and even marine forecasts for the nearby Pacific Ocean. All forecasts say that the wind is coming from the east at 25 mph. This information makes it easy to determine the direction of takeoff.

However, when you arrive at the airport, you are surprised to observe that the simple windsock beside the runway shows that the wind seems to be coming from the west, not the east as all the forecasts predicted. After you have warmed up the engine and completed the preflight checks, you check the windsock one more time as you taxi towards the runway. The windsock still indicates the wind is coming from the west instead of the east. As the pilot of this expensive plane that took you two years to build, you are faced with a real dilemma. Do you follow all the forecasts from the latest, most advanced weather forecasting tools and software from well-respected government sources? Or do you take off in the direction indicated by a simple piece of red cloth fastened to a ring on top of a pole at the airport? What choice would you make? If you were a Boeing 747 pilot for Air Canada, with 5,000 hours of experience, would your decision be any different?

Physicists, engineers, and other experts use formulas and equations to design bridges, buildings, and airplanes that are reliable because they are dealing with materials that always react to various conditions in a predictable fashion. However, the smartest people or fastest computers in the world cannot create formulas or equations to accurately determine who will win a sporting event, an election, or even the latest episode of the TV series *Survivor*. They also cannot create models that accurately forecast what the weather will be like weeks or months into the future, what interest rates will do, or how stocks, commodities, real estate, or currencies will behave. The reason for this is that nature and human behavior are not entirely predictable.

It seems as though human nature has not changed much over time. The *Proverbs* of Solomon and the sayings of Confucius from the fifth century B.C. are still relevant today. Author Philip Yancey wrote, "I once resolved to read all 38 of Shakespeare's plays in one year…I expected to learn about Shakespeare's world and the people who inhabited it, but I found that Shakespeare mainly taught me about my world." Art Huprich, Senior Vice President and Senior Market Technician for Raymond James Equity Research, developed a list of investment rules. One of his rules is, "There is nothing new on Wall Street. There can't be because speculation is as old as the hills. Whatever happens in the stock market today has happened before and will happen again, mostly due to human nature." While human nature has not changed much, it is not always predictable. Because human nature follows general guidelines and typical patterns, markets follow certain patterns and respond to events in a similar fashion. Thus, it is impossible to pin down exactly when markets will respond, for precisely how long they will react in a certain way (how long a trend will last), or how much prices will move. Consequently, it is impossible to predict exactly how and when the masses will behave in a certain way in economies and markets. This is why Mark Twain reportedly said,

> "History does not repeat itself, but it does rhyme."

Therefore, as mentioned earlier, analyzing human behavior in markets and economies is more of an art than a science. Market specialists have tried to create formulas and equations for how markets will move. Like long-range weather forecasts, making forecasts or predictions based on economic statistics will always be more of an educated guessing game than an outcome on which investors can rely. Consequently, it is far better for market participants to rely on how markets are actually behaving than to count on predictions from traditional analytical tools, news releases, company projections, and analyst opinions. Here is what John J. Murphy, the father of intermarket technical analysis, said in a book entitled *Technical Analysis of the Futures Markets* (New York Institute of Finance, 1986):

> "It follows then, that if everything that affects market price is ultimately reflected in market prices, then the study of market price is all that is necessary."

A moving average crossover is one of the best tools an investor can use to study prices. It shows investors how markets are really behaving so that they can act appropriately. Let's look at moving averages first and moving average crossovers later. Moving averages are not forecasting tools. They are like a windsock or a Global Positioning System (GPS) device. A GPS unit does not predict where you will be in the future. It only tells where you are now. It is not attempting to predict the future. Neils Bohr said, "Prediction is very difficult, especially if it's about the future." It is much simpler and easier if one does not attempt to predict the future. Like a GPS, moving averages do not predict the future either. They only tell us what people are doing with their money at the present time. However, that is what makes them reliable—they show us what individual and professional investors are actually doing with their money every day or week, based on all the variables. Forecasts and market predictions only tell us what experts think people should be doing with their money. There is a huge difference between the two!

Figure 6.2: A weather system on a yacht. Photo by Dave Harder

All that is needed to determine the current weather is a thermometer, barometer, weather vane, and a rain gauge. If one wants to try to provide a forecast for the future, much more sophisticated equipment is required. It looks very impressive and is difficult for an ordinary person to use, but studies show that even specialized equipment does little to increase the accuracy of forecasts for more than two days into the future. Many times investment strategies are the same way. We often believe that more sophisticated investment systems are superior to simpler strategies, yet that is not usually the case.

A moving average (MA) is very simple. (See the examples in Figures 6.3 and 6.4.) It is the average price for an asset over a certain period of time. For example, a 200-day MA is simply the average price for an asset over the last 200 trading days. Each new day the closing price of an asset is added to the total number, and the closing price 201 trading days earlier is subtracted. Many market watchers use 200-day moving averages as a guide. If the price of an asset rises above the 200-day MA, it is confirmation that the price trajectory is up. If the price declines below the 200-day MA, it is confirmation that the price is weak and in a downtrend.

Investors who use this tool buy an investment when the price rises above the 200-day moving average and sell when it declines below the 200-day MA. No indicator is perfect, including moving averages. Moving averages do not give a signal to buy at the exact low or sell at the exact high. Because a moving average evens out price volatility, there is a lag time before it gives a buy or sell signal. While this can be frustrating, it enables investors to capture most of a trending upside move—and trends can last longer than we can ever imagine. Edgar S. Genstein said, "You should sell when you wish you had sold sooner, never when you think the top has arrived. That way you will never get the best price…But some of your profits will be large and your losses should be quite small. In order to be successful, investors have to be content with being approximately right instead of precisely wrong. This can be difficult to accept for those who want everything done just right. Accounting is exact—investing is not."

From the time we are young we are told that the object of investing is to buy low and sell high. This is a misconception. Just because enough people have repeated it long enough does not mean it is true. As mentioned in the preface, the late financier Bernard Baruch stated, "Don't try to buy at the bottom or sell at the top. It can't be done—except by liars." The object of investing is to buy when prices have already started an uptrend and to sell when they have already started a downtrend. Investing is like being a defender on a soccer team. A defender pulls back into his own end when the opposing team has possession of the ball and is advancing. It is only after his teammate has possession of the ball and the defenseman is quite certain that the ball is going to move to the opposing end that he runs ahead to keep pace with the ball. A defender does not run toward the opposing goal just because the ball has been in his own end too long, or because a weaker player has the ball and he thinks he might lose possession of it. He remains alert and patiently waits until the ball is actually moving away from his own end in a convincing fashion before he moves away from his own goal. Wayne Gretsky said, "Skate where the puck is going." That is a good analogy for investing, too.

> Invest where the money is going, not where you think it might go.

Trying to buy at the exact low or sell at the exact high is even more difficult than trying to pick the hottest and coldest days of the year to the exact hour. No one I know tries to do that, and nobody expects anyone else to do that. A farmer does not wait to plant crops until the coldest day. In most cases, he or she waits until the weather has warmed up enough that the risk of frost is over. Markets or stocks can be very volatile on the day of the exact high or low. Some investors always bemoan the fact that they were not advised to sell right at the high or buy at the low. They have no idea how impossible that is.

Even if one is following the trends, the price can move above and then back below a moving average in a short period of time. This is called whip-sawing. Keep in mind that people pay a price to buy insurance for many things in life. The chance of sometimes having to reverse course quickly at a loss is the price of having a circuit breaker that provides portfolio protection. However, in most cases, using the 200-day MA as confirmation can enable investors to capture most of a longer-term upside move and to avoid most of a longer-term decline. Shorter-term moving averages can also work in the short term. A Buddhist proverb says, "If we are facing the right direction, all we have to do is keep on walking."

Figures 6.3 and 6.4 show the price action and 200-day MA of the Dow Jones Industrial Average (DJIA) from 1925-1932. The black line is the DJIA and the red line is the 200-day MA. The arrows show when the DJIA crossed above and below the 200-day MA. Using just this simple indicator and absolutely no other input would have enabled an investor to capture most of the upside move of the DJIA from the 150 level in 1926 to over 350 in 1929. A sell signal was triggered when the DJIA fell to the red MA at the 325 level a month before the famous 1929 Stock Market Crash.

Figure 6.4 shows that the DJIA stayed below the 200-day MA for three years as it fell 78% from 325 to the 70 level in 1932. If an investor had been stranded on a deserted island from 1925 to 1933 and only had this one indicator to look at for a few minutes a week, he or she could have had excellent results.

Figure 6.3: Chart of 200-Day Moving Average for the DJIA 1925-1929. Source: Thomson Reuters

Figure 6.4: Chart of 200-Day Moving Average for the DJIA 1928-1932.
Source: Thomson Reuters

Investors may also combine a shorter-term moving average with a longer-term moving average, which may provide a trend change signal. For example, a buy signal would be triggered if a 50-day MA crossed above the 200-day MA. This is called a moving average crossover. When this happens on a major stock market index, it is referred to as a golden cross, indicating that prices are starting a major trend to the upside. In a February 11, 2012, *Wall Street Journal* article, Brenda Conway and Tomi Kilgore said, "Since 1975, the S&P 500 has been higher a year after the appearance of a golden cross 94% of the time, according to Schaefer's Investment Research, with an average gain of almost 13%. The NASDAQ Composite has risen 91% of the time." The Dow Jones Industrial Average experienced a golden cross at the start of 2012. The S&P 500 and NASDAQ Composite produced a golden cross in late January 2012. The Russell 2000 Index, Euro STOXX 50, and U.K.'s FTSE 100 hit the golden cross in early February 2012.

Conversely, when the 50-day MA for a major market index such as the S&P 500 declines below the 200-day MA, it is called a death cross. Sometimes serious declines occur after this happens. The most recent death cross occurred during the European Debt Crisis on August 11, 2011, when the S&P 500 was already 15% below the summer high. In an August 12, 2011, article Simon Maierhofer stated, "There were some false alarms, but the damage of the misfires was miniscule compared to the benefit of the warnings which is reflected in the 19.7% average gain of a winning trade (7.6% average for a losing trade). To sum it up in one sentence, the SMA crossover is correct 6 out of 10 times with a risk/reward ratio of 3:1 in favor of the investor. One interesting little factoid about the 2000 and 2007 death cross is that the signals—albeit late—occurred right before the next powerful decline." North American equity markets did not fall much more than 20% from the 2011 highs, so the death cross was not very accurate in 2011. The death cross is not as reliable as the golden cross.

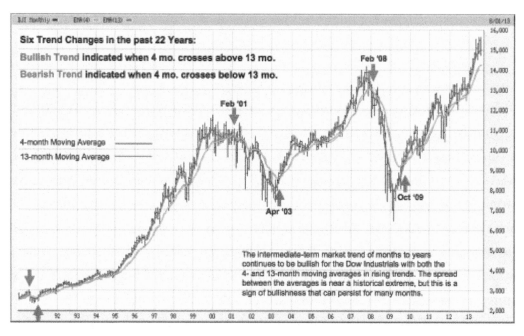

Figure 6.5: Chart provided courtesy of Bigcharts.com and Bob Dickey, Technical Analyst

Figures 6.5 and 6.6 show examples of a moving average (MA) crossover. The red line is a 4-month moving average and the green line is a 13-month moving average. When the red MA crosses above the green MA, it is a buy signal. Figure 6.5 illustrates these signals from 1991 to 2013. Figure 6.6 shows the signals from 1970 to 1990. There are many variations of moving average crossovers, using different periods of time. The shorter the time periods, the quicker a buy or sell signal is triggered. The negative aspect of a quicker signal is that there will be more trading activity and a greater chance of being whipsawed. If one chooses to use a longer time frame for the moving averages, there will be less trading activity and less likelihood of being whipsawed.

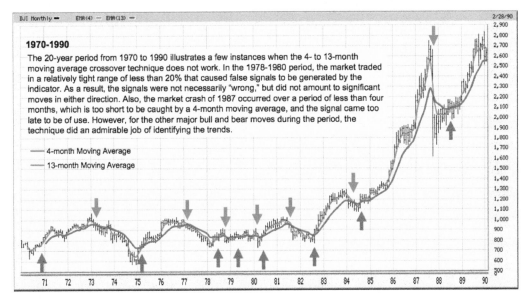

Figure 6.6: Chart provided courtesy of Bigcharts.com and Bob Dickey, Technical Analyst

The charts above point out another major benefit of using moving average crossovers: they work in any type of market environment! There was almost no fundamental research warning of a market decline during 2008, which confirms that investors cannot rely on fundamental research to provide warnings of increasing risk. When stock prices fell to so-called attractive valuations in September 2008, prices still fell much further. How cheap is cheap? Value investing did not work very well in 2008 either. Before investing in mathematical models, portfolio managers knew that these types of disciplines only worked 99% of the time. When the "one percent of the time" period arrived in 2008, they failed. What is the use of wearing a seatbelt if we know it will fail in a serious accident?

Quantitative and qualitative strategies also failed in 2008, as almost every asset fell sharply while the U.S. dollar, government bonds, and the Japanese

Yen rose. Investors must use tools that they can count on to work all of the time, especially during the one percent of time when there is extreme volatility. They should also work during an outlying event or surprise like the Financial Crisis. The quote below verifies that moving average crossovers worked during one of the longest bear markets from 2000 to 2003, and during one of the most severe bear markets from 2007 to 2009. John Murphy has said, "One of the great strengths of technical analysis is its adaptability to virtually any trading medium and time dimension." Consequently, moving average crossovers are one of the most basic and useful tools of technical analysis.

Moving averages provide investors with a discipline to follow in order to implement sound strategies. Everyone knows the saying, "Buy low and sell high." How low is low? Is a 10% correction low enough to buy? Should one wait for a bear market of 20% or more? What if there is a huge decline of more than 35%, or more than 50%, as in 2008-2009? Moving averages can help investors to be patient and to wait until selling is exhausted. This is the necessary requisite for markets to rise. How high is too high? After 1999, oil prices quadrupled from $10 to $40 some years later. John (Jack) Bogle, the founder and retired CEO of The Vanguard Group, said, "When reward is at its pinnacle, risk is near at hand." Was $40 too high for oil prices? Was $80 overvalued? No. Prices climbed to more than $140 in 2008. Selling at $80 could have tempted investors to succumb to the pressure of missing out on a big move and to buy back in at $140, when analysts were saying prices would rise to $200. Instead of making a profit, that would have put investors in a position to suffer from losses as oil prices proceeded to fall by more than $100 per barrel, from $145 to below $40 in just a few months during the last half of 2008. Just imagine how painful that would have been!

Experts say it is prudent to hang on to winners and to sell losing positions. However, how much should an investment fall before it is sold? Moving average crossovers can provide clear points for selling or buying.

Warren Buffett has said that investors should be fearful when others are greedy, and greedy when others are fearful. That is very wise advice. However, how much fear is enough fear? There was a high degree of fear in the summer of 2001, when stock prices had already declined for almost a year after the technology boom came to an end. Then terrorists attacked the U.S. on September 11, 2001, and created even more fear, which resulted in even lower share prices. Could there ever be more fear than there was after September 11, 2001? We don't know for certain. Even so, from the close of trading on September 17, 2001 (the first day of trading after the terrorist attacks) to the close of trading a year later on September 17, 2002, the S&P 500 fell 15.9%.

In the fall of 2008, the Volatility Index (or Fear Index as it is often called) continued to rise until it was higher than at any time after the 1987 Crash. The moving average crossovers illustrated in this chapter stayed negative from the summer of 2008 until April 2009, helping investors determine when fear had peaked and when it was safe to buy again.

In the following pages, you will see examples of the moving average crossovers I prefer to use for various investments. The long-term moving average crossovers use three-week and nine-week moving averages. These moving average crossovers are proprietary tools that are enhanced in order to reduce the overall number of signals as well as the number of false signals.

For a moving average, one bar is subtracted and added each month. When the bars turn green, it is a buy signal. When the bars turn from green to red, it is a sell signal. When the bars become shorter, there is greater likelihood of a trend change. The data for these charts is compiled by Thomson Reuters.

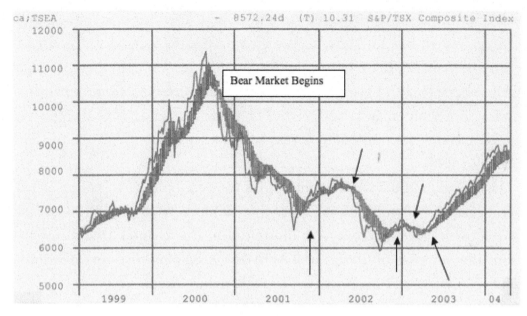

Figure 6.7: Long-Term Moving Average Crossover for S&P/TSX Composite Index 1999 to March 2004. Data for chart compiled by Thomson Reuters

Figure 6.7 is a chart of a long-term moving average crossover for the Canadian TSX Index (the Toronto Stock Exchange Index which is now named the S&P/TSX) from 1999 to 2004. The long-term trend indicator for the DJIA, NASDAQ, and S&P 500 also followed this pattern very closely. Each bar represents one week. Every week, one bar is removed from five years ago and a new one is added for the current week. The trend remained positive (green) for two years, from the fall of 1998 until after markets peaked in September 2000. In spite of strong rallies in January and April 2001, the longer-term trend remained negative (red) until late October 2001. The sell-off after the terrorist attacks on September 11, 2001, actually ended the year-long decline from the September 2000 peak to the lows printed on September 21, 2001, only a few business days after the New York Stock Exchange reopened for trading. The arrow shows when the long-term trend turned positive again in November 2002. The lack of a double bottom in a bear market was a sign that the decline was not over. Nevertheless, North American markets rallied for six months before the final leg of the longest bear market since 1975 ensued. North American indices experienced a 20% drop near the final bear market lows at the end of July 2002. The TSX dropped to a lower low in October 2002, but the S&P 500 October low was very close to the July 2002 low, finally forming a double bottom. Markets only made slow upside progress until late January 2003, since the United States was planning to attack Iraq. Once again, markets dipped slightly into March 2003. Then, when investors were on tenterhooks due to the threat of the SARS (Severe Acute Respiratory Syndrome) virus and the invasion of Iraq, global markets started moving higher in a steady fashion. Although it seemed impossible to believe at the time, global stock markets were starting a five-year rally with no corrections greater than 10%. The moving average crossovers were not perfect; however, they were very helpful in determining the major turning points over a most challenging two and a half years.

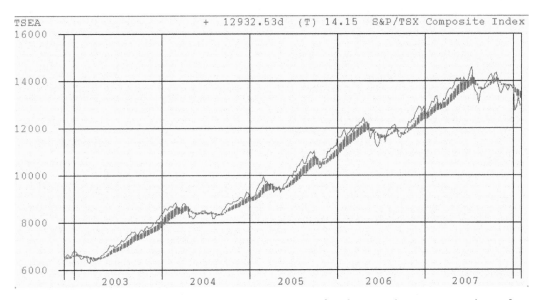

Figure 6.8: Long-Term Moving Average Crossover for the S&P/TSX Composite Index 2003-2007. Data for charts compiled by Thomson Reuters

The Long-Term Moving Average Crossover (LTMAC) for the S&P/ TSX was positive (green) for twelve months from March 2003 to March 2004. After some minor volatility during the summer of 2004, the LTMAC remained positive for almost two years until spring 2006. After a minor dip in the summer of 2006, the LTMAC turned positive and stayed positive for another twelve months until the summer of 2007. This enabled investors to capture much of the upside from March 2003 to 2007.

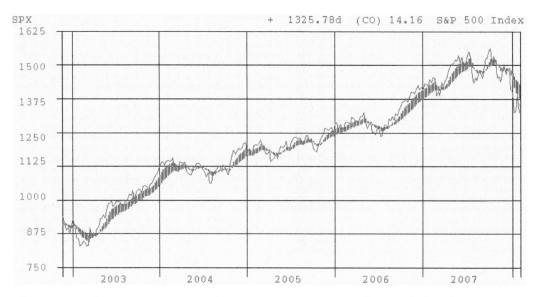

Figure 6.9: The Long-Term Moving Average Crossover (LTMAC) for the S&P 500 Index 2003-2007. Data for charts compiled by Thomson Reuters

The LTMAC for the S&P 500 Index was very helpful during the March 2003 to 2004 rally. However, from 2004 to the summer of 2006, investors were whipsawed by too many buy and sell signals. It often works best to act on a buy or sell signal if the LTMAC changes for the S&P 500 and another major market average such as the S&P/TSX Index or the iShares S&P Global 100 Stock Index Fund.

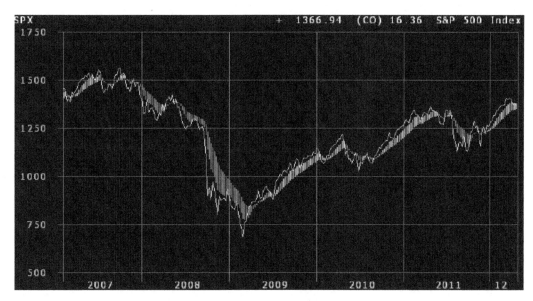

Figure 6.10: Long-Term Moving Average Crossover for S&P 500 Index from 2007 to March 2012. Chart data compiled by Thomson Reuters

The background color for the charts in the weekly Harder updates was changed from yellow to black a few years ago to enable the red and green bars to stand out more. This chart in Figure 6.10 shows the long-term moving average crossover for the S&P 500 Index from 2007 to 2012. When the chart turns green, it is a buy signal. When it turns red, it is a sell signal. If I were on a deserted island and could have only one piece of information for making investment decisions for equities, the indicator for the S&P 500, the LTMAC shown in Figure 6.10, would be my choice.

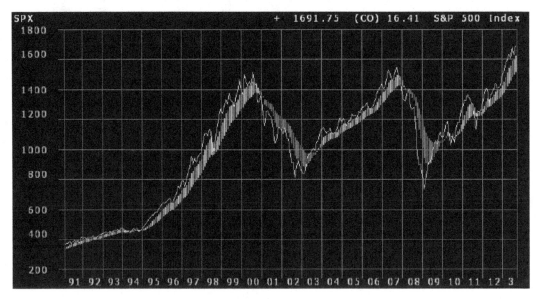

Figure 6.11: Very Long-Term Moving Average Crossover for the S&P 500 1990-2011. This chart is a good indicator for determining very long-term trend changes, capturing most of the upside and avoiding most of the downside. The Very Long-Term Moving Average Crossovers use moving averages for three-month and nine-month periods. Chart data compiled by Thomson Reuters

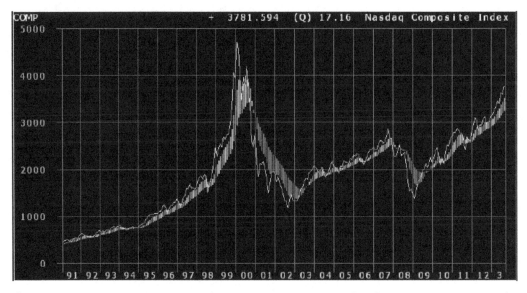

Figure 6.12: Very Long-Term Moving Average Crossover for the NASDAQ Composite Index 1990-2011. Chart data compiled by Thomson Reuters

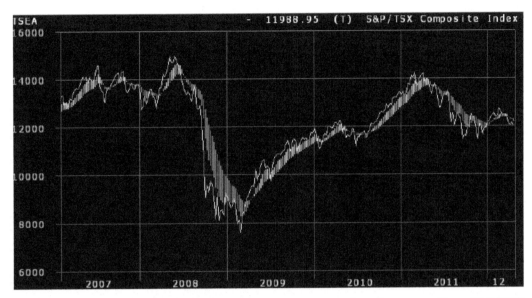

Figure 6.13: Long-Term Moving Average Crossover for the Canadian S&P/TSX Composite Index from 2007 to March 2012. Chart data compiled by Thomson Reuters

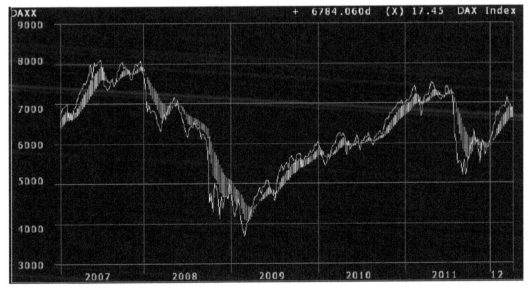

Figure 6.14: Long-Term Moving Average Crossover for the German DAX Index. Chart data compiled by Thomson Reuters

The LTMAC produced a sell signal for the DAX in early 2008 and mid-2011. It triggered a buy signal after the bear market low in early 2009, and again in January 2012. There were only five trend changes during this period, and they were all accurate, making the DAX Index one of the best proxies for the trend of global equity markets during this period.

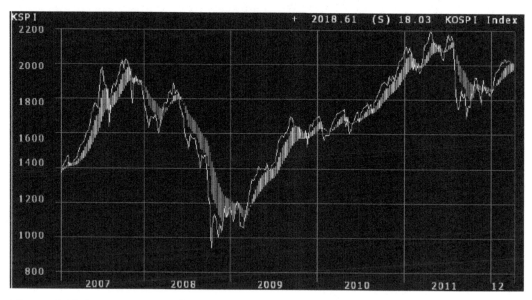

Figure 6.15: Long-Term Moving Average for the Korean Stock Exchange KOSPI Index in South Korea. Chart data compiled by Thomson Reuters

While the magnitude of the trend may vary, global markets have generally moved in the same direction for the last hundred years. (The Japanese Nikkei 225 Index has been an exception since 1989.) It was a rare exception when U.S. equity markets rose approximately 10% from June 2011 to June 2012, when most other global markets fell close to 10%.

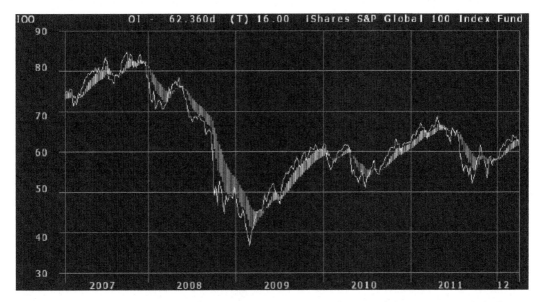

Figure 6.16: Long-Term Moving Average Crossover for the iShares S&P Global 100 Index Fund ETF, representing 100 of the largest companies around the world. Chart data compiled by Thomson Reuters

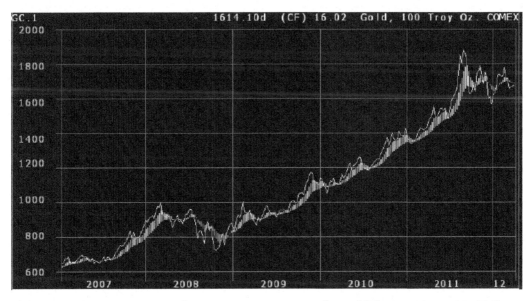

Figure 6.17: Long-Term Moving Average Crossover for gold from 2007 to 2012. Chart data compiled by Thomson Reuters

Notice how this LTMAC for gold in Figure 6.17 remained positive for almost three years from the $800 level in late 2008 to the $1,700 level in late 2011 in spite of volatility. Trading too frequently can reduce returns. In the authors' opinion, the LTMAC strikes the best possible balance between buying and holding and active trading. Before I started my career in the world of finance, I bought and held some gold futures contracts from late 1979 to early 1980, when gold was in the final stages of its long-term uptrend. When I called my commodity broker to sell and take some big profits, he told me that I was the only one of his clients who had really made any money from the big rise in gold prices. All of his other clients were just too reactive and had jumped in and out, thus giving away much of their profit.

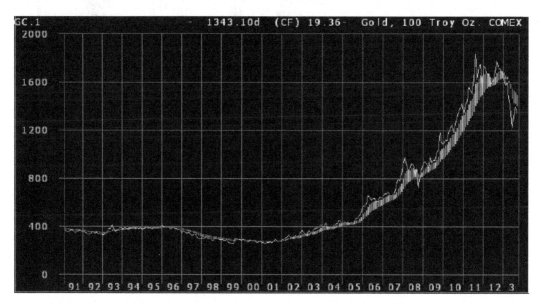

Figure 6.18: Very Long-Term Moving Average Crossover for gold from 1991 to April 26, 2013. Chart data compiled by Thomson Reuters

Notice how the Very Long-Term Moving Average Crossover for gold has provided only two buy signals (1993 and 2001) over this 22-year period. It has also produced only two sell signals. The first sell signal was triggered in 1996, and the second sell signal occurred on April 26, 2013, when a red bar appeared for the first time since 2001. Look carefully at the right hand side of the chart in Figure 6.18 at the $1,600 level to see this. Gold bullion ended that week at a price of US$1,453.60, as you can see at the top of the chart. This indicator suggests that the decade-long uptrend could be over. Gold seems to have 16- to 18-year uptrends and downtrends. In this day and age, these periods are like epochs. There are times to own gold or increase gold holdings, and there are times to sell or reduce positions. This indicator provides a good discipline for making those decisions. If the long-term rise of gold is over, investors and precious metal mining executives need to plan for a more challenging environment. If there is merely a pause in the longer-term uptrend, this indicator will turn positive again. It is better to face reality than to be an eternal optimist.

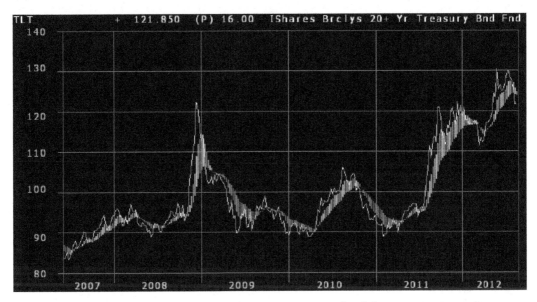

Figure 6.19: Long-Term Moving Average Crossover for iShares 20+ Year Treasury Bond ETF (Exchange Traded Fund). Data compiled by Thomson Reuters

The ETF in Figure 6.19 (TLT) owns long-term U.S. Treasury bonds that mature in 20 years or more. Long-term U.S. bonds have been volatile over the years, so there have been many buy and sell signals. No indicator is perfect for every investment all of the time. Even so, the chart in Figure 6.19 has been a good indicator that the environment for riskier assets is increasing. Cash can be invested in longer-term bonds when this indicator turns green and sold when it turns red.

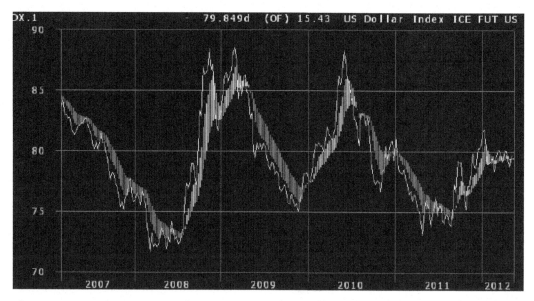

Figure 6.20: Long-Term Moving Average Crossover for the U.S. Dollar Index. Chart data compiled by Thomson Reuters

The LTMAC in Figure 6.20 has produced few signals and has still captured most of the gains and avoided most of the losses for the U.S. Dollar Index from 2007 to 2012.

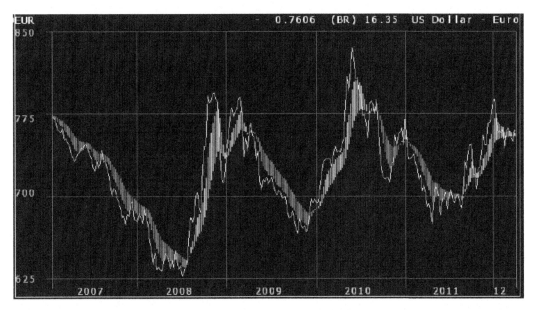

Figure 6.21: Long-Term Moving Average Crossover for the U.S. Dollar compared to the Euro. This chart is very similar to the one in Figure 6.20. Chart data compiled by Thomson Reuters

There was a famous quote by the late Sir John Templeton: "Bull markets are born on pessimism, grow on skepticism, mature on optimism and die on euphoria." This is such an astute statement that it will be mentioned again in the chapter "The Cycle of Market Emotions." However, at exactly what point is there enough pessimism? When does optimism shift to euphoria? There was euphoria in 2000. There was euphoria in the U.S. housing market in 2006. However, there was not a hint of euphoria for stock markets in 2007 or 2008 before global stock markets collapsed.

When does normal crowd behavior make the transition to irrational behavior? There are a few traders who have the skill or the sixth sense that enables them to determine that. Sometimes they can sell close to the high or buy very near a low. However, for most others, it can be difficult to detect when investors are stampeding to buy or sell. Just because markets are exhibiting signs of herd behavior does not mean prices will necessarily reverse direction either. Moving average crossovers alert investors after prices have reached a peak when people have been buying in an irrational manner.

They also notify us after values have reached a low when individual and professional investors have been selling in an irrational manner. (Sophisticated investors are not immune from getting caught up in irrational behavior.) Baron Rothschild was a member of the Rothschild banking family and an 18th century nobleman who made a fortune buying investments during the panic after the Battle of Waterloo. He is credited with saying, "Buy when there is blood in the streets, even if it is your own." Sometimes a market sell-off in response to a military conflict does indeed create a buying opportunity. However, on other occasions, financial markets can continue to decline until there is a resolution. Buying stocks automatically every time the markets fall for a few days after there is a crisis somewhere in the world is not a prudent strategy, especially if equity markets are already in a longer-term downtrend. It is much safer to ensure that the market's momentum is acting in one's favor before making a decision to invest when, tragically, there has been "blood in the streets." Consequently, moving average crossovers provide a reliable tool anyone can use to identify emotional turning points and determine when to be a contrarian investor. Expert traders can also use moving average crossovers as an unemotional safety check to ensure they have not missed a major turning point for an investment when there have been signs of extreme optimism or pessimism.

As mentioned above, moving average crossovers provide a decisive signal when there has been enough pessimism to flush out all of those who want to sell, which is a necessary prerequisite for a new bull market to be born. Sometimes it only takes a 3% to 5% correction to eliminate excess enthusiasm. During long bull market runs like 1982 to 1987 and 2003 to 2007, the S&P 500 never corrected much more than 10%. Consequently, in 1987 and 2008, markets needed to correct 40% or more in order to create enough pessimism to exhaust the selling so that markets could turn up again.

Stock trading legend Jesse Livermore (1877-1940), also known as the Great Bear of Wall Street or the Boy Plunger, became famous for making and losing multimillion-dollar fortunes in the 1900s. Many of the lessons he learned were passed on in a popular book, *Reminiscences of a Stock Operator*, written by Edwin Lefevre. Livermore had this to say about fear and greed:

"The successful investor has to fight these two deep-seated instincts. He has to reverse what you might call his natural impulses. Instead of hoping, he must fear; instead of fearing he must hope. He must fear that his loss may develop into a much larger loss and hope that his profit may become a big profit." By making and losing fortunes trading his own money, Livermore concluded that the most money is made by following the longer-term, major trends, not day-to-day fluctuations. Baron Rothschild remarked, "You can have the top 20% and bottom 20% and I will have the middle." Livermore went on to say, "The point is not so much to buy as cheap as possible or go short at top price, but to buy or sell at the right time." Since longer-term moving average crossovers, like those shown on these pages, identify longer-term trends, and produce a clear signal for when to buy or sell, they can give investors confidence at the right time, not the wrong time. They can also show an investor when he or she should have fear and act on it. Most importantly, they often enable investors to determine the major long-term trends and thus when to buy or sell as close to the right time as is reasonably possible in this day and age.

The first time I used the long-term moving average crossovers was in 2002. Let me provide some background. In 1994, I recommended the shares of a small fuel cell company called Ballard Power Systems to my clients. Most of my clients invested less than 10% of their portfolio in this company, which had links to Daimler Benz and Ford Motor Company. By the time technology stocks had peaked in March of 2000, the price of the shares had increased from CDN$3.30 to $200, including a three-to-one share split. A client who invested $100,000 in this stock in 1994 had a position worth $6 million at the peak in 2000.

After the technology bubble burst, the share price of Ballard Power Systems fell sharply. Having started my career as an Investment Professional in 1981, I had experienced the grueling recession and bear market in 1982, the shocking crash of 1987, and the doldrums of the early 1990s. As another bear market unfolded in early 2001, I knew I had to do something different. In the 1990s it was easy to just buy, hold, and prosper. It seemed as though the time for counting on that strategy had ended. After Nobel-Prize-winning economists and well-respected traders almost created a financial crisis with the collapse of Long-Term Capital Management (LTCM) in the summer of 1998, I had to create an investment discipline that was simple and reliable in any type of market conditions.

When I attended Trinity Western College (now called Trinity Western University) in Langley, B.C., from 1973 to 1975, I heard a guest speaker who was the top psychologist for General Motors. He encouraged us to find something we enjoyed doing and to be better at it than anyone else. With this encouragement in mind, I studied every market timing tool or indicator I could find and tried every investment method that held promise. After twenty years of doing this, I felt somewhat like Thomas Edison when he said, "I have not failed. I have just found 10,000 ways that do not work." I had to find a disciplined way to make prudent market decisions for my clients. Making decisions during the 2001 bear market was like working in sudden death overtime. Clients, friends, and family members were relying on me. They deserved the best advice I could possibly offer them. In addition, I did not know how many more times my mind and body could go through the stress and anguish of a bear market. In response, I considered all of the variables that affected investing and distilled them. After doing this analysis, I came to the conclusion there is one important factor which supersedes them all.

After this intense study, it was time to apply what I had learned. The shares of Ballard Power were in an uptrend along with most other stocks soon after the September 11, 2001, terrorist attacks. Based on what I discovered, the outlook turned negative for Ballard Power shares in January 2002 when the shares were at CAD$52.00, 75% below the record high of over $200 almost two years earlier. After holding the shares and following the company very closely for eight years, I now had to make a very difficult decision in my clients' best interest. Knowing that I could always buy back if the trend changed for the better, I sent a letter to all of my clients who owned the shares, advising them to sell. At the $50 level, the shares had still appreciated 1,500% over eight years.

Looking back, I am thankful that I applied the lessons I had learned, because the share price eventually drifted down to less than $1.00 per share! The discipline I had developed also suggested that the risk of a decline in North American market averages increased in March 2002. Even though it seemed like the bear market had come to an end in September 2001, I recommended that my clients move most of their equities into cash in Canadian dollars at that time. After that, the S&P 500 fell 26% during July 2002. Finally, a dream had come true. While there was "wailing and gnashing of teeth" amongst investors and portfolio managers in July 2002, I was able to relax and sit by the beach. Recalling that time, an experienced money manager from Toronto said that the only thing missing was a swarm of locusts around his office tower. Soichiro Honda has said, "Success represents the 1% of your work which results from the 99% that is called failure." In the summer of 2002, I realized that I was closer to discovering the essence of investing than I had ever been before.

In March 2010, Jon Corzine, former CEO of Goldman Sachs and former governor of New Jersey, was appointed CEO and Chairman of MF Global, a major global commodity brokerage firm. He was a very experienced trader. The management at this multinational futures broker and bond dealer thought they could take advantage of the fear investors had about higher risk European government bonds. They followed Mr. Buffett's advice to become greedy when others were fearful and Mr. Templeton's advice that bull markets are born on pessimism. They presumed that European authorities would support these bond prices. However, the bonds MF Global purchased kept falling in price. By October 2011, the losses were so severe that MF Global was forced to declare bankruptcy. It ranked as one of the ten biggest bankruptcies in U.S. history. This experience is just one more high-profile example illustrating how important it is that investors ensure that the trend has changed in their favor before making a major investment, even when fear and pessimism are so thick they can be cut with a knife.

The NASDAQ almost tripled in the three years after Alan Greenspan believed that there was irrational exuberance, or greed, in late 1996. The long-term moving averages allowed investors to stay invested for almost the entire powerful advance from 1996 to November 2000. This captured most of the gains from 1996 to 2000 and missed most of the declines from 2000 to March 2003. Moving average crossovers can provide investors with the tools to implement age-old guidelines of investing in a disciplined manner.

Many investors are tempted to invest more money if prices fall below the original cost of an investment. This strategy is called averaging down, because investing more money in the asset lowers the average cost of the earlier buys. Howard Gold said, "If a stock is a good investment at $20, it's a steal at $10." That is a dangerous statement to make. How does one really know if it is a good investment if it has dropped that much? Averaging down has been a major factor in most trading disasters. The only time an investor should add to a losing position is after the moving average crossovers have confirmed a change in the trend. This is the only condition that supports adding capital to a losing position. Michael D. Sheimo, an author of several books about investing, wrote,

"It is better to average up than down."

Remember that trends can last much longer than anyone expects, so wait for an actual trend change instead of trying to anticipate it. Since 1958, Richard Russell has written *Dow Theory Letters*, the oldest investment newsletter written by one person. According to him, "A bull market bails you out of mistakes. Bear markets make you pay for your mistakes." Investors who buy or average down in a bear market often pay a higher price than most other investors.

Some investors think that their portfolios will be insulated from market volatility because they have invested in some of the largest, safest companies in the world that sell products consumers will continue to buy even if the economy deteriorates. This type of thinking ignores the fact that when markets fall, the biggest and best companies might actually be the easiest for investors and portfolio managers to sell in order to quickly raise some cash. In most bear markets, few investments escape the carnage. After having experienced this kind of scenario, traders circulated the saying, "When police raid the house of ill repute, they take the piano player too." During most bear markets, there is nowhere to hide other than cash.

Contrary indicators, such as insider buying or selling and investor sentiment, are also very helpful for investors. (Directors and officials of a company are called insiders. If they buy or sell shares in the company they are connected with, they must file reports with government regulators.) For decades, *Investors Intelligence* in New York has been providing advisory sentiment figures for investors. I have been a long-time subscriber. It provides weekly data showing the percentage of investment newsletter writers who are optimistic or pessimistic. Information about advisory sentiment, investor sentiment, and insider buying or selling is useful as a guide. Even so, market trends can continue for long periods of time before they respond to extreme levels of bullish or bearish sentiment or high insider buying or selling. Using moving average crossovers together with these useful tools can enhance investors' ability to be more accurate in determining a prudent time to buy and sell.

When investors meet with investment professionals, they sometimes complete a Risk Tolerance Questionnaire and receive a Financial Plan. This plan will state how much a person will need to put aside for retirement to achieve his or her goals, or what the return of an investment portfolio should be over time. Since equity markets had performed so well throughout the 1980s and 1990s, the acceptable rate of return to use for long-term returns in the year 2000 was 10%, and even went as high as 12%.

However, markets performed very poorly from 2000 to 2012. Consequently, by 2012 the acceptable rate of return to use for long-term equity returns dropped to 6% or even less. Remember, human beings have the natural tendency to extrapolate current trends into the future. Very long-term data suggest that 8% is a more accurate figure. Investors who received a financial plan in 1999 showing they had enough savings to retire in 2000, and did so, might well have experienced quite a shock ten years later. They found that the financial plan they thought was accurate was not very reliable. Lower than expected returns, extreme volatility, and current events have caused investor anxiety for many years. Long-term plans are easy to agree to and follow when there is smooth sailing. However, when markets fall and the news is bleak, some investors cannot withstand the emotional pressure to sell. Usually, these investors end up selling very close to the low.

Long-time stock market analyst Bob Farrell was the Chief Strategist at Merrill Lynch & Co. from the late 1960s to the late 1990s. He wrote his famous "10 Market Rules to Remember" from his experience. His rule number 6 is,

"Fear and greed are stronger than long-term resolve."

Santa Clara University finance professor Meir Statman said, "Investors can be their own worst enemy, particularly when emotions take hold. Gains make us exuberant; they enhance well-being and promote optimism." His research on investor behavior shows that "losses bring sadness, disgust, fear, regret. Fear increases the sense of risk and some react by shunning stocks." The disciplined use of moving average crossovers can help investors to have the confidence to go against their feelings and reduce exposure to risk after prices have peaked. Unless they have many years of experience, a number of investors who say they are "in it for the long term" when conditions are favorable will suddenly change their minds and sell near the low when markets fall sharply. *Forbes* magazine editor Steve Forbes reiterated this when he said,

"Everyone is a disciplined long-term investor until the market goes down."

It is much better to use long-term moving average crossovers to reduce long positions when they turn negative slightly below the highs than to do nothing and stand by while an investor forces his advisor or portfolio manager to throw in the towel at the worst point, well below the highs.

Moreover, investors are more likely to continue to have confidence in an investment professional who at least takes some action to reduce long positions in response to this discipline than in someone who is always providing an optimistic forecast in the midst of a long or severe bear market. Moving average crossovers can help investors deal with fear and greed so that they can stick to their long-range plans and maintain their long-term resolve. An investor is much more likely to stick to the discipline of a financial plan if a portfolio manager has a discipline which manages the risk and volatility of the portfolio. Moving average crossovers provide this discipline. Taking at least some action can be better than just buying, holding, and suffering. A later chapter, "It is Time for a Revolutionary Change in Portfolio Management," offers advice on when it is critical to act on moving average crossovers.

Suggesting that investors should always have a certain asset mix, such as 60% equities and 40% fixed income, for example, is like asking everyone in New York to wear a pair of jeans and a long-sleeved shirt all year round. Wearing a pair of jeans and a long-sleeved shirt would be comfortable most of the time. However, there would be times in the winter when a person would be very cold, and times in the summer when he or she would find the heat unbearable. Maintaining a 60% equity position during a severe, long-term sell-off like the period from 2000 to 2003 can create so much discomfort that investors are almost forced to take action of some sort.

On the other hand, does it really make sense to have a high degree of funds in cash or bonds when equity markets are performing very well and paying attractive dividends? We change the way we dress with the seasons to be comfortable. It also makes sense to change the asset allocation of a portfolio with market conditions in order to be comfortable. However, one must follow a very disciplined approach in doing this. In the writers' opinion, following moving average crossovers provides the best strategy. Will this approach outperform a buy-and-hold approach? It may not. However, it will likely produce better returns for investors who might otherwise sell or buy at the wrong time by acting on their emotions or media reports. A 2009 study conducted by DALBAR analyzing the period from January 1, 1989, to December 31, 2008, showed that equity mutual fund shareholders earned an average annual gain of only 1.87% compared to gains of 8.35% in the S&P 500. A more recent Quantitative Analysis of Investor Behavior (QAIB) study by DALBAR in 2013 concluded that the twenty-year returns for investors using equity mutual funds had improved to an average annualized gain of 4.25% per year compared to a return of 8.21% per year for the S&P 500 Index. For the same period, investors in fixed income mutual funds earned only 0.98% per year, on average, compared to a return of 6.34% for Barclays Aggregate Bond Index. While investors are being active, this information verifies that they seem to be buying and selling at the wrong time. Following moving average crossovers has the potential to substantially improve the long-term results above 1.87% or 4.25% over twenty-year periods like this, even if this strategy slightly underperforms the market averages.

Surgeons, accountants, engineers, and construction workers can follow plans with precision and have confidence that their work has been completed to a high standard. Portfolio managers can follow all the accepted procedures to create an investment portfolio for a client only to have it seem totally inappropriate months later. In contrast to accounting and engineering, investing isn't about being right all the time. It is about being right more often than we're wrong. Moving average crossovers can help investors handle inevitable mistakes in a disciplined fashion.

Moving average crossovers are momentum-based indicators that change as the trend of the market changes. They are not affected by models, forecasts, or what people expect the market to do. They show us how investors all around the world are reacting after considering all the inputs into decision making, including emotions. That is what really matters. Based on decades of experience, our opinion is that moving average crossovers are the best indicators to determine the length of market trends and changes in market trends.

How important is it to be aware of market trends? There is a saying that the three most important factors to consider when purchasing real estate are location, location, location. In investing also, one factor is most important, and that is to follow the trend. Before quote screens were commonplace in the late 1970s, a ticker tape rolled out of a machine so that people could read it and follow market moves. Financial expert Stan Weinstein has been pounding the table saying "Don't fight the tape" for decades. What he meant was, do not fight the trend you see when looking at the evidence of the market's direction. Edgar S. Genstein has written, "The absolute price of a stock is unimportant. It is the direction of price movement that is important."

In the popular 1990s book *Winning on Wall Street,* respected author and analyst Marty Zweig emphasized the phrase, "The trend is your friend." In an August 21, 2011, article in the *Washington Post*, Barry Ritholtz said, "But what investors really need to understand comes down to one word: trend." He also wrote, "The trend is your friend—until that nasty bend at the end." Commandment #1 of Art Huprich's investment rules is: Thou Shalt Not Trade Against the Trend.

More than fifty years ago, economist John Maynard Keynes stated what can happen when investors act against a trend that they think may have lasted too long:

> "The market can stay irrational longer than you can stay solvent."

In other words, a market trend can sometimes continue much longer than anyone ever expected. By the time the trend changes, those who may eventually be right have lost all their money. Consequently, following the trend is the cardinal rule of investing. It is interesting, and sad, that most trading disasters, including those mentioned in this book, come as a result of ignoring this very simple (but not easy) premise. History and experience show us that knowing what to do is more difficult than actually doing it!

While trading disasters make the headlines, accounts of missing out on huge profits do not garner the same attention. Nevertheless, I have heard many stories from people who still feel the pain of regret decades after they were so close to cashing in on a major windfall but missed it. The thoughts of what could have been can linger for a very long time.

In a March 12, 2013, *Globe and Mail* article entitled "The Five Biggest Mistakes of Growth Investors," journalist Chris Umiastowski describes a personal experience of selling too soon: "Around 2003, early in my career as a Bay Street analyst, I bought Apple Inc. for the first time. The company was well into its iPod boom but had yet to unveil the iPhone and iPad. I sold the stock after a quick 50-percent gain, simply because I had made a great profit. I eventually bought the stock again when the iPhone was announced in 2007. This time I had a long-term perspective in mind. Despite Apple's big drop recently, I'm up 160% on my stock, which is 17 percent annualized. Not bad. If I had just stuck with my initial investment from 2003, I'd be up about 23 times more than I am now. My initial $10,000 investment in Apple would be worth about $600,000." Using long-term moving average crossovers to manage positions like this can give investors the confidence to stick with an investment that is producing spectacular gains until the long-term trend has deteriorated. The fact that there is a "circuit breaker" to use for a sell discipline can remove some of the anxiety that occurs when there are huge profits and everyone is suggesting it is time to sell. Are the long-term crossovers perfect? Of course not. At the time of a transaction, investors often lament the fact that they are purchasing a stock well above the lows or selling well below the highs. However, if the trade is successful, over time their attitude changes to profound satisfaction that a good decision was made.

For example, the short-term moving average crossover for crude oil changed from positive to negative when the price had dropped from its peak of $147 to $129.29 on July 17, 2008. The long-term moving average crossovers for oil also turned negative when oil prices dropped to $115 per barrel. If the traders at SemGroup had waited for the moving average crossovers to turn negative before entering their short positions, they would have earned substantial profits.

Figure 6.22: Long-Term Moving Average Crossover for Crude Oil from 2007 to 2012. Each bar represents one week. Notice how helpful this chart was in determining the major trend, even though it turned positive above the lows and negative below the highs. Chart data compiled by Thomson Reuters

Figure 6.23: Very Long-Term Moving Crossover for Crude Oil from 1990 to 2012. This very helpful, simple tool enabled investors to capture most of the upside from 1990 to 2012, and to avoid much of the downside during the 1990s and in 2008. Chart data compiled by Thomson Reuters

SemGroup might have reaped billions in profits had they waited for the moving average crossovers to turn negative before adding more funds to their trading strategy. Instead, they lost everything—everything! The real-life situations mentioned in this book have taught us that no corporation or individual is immune from suffering an insurmountable loss, no matter how large, wealthy or powerful they are. If investors want to go against the trend and try to "swim upstream" or "stand in front of a freight train," they should do it with a small amount of money so that they can at least live to fight another day. Warren Buffett's purchase of $5 billion of Goldman Sachs shares in September 2008 was not as good a move as it could have been because he took a risk and bought too early. However, it was a relatively small purchase given the overall size of the portfolio he was managing. As a result, it did not cause him too much grief. He handled the situation well, in that he did not buy more and more shares as the prices dropped. He also earned an attractive rate of interest while he held the shares.

Figure 6.24: Long-Term Moving Average Crossover for Goldman Sachs Group Inc. Chart data compiled by Thomson Reuters

The moving average crossover indicators for Goldman Sachs Group Inc. indicated that the share was in a steady downtrend from late 2007 until early 2009. Warren Buffett invested in the shares at $133 in September 2008. If he had waited for this trend indicator to turn positive, he could have purchased shares at a lower price of $100 and avoided the scary ride below the $60 level in November 2008. Investors who followed the timing of the "Oracle of Omaha" and invested in other financial giants like Bank of America and Citigroup on September 24, 2008, were still suffering by the end of 2012. Shares of Bank of America fell off a cliff from $33.07 on September 24, 2009, to penny stock status of only $2.53 in February 2009. The price recovered to $11.61 by the end of 2012. The stock price of Citigroup resembled an elevator shaft as it fell from $189.60 on September 24, 2008, to a low of $9.70 and clawed its way back to $39.56 by the end of 2012. As Warren Buffett said in his 2000 address to shareholders,

"You never know who's swimming naked until the tide goes out."

During the Financial Crisis, financial titans such as AIG, Lehman Brothers, and Merrill Lynch were also "swimming naked." Investors soon discovered that Bank of America and Citigroup were not "wearing much" either.

Apple Inc. has been one of the most popular U.S. companies to invest in from 2008 to 2012. There were some minor hiccups for Apple in late 2012. However, the company's products are still selling well. Nevertheless, the share price of Apple Inc. fell sharply in the fall of 2012 after the shares just became too popular with investors. The Long-Term Moving Average Crossover for Apple Inc. turned negative for the first time in years on October 6, 2012, at a price of US$629.71. While the share price was down close to 10% from the high, it was still a good time to reduce long positions. The Long-Term Moving Average Crossover turned positive for Apple Inc. on August 6, 2013, when the price closed at US$465.25.

Figure 6.25: The Long-Term Moving Average Crossover for Apple Inc. turned negative on October 6, 2012, at a price of US$629.71 and turned positive again on August 6, 2013, at a price of US$465.25. One green bar appeared on August 6, 2013, indicating that the selling had been exhausted. This indicated enough shares had moved from weak hands to strong hands to the point that there were more buyers than sellers. The share price had declined US$164.46 or 26.1% from the October 6, 2012, sell signal. Using this indicator with a portion of one's position is a prudent strategy. Chart data compiled by Thomson Reuters

Many experts encouraged investors to buy more Apple shares as they were declining. It was safer to wait until there was a sign the selling was exhausted before buying.

Never add to a losing position unless the moving averages turn up—never, ever. A losing position suggests that the trend is not moving in your favor. If any action is to be taken in such a situation, it is to sell soon, not to throw more good hard-earned capital after bad. It is usually a mistake to average down. Most trading disasters occur because of this. The authors have learned this lesson well.

In 2011, I made a stupid mistake. One day, I took off my glasses so that I could put on contact lenses because I wanted to go for a long run. For me, contact lenses are more comfortable than glasses when I am running. Earlier in the day, I had put my contact lenses into a cleaning solution containing hydrogen peroxide and phosphoric acid. I did not realize they were not in the container long enough to neutralize the chemicals. Consequently, when I took out the first contact lens and put it in my right eye, it burned so much I could hardly stand it. I finally held my eyelids open with one hand and took out the contact with the other. Then I quickly grabbed the saline solution to rinse the burning chemicals from my eye. However, after doing this for ten seconds or so, my eye seemed to burn even more. At that point I slowed down long enough to look at the bottle I was holding in my hand. I realized I was rinsing my eye with the cleaning solution instead of the saline solution! In my haste I had grabbed the wrong bottle with acid in it, even though the bottle had a red top. The burning sensation finally went away after I rinsed my eye with the saline solution. The results of adding to a long position as it falls, or a short position as it rises, can be as painful as reaching for the wrong bottle of contact solution and putting acid in your eye. It often results in larger losses which can make your head feel like it is burning, just as my eyes were. Since this experience, I always keep the cleaning solution under the sink, away from the saline solution on the counter, so that I do not take it by mistake in the future. Investors need to take mental action ahead of time to ensure that the strategy of adding to a losing position is avoided until the trend moves back into favor again. Put the notion of averaging down under the counter, or even in the garbage!

It is our hope that readers will not repeat the mistakes others, including us, have made. No matter who you are, strive to always use a moving average crossover to ensure that the position you are contemplating is in line with the trend. After that point, spend a few minutes every week to ensure you remove the position if the moving average crossover indicates that the trend has changed. It is that simple. While this strategy is simple in theory, it still takes intestinal fortitude as well as a healthy dose of discipline to follow the indicators and act on them. We all know how to lose weight: eat less. Sticking to the discipline is the hard part. Selling an investment just after the price has declined when the outlook still seems so promising is not easy. It is not easy either to purchase an investment after it has already rebounded from a sharp sell-off when all the experts still say that more carnage is just around the corner. It requires a lot of courage and discipline to stick with any strategy. At least this strategy works well, even when the going gets rough, as it did after 2000 and 2007. That is more than can be said for almost all other investment disciplines.

Going against the trend is like spitting into the wind. In most cases, it ends up being a messy, uncomfortable, embarrassing experience. All seasoned traders and investors eventually learn this lesson the hard way. The trading disasters mentioned in this book are just a small sample of some of the high-profile losses incurred by those who thought that they were smarter than the markets.

Stock trader Jesse Livermore first became famous when he shorted stocks (selling short enables an investor to profit when asset prices fall) during the Panic of 1907 and made $3 million. After that major success, he lost 90% of his money when he speculated in cotton and invested more money as prices dropped. He declared bankruptcy in 1912 with $1 million in debt after stock markets made no progress for four years. Mr. Livermore became wealthy again during the bull and bear markets that followed, enabling him to repay his creditors. He owned mansions all over the world, complete with staff, limousines, and a yacht. This investing legend made millions during the

Roaring Twenties and his net worth reached $100 million when he shorted stocks during the 1929 Stock Market Crash as most investors incurred severe losses. When he died at the age of sixty-three in 1940, his net worth was $5 million. When an investor with the experience of Jesse Livermore speaks, it is imperative that we pay full and complete attention to what he says. He learned,

"Markets are never wrong—opinions are."

He did not mean that markets always act in a rational manner or that asset prices always reflect their true value. The lesson he has passed on is that the market price of an asset is the final verdict. No matter how convinced an investor is in his or her convictions, the market price determines the success or failure of a venture. One's opinion, extreme undervaluation, high corporate cash levels, or a world-famous brand name are meaningless. When a client looks at his or her portfolio statement, when an institution states quarterly results, or when margin clerks (employees who force clients who have borrowed money for investing to contribute more cash to their account or to sell their holdings due to falling asset prices) evaluate debt levels, these are all based on only one piece of information—the actual market price. Absolutely nothing else matters. Since so much rests on the price of an asset, investors must grant it the respect that it deserves. It is not easy, but investors must respect the trend of market prices, as the direction of prices will ultimately determine the success or failure of an investment strategy.

Warren Buffett shared an interesting story in the 2012 Annual Report for Berkshire Hathaway. A senior citizen received a call from his wife as he was driving home. "Albert, be careful," she warned. "I just heard on the radio that there's a car going the wrong way down the Interstate." "Mabel, they don't know the half of it," replied Albert, "it's not just one car, there are hundreds of them." Making investments based on the premise that the trend will change can be as dangerous as driving the wrong way along a highway during rush hour. Successful money manager Ron Miller said, "The problem with being an early contrarian is that the blood on the street will be your own." It is prudent to have an opinion that is contrary to the crowd. As Mark Twain said, "Whenever you find yourself on the side of the majority, it is time to pause and reflect." However, when does one act after pausing and reflecting? It is not prudent to act against the crowd until moving average crossovers provide confirmation that prices are moving in a direction opposite to what the consensus expects.

In Humphrey Neill's book *The Art of Contrary Thinking*, the man *Life* magazine called the "father of contrary opinion" wrote,

"The public is right during the trends but wrong at both ends."

The public can sometimes be right for years before the trend changes. Selling just because an investment is popular is not the best policy to follow. Selling short just because public interest is high can be deadly as well.

Technology has produced so many automatic safety features—for example, detectors, parking sensors, and anti-lock brake systems (ABS) for vehicles—that there is a tendency for investors to believe they will automatically receive clear warning signs before market prices fall or start rising again. Victorian-era philosopher Herbert Spencer believed, "The ultimate result of shielding men from the effects of folly is to fill the world with fools." One wonders if liberal bankruptcy laws and corporate bailouts are filling the world with more fools than there have been before.

Figures 6.26 to 6.30 show some of the signs on the "Highway Thru Hell," located an hour away from where I live, warning drivers of almost every hazard they might encounter while traveling this route. There are many more warning signs for drivers now than when the highway was first constructed. Drivers had to be more observant and use common sense to travel safely.

Figure 6.26: Sign from Highway Thru Hell. Photo by Dave Harder

In August 2012, the Discovery Channel began an original television series called "Highway Thru Hell." The Discovery Channel describes the Coquihalla Highway, a one-hour drive east of Chilliwack, B.C., as "having steep hills, lethal drop-offs, killer rockslides, and wicked weather." It can easily snow a meter or more in one day. I took the pictures in Figures 6.26 to 6.30 on a recent trip along the Coquihalla Highway. Figure 6.27 is a sign warning of a long hill ahead.

Unfortunately, there are still no obvious warning signs that a market correction is coming until it is well underway or near its end.

Figure 6.27: Sign from Highway Thru Hell. Photo by Dave Harder

There are no outlines showing investors how bad and how long the next bear market is going to be.

Figure 6.28: Sign from Highway Thru Hell. Photo by Dave Harder

There usually are no warnings that there is going to be some wild market turbulence "around the corner."

Figure 6.29: Sign from Highway Thru Hell. Photo by Dave Harder

The Coquihalla Highway has runaway lanes beside the highway on long, steep declines to stop heavy trucks in case the brakes fail. However, in markets, there are no runaway lanes where an investor can decide that since he has lost control, he can just take a diversion and opt out without incurring losses. One can never turn back the clock when investing.

Figure 6.30: Chain Off on Highway Thru Hell. Photo by Dave Harder

This particular Chain Off Area sign means that the downhill section has come to an end, so it is safe to take the chains off the tires if there is no snow on the road. When it comes to investing in any type of asset, there are few telltale signs that the period of declining prices has come to an end since conditions have improved. The best "road signs" for investors are moving average crossovers.

A successful investor must do two very basic things. First, he or she must change positions when the trend changes. Investors must buy or cover short positions only when the trend turns up. Conversely, investors must sell or sell short only when the trend turns down. CNBC's Bob Pisani interviewed a seasoned trader on the trading floor of the NYSE who said,

"Markets don't change when fundamentals change. They change when beliefs change."

It appears that many investors and analysts still prefer to focus almost entirely on seeing more positive or negative fundamental information to discern a change in the trend. However, if markets change when beliefs change, what can investors use to show them this has happened? Indicators that follow the trend of prices show investors if money is flowing in or out of an asset or a market. When the money flow reverses direction in a major way over many weeks, this shift shows that beliefs have changed.

It is not easy to buy when the long-term trend turns positive and it seems like there is still much risk and uncertainty. Conversely, it does not seem as if there should be any urgency to sell when the long-term trend turns negative and the investment environment still seems very positive. However, as a result of being involved with the markets every day for several decades, I have discovered the following:

It does not matter how good or how bad the news is. All that really matters is how much of the good or bad news is already reflected in current market prices.

I have also observed many global crises and extremely negative economic or market events since the 1970s. In reference to North America and most developed countries, I have concluded,

As a problem gets worse, more and more energy is devoted to solving it.

For example, when a problem is making headlines all over the world, it has everyone's attention. This motivates the public to demand action, which, in turn, encourages politicians, government officials, and central banks to respond. When elected officials are under pressure to react to the public's concern, the problem is probably closer to being solved than it is to becoming worse. When everyone is very aware of a serious issue, think of the comment from Jim Rogers: "The more certain it is, the less likely it is to be profitable." Legendary Legg Mason mutual fund manager Bill Miller said, "When it is in the papers, it is in the price." Investors should not let serious problems dissuade them from buying once the long-term trend in prices has improved.

Investors must stick with the trend until it ends. Famous money manager Peter Lynch said, "Far more money has been lost by investors preparing for corrections, or trying to anticipate corrections, than has been lost in corrections themselves." Moving average crossovers are the best tools to stick with the trend "until it bends." They are also one of the best indicators to show when the trend "bends." Throughout our careers, there have always been some experts warning that financial markets and currencies are on the verge of collapse. As the end of the Mayan calendar was approaching in late 2012, Senior NYSE Floor Trader for UBS, Art Cashin, said, "The end of the world only happens once. You have to time that trade very carefully."

The authors have learned that one of the most difficult things to do is to sell at a loss. My wife, Marianne, has a female giant schnauzer which had ten puppies in November 2012. The runt of her first litter was much smaller than the rest, and we were not sure if it would survive. We contacted the veterinarian to see what we should do. We were told that it was best not to interfere because the mother has a strong sense of whether a puppy will survive. Without any training or guidance, dogs naturally push away the sickly pups so they cannot feed. In this way, they can focus on the healthy puppies. Dogs are "programmed" to cut their losses.

In this case, the mother would put the runt in her mouth and walk away with it. We did not know if she was trying to give it extra attention or if she was attempting to take it away. As it turned out, she was giving it special attention and the little runt survived.

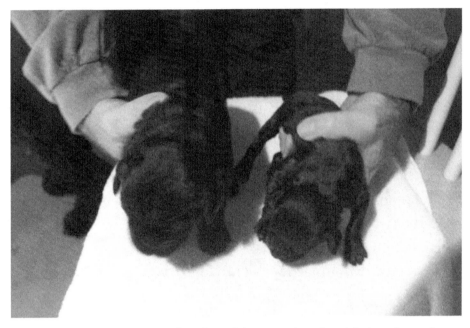

Figure 6.31: This picture shows the size of the runt (on the right) and another puppy (on the left) two weeks after they were born. Photo by Marianne Harder

On the other hand, when humans have a baby, they do everything possible to enable the baby to survive, no matter how premature or sickly it is. We are designed to endure and persevere. For example, humans are the only living beings that will run a marathon (26.2 miles or 42 kilometers) without stopping. I know what it is like to persevere through marathons and triathlons, but that does not compare to what Dr. Janice Dorn has endured. She lost both her parents when she was a teenager. Then, on New Year's Eve in 1990, her lungs collapsed and she stopped breathing. She remained in the hospital for seventy days, much of that time in critical intensive care, after the doctors determined she had Adult Respiratory Distress Syndrome. She had two near-death experiences. Her chances of survival were less than 1 percent. Dr. Dorn was told that she would be confined to a wheelchair and be a respiratory cripple for the rest of her life. However, over the following two years she taught herself to speak, walk, run, and even dance again. She also had to struggle for years to overcome an addiction to the powerful opiate drug, Demerol, which was given to her in massive doses during her hospitalization. The details of this experience were recounted in her book, *Personal Responsibility: The Power of You,* in the chapter entitled "As I Lay Dying."

The natural instinct of humans is to hang on to life no matter what happens. This serves us well in most things, but it does hinder us from selling our investments at a loss. Enduring and persevering through pain and suffering are natural and commendable traits in the pursuit of long-term gains. However, enduring the mental anguish and financial loss of a losing position is not commendable. Hesitating to get out of a losing position is one more area where human nature works against making prudent investment decisions. As strange as it may seem, dogs may be better at cutting their losses than some seasoned investors.

Many experts give projections for the next year or so, especially at the beginning of a new year. However, since markets are driven by human behavior, which is not always predictable, no one can predict how far a market will move, or which direction it will take, with any degree of certainty. When the long-term moving average crossovers I use give a buy or sell signal, clients will often ask me how far I think the trend might go. I always say that the trend will continue until the moving average crossovers change. My comments are often received with a puzzled look, since most market experts respond to a request of that nature by giving a longer-term projection. I maintain that my answer is really the only accurate response to such a request. A highly respected trader (and friend) responded this way when he was asked to give a market projection during an uptrend on February 8, 2012: "When we are asked in press interviews how far we think prices can rise, we say only this ... and this is the 'wisdom' of three and one-half decades of being involved in the markets on a daily basis and with our money always at risk ... Prices will continue to rise until they stop. We can say nothing more and although we know some shall consider this uncommon idiocy and others shall consider it cowardice on our part, those who've been involved with markets shall know this to be wisdom learned of hard knocks over time."

Truer words have never been spoken. Investors expect analysts and economists to provide price targets and forecast the future. The analysts and experts do their best to comply with this. Regulators hear stories from investors who have lost money when they made investments based on the projections in company research reports. To protect individual investors from putting too much confidence in the predictions they desire, North American securities regulators now demand that research reports on an individual company have five pages of disclaimer in fine print, attached to a two-page summary.

Since human behavior is not entirely predictable, any forecast or projection should be compared to the signal that the moving average crossovers are giving. If forecasts and predictions do match the current trends, then investors must watch the moving average crossovers to make sure that they can act if the trend changes.

> Trends can change for many reasons, including an unexpected event.
> Rely on what the money is doing, not on what people say it should do.

Count on moving averages and moving average crossovers to show you the trends. Keep this in mind the next time you hear a group of experts freely providing target prices for stocks or equity markets for the coming year.

As human beings, we have always been interested in predictions about the future. As a result, experts will continue to issue price targets and projections because investors demand them. We have found, for the most part, that forecasts improve as the markets improve. The more prices rise, the more price targets tend to increase. For example, when oil prices reached $130 in 2008, many media reports highlighted the report of a Goldman Sachs energy analyst when he raised his target price for oil to $200. As mentioned earlier, prices peaked at $147 and dropped like an elevator shaft to $33 by the end of 2008.

A while after prices start to decline, price targets tend to be reduced. The longer prices decline, the more bearish the analyst community becomes. At the price low, almost every expert is forecasting much lower prices for the foreseeable future. Consequently, forecasts and projections primarily reflect what has happened in the past, not what will happen in the future. In the vast majority of cases, forecasts merely extrapolate the most recent experience of the markets into the future. This will always be the case because no one knows precisely how humans will react in every circumstance. In addition, few analysts or research firms want to stick their necks out and deviate too much from what everyone else is saying. This tendency ensures that they will be just as right or wrong as everyone else. That is good for job security. There are a few analysts, such as banking analyst Meredith Whitney, who are willing to issue controversial forecasts. Meredith Whitney made a name for herself in 2007 when she wrote a very pessimistic report on Citigroup. The collapse of Citigroup share prices during the Financial Crisis showed that her opinions were accurate. After the Financial Crisis, she gained such a following that she was able to start her own firm, Meredith Whitney Advisory Group LLC. Unfortunately, Meredith Whitney closed her research firm in October 2013 to start her own hedge fund, after her predictions of a sharp decline in U.S. municipal bond markets did not materialize. It seems as though she is just one of many market experts who made one great call on the market but was unable to follow up with another.

A Eugene, Oregon, think tank called Decision Research has polled investors seven times since 2008. In a February 11, 2012, *Wall Street Journal* article, "This is Your Brain on a Hot Streak," columnist Jason Zweig wrote, "These surveys have shown that investors' forecasts of future returns go up after the market has risen and down after it has fallen. William Burns, an analyst at Decision Research, says investors' forecasts of the market's return over the coming year were heavily swayed by how stocks performed in the previous month. They might not have had a choice. The investing mind comes with built-in machinery that sizes up the future based on a surprisingly short sample of the past." In my experience, this does not just hold true for individual investors. Market experts and research analysts are affected in the same way. This proclivity is just another example of how our basic instinct inhibits our ability to make wise investment decisions.

Having said this, some experts might be accurate with market forecasts for a long period of time when certain cycles are in place. (The significance of market cycles will be addressed in a later chapter.) However, those who are accurate for a long time when a particular trend is in force rarely change their views when the trend ends. In most cases, that is usually when the winning streak for an analyst also comes to an abrupt end. Therefore, it is critical for investors to follow a discipline of using moving average crossovers so that they can sell within 10% or so of a top when an uptrend ends, or buy within 10% or so of a low after a downtrend ends.

Often the share price of a company engaging in fraudulent activity will decline before investors are aware of it. In several cases, moving average crossovers have alerted investors of a downtrend before the public knows any information about the fraud. When the Prime Minister of Luxembourg, Jean-Claude Juncker, was dealing with the European Debt Crisis in July 2012, he said,

> "When it becomes serious, you have to lie."

Moving average crossovers are one of the few tools that can turn negative before the worst losses occur when there is a case of fraud or false information. (See the moving average crossovers in Figures 6.32 and 6.33, which turned red and alerted investors of a downtrend before fraud destroyed most of the share value for Olympus Corporation and Sino-Forest Corporation in 2011.)

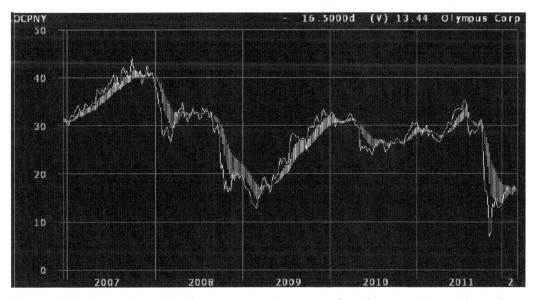

Figure 6.32: Long-Term Moving Average Crossover for Olympus Corp. Chart data compiled by Thomson Reuters

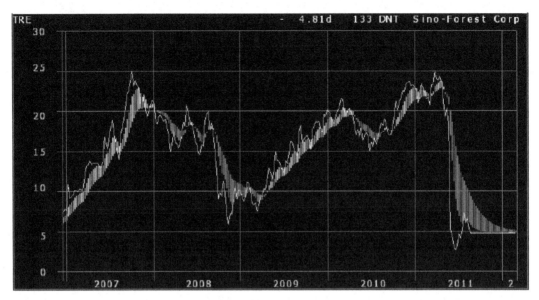

Figure 6.33: Long-Term Moving Average Crossover for Sino-Forest Corp. Chart data compiled by Thomson Reuters

Sometimes market prices will fall continuously, even when the news seems to be positive. This shift does not matter—follow the indicators and ask questions later. In many cases, a quarterly report will announce that sales or revenues have declined well after the share price has already declined. Many times, market prices will skyrocket for weeks just when it seems as if they are going to collapse after a long decline. If moving average crossovers turn positive when the outlook is still bleak, buy and find out the reason later.

Since following the trend and changing with the trend are of utmost importance, we must have the best tools to help us do that. Again, in my experience, moving average crossovers are the best indicators, even though they are not perfect. Moving average crossovers have a major attribute—they provide clear signals! They act like traffic lights. One does not have to spend much time every week or so watching the moving averages. However, like a traffic light, once the trend indicator changes, a decision has to be made. If investors do not have a trigger or a "fuse that blows" at a specific point, prices can continue to drift in the same direction while losses mount. We have learned the hard way that any combination of pride, self-confidence, too much reliance on information (which may or may not be accurate), procrastination, denial, hope, greed, fear, or shock can easily cause an individual to put off making a decision. Confidence that a trend change must be just around the corner because prices cannot keep moving in the same direction any longer can motivate investors to hang on. In contrast, a discipline of following the clear, definitive signals of moving average crossovers can provide the incentive for investors to take action.

Many have heard of the boiling frog story. If a frog is thrown into a pot of boiling water, he will jump out of it. However, apparently a frog will not jump out of a pot where cold water is slowly heated to the boiling point. The result is that the frog is boiled to death. If investors do not have a clear trigger point or a line in the sand to force them to make a buy or sell decision, they can end up like a frog in boiling water. Negligible losses are ignored because they are of minor consequence. When losses increase, it seems as if prices have dropped as much as they have in previous years before they turned around again. When the losses multiply, to take such a major loss is too much to bear—surely it cannot increase any further. When losses do increase even more, they can lead to financial death. This was the psychological progression of the trading disasters discussed previously.

It is never easy to sell if there is a loss, or if prices have already declined a little from their highs. However, if investors have a discipline that they know will work in every situation and that gives an unequivocal signal to buy or sell, it can give them the confidence to take action. In that way, a small loss will not morph into a giant loss, and investors will still have the bulk of their capital left to invest when the next opportunity arises. Remember that it is impossible to make the right investment decisions all of the time. The main objective of investing is to be right more often than wrong.

When the media interview analysts and market experts, they are often asked if they are bullish or bearish. They usually respond to the question, giving some reasons for their view. Again, that is not the best response. Investors, money managers, analysts, and experts should not be bullish or bearish. They should try to be neutral. The main objective of investing is not to do one's analysis and come to an optimistic or pessimistic conclusion. The main objective is to invest with the trend. The Dalai Lama said,

"The mind is like a parachute. It works best when it's open."

It is much easier to follow the trend if one tries to remain open-minded to any eventuality rather than having a preconceived notion of where prices are headed. Markets don't care what anyone thinks. They will do what they do when they do it, and no person can impose his or her will on the markets.

One group of investors known to be bullishly biased is the one that truly believes in a bull market in precious metals (gold and silver). These individuals, often called the somewhat derogatory "gold bugs," believe that gold prices should always be higher than they are because they think paper currency is worthless due to high levels of government debt. Everyone is entitled to his or her opinion, but there is a price to pay for not respecting the price trend of an asset. After gold prices peaked in 1980, market forces effectively banished gold bugs to "wander in the desert" for twenty-eight years as they waited for prices to finally move above the previous highs. At the time of this writing, the price of silver is still below the high attained thirty-two years ago. Although it is shiny and beautiful to look at, the hard reality is that silver paid no interest or dividends over all that time.

Various forms of research, such as relative strength, can be helpful to ascertain which stocks or market sectors are the weakest or the strongest. This information is discussed in the chapter "It's All Relative." Even with that information, the most important priority is to determine the trend of an asset and follow it. Pride and overconfidence can seduce investors into thinking that the markets will follow the scenarios they have created in their minds. That is backward thinking. Instead, investors need to remain neutral, and match their strategies to the trend, not the other way around. The traders at Amaranth and SemGroup are good examples of what happens when investors focus on their own preconceived notions of what the market should do, instead of what the money is really doing. Investors should not work toward the goal of becoming bullish or bearish. They should work towards the goal of following the trend and being right.

Even the most powerful and successful people in their field can end up being wrong, and can suffer catastrophic financial and psychological losses if they do not listen to the message of the markets. No one is immune. There is no forecasting model that works all of the time. Recent market activity shows that it is becoming more and more important for all investors to do a "windsock test" by looking at moving average crossovers. In this way, investors can have more confidence that they have come to the right conclusion, have their timing right, and will avoid getting caught on the wrong side of an unexpected event.

In his book *The Battle for Investment Survival*, Gerald Loeb wrote, "The really great fortunes were made by concentration, not diversification." Economist Mark Skousen wrote, "To make it, concentrate; to keep it, diversify." There are many executives and employees who have a large portion of their nest egg invested in the shares of the company they work for. That is all well and good until the company runs into difficulty as Enron, Nortel, Lehman Brothers, and many others have done. In most cases, it is not possible or advisable for insiders or employee shareholders to actively trade positions. However, there are times—for example, after oil prices have had a large increase—when it may be prudent to take some action to protect a portion of the portfolio in case there is a sizable loss. Accidents happen when there is a bear market. Investors can choose the least active option for this situation, as explained in the chapter "It is Time for a Revolutionary Change in Portfolio Management."

I have a client who allowed me to share his story from many years ago. He started a transportation company which was very successful. A conglomerate offered to buy the company from him in exchange for shares in the conglomerate. Soon after this, conglomerates fell out of favor with investors, and the shares he received lost 95% of their value. Since the transportation company was still doing well, he borrowed enough money from the bank to buy it back again. It has kept growing ever since and is still operating today.

Many young entrepreneurs sold their Internet and technology companies to larger companies in exchange for shares in the late 1990s. Living in a period when buy and hold was the mantra and having never experienced a devastating bear market, they viewed this as a good strategy. After the technology bubble burst in late 2000, a good portion of these entrepreneurs had much less to show for their efforts. Starting and operating a business is totally different from investing. Those who sell a business should try to receive as much cash as possible for it instead of securities. If shares are received as payment, a sell discipline should be in place to preserve a large portion of the value the seller received. Moving average crossovers are a good tool for such a discipline.

George Soros said that "to make big money, you have to bet on the unexpected." Sometimes, individuals or investment firms concentrate on one or two securities in order to try to make a "fortune." Moving average crossovers and relative strength data can be some of the most useful tools to increase the odds of being successful. They can also be some of the best tools to act as a fuse that blows when something unexpected is going wrong. Handling a concentrated position requires special care!

After analyzing many investment systems between 1978 and 2000, I came to the conclusion that the long-term moving average crossovers were the easiest to understand and follow. More importantly, they also seemed to be more reliable than anything else. They are not complicated. Often, simpler is better. The failure of so many complicated systems from 1998 to 2011 confirms this principle.

When I started using these moving average crossovers after 2000, few seemed to respect them. My conclusions were supported by a study produced by Myles Zyblock, former Chief Institutional Strategist and Director of Capital Markets Research for RBC, on May 11, 2011. Myles Zyblock starts his report with this statement, "Momentum gets a bad rap. It is often viewed as a reflection of consensus thinking, or beta chasing, and a strategy highly prone to sustained or crushing risk reversals. Our data tell a different story and one so favorable that we'd encourage investors to take a closer look at momentum's attributes." (Moving averages and moving average crossovers follow the trend of momentum of the markets so they are classified as a momentum indicator.)

The report states, "Momentum is a leadership strategy. It has outperformed on an absolute and risk-adjusted basis through time and over various market and economic cycles. Take the 1930s, which was defined by extreme circumstances, yet momentum outperformed the composite by 280 bps, growth by 70 bps, and value by 810 bps per annum." (bps stands for basis points. One basis point is 1/100th of a percent. 100 basis points is 1%.)

Momentum-based indicators are also less volatile than the markets and other strategies. Myles Zyblock writes, "Momentum is not a high beta strategy. Beta on the high momentum index is 0.92 versus 0.94 for growth and 1.21 for value using data back to 1930." (A beta of 1.00 means that it matches the market averages. Anything below 1.00 is less volatile, and anything over 1.00 is more volatile than the market averages.)

Markets often have periods where growth stocks (stocks that have above-average growth in earnings, sales, or revenues) outperform value stocks and vice versa through a business/earnings cycle. Yet momentum stocks outperform value and growth stocks throughout earnings cycles. Myles Zyblock states, "Growth outperforms Value as S&P 500 earnings decelerate. Value outperforms Growth as S&P earnings accelerate. Yet, the performance of High Momentum marginally dominates Growth in earnings decelerations and Value in earnings accelerations." Zyblock states that, over the very long-term, "The data from 1930 indicates that a High Momentum portfolio has delivered a compound annual growth rate of 13.1% versus 11.6% for Value, 9.4% for the S&P 500 while Growth brings up the rear at 8.9%. The ordinal ranking across these various style benchmarks is preserved in a risk-adjusted basis, as measured by the Sharpe Ratio." The report concludes that value managers, core managers, and growth managers should have some exposure to momentum strategies.

When it comes to investing your hard-earned money, or the money entrusted to you, what are you going to rely on as your guide? After doing all of your analysis, are you going to rely entirely on your own interpretations and conclusions to guide your investment decisions, or are you going to check the "windsock" (momentum indicators) of the markets to make sure you are on the right track? Are you going to use investment principles that are general in nature, or those that offer decisive signals? Do you want to base all of your investment decisions on a sophisticated discipline that works most of the time, or a basic indicator that functions as it is supposed to all of the time? Do you want to incorporate the best performing investment style into your decision-making process or ignore it?

It is hard enough to figure out what is going on in the markets without our emotions getting in the way. From time immemorial, there have been boom-and-busts, bubbles, and depressions. Our emotions, human nature, and basic instincts usually work against us when it comes to dealing with how markets of any sort function. Moving average crossovers provide an objective discipline to follow that offers investors a solution for taking the emotions we all deal with out of the equation. Moving average crossovers do not offer any indication of the magnitude or duration of a move. They are not perfect since they often give a buy signal after prices are up from the lows and a sell signal when prices have already declined from the peak. However, all in all, we believe they rank among the best tools for every investor. There is a saying, "What wise men do in the beginning, fools do in the end." If one cultivates the ability to overcome one's emotions and follow moving average crossovers, one can be the wise person taking action not at the very start of a move, but near the beginning of a trend, as opposed to at its end. Using moving average crossovers can enable unsophisticated investors to act with the wise.

Legendary asset manager Jeremy Grantham has published "10 Investment Lessons." His first lesson is, "Believe in history. All bubbles break; all investment frenzies pass. The market is gloriously inefficient and wanders far from fair price, but eventually, after breaking your heart and patience…it will go back to fair value. Your task is to survive until that happens." Surviving flat markets over the period from 2000 to 2012 required more patience than many could muster. Moving average crossovers can enable investors to take action from time to time, making it easier and less stressful to be patient.

Grantham's second lesson is, "Neither a lender nor a borrower be." He states, "Leverage reduces the investor's critical asset: patience. It encourages financial aggressiveness, recklessness and greed." The authors have learned this lesson the hard way. Having a sizable cash down payment to leverage a real estate investment where rental income will cover expenses can work well as long as the real estate market is not overheated. Otherwise leverage must be handled with the highest level of care.

History shows that moving average crossovers are very reliable, decisive indicators that work all of the time, even when almost every other indicator fails. Not only are they easy to use, they provide better long-term results than other major investment disciplines. In contrast to all the other investment systems mentioned previously, moving average crossovers are like airbags and seatbelts that you can count on even in a most disastrous event. Always remember, "the trend is your friend until the end when it bends." The first and most important criterion that every investment decision must meet is that it follows the trend. The chapter, "It is Time for a Revolutionary Change in Portfolio Management" addresses how to use momentum indicators as well as the other ideas mentioned in the following pages.

Respecting the trend of prices is not just important for individual and institutional investors. It matters to society as a whole. This is what George F. Warren and Frank A. Pearson wrote in their book *Prices*, which was published in 1933:

> A knowledge of the laws of prices is essential for personal business success because every business transaction involves a guess as to the future of prices. Such knowledge not only is essential for the individual but also vital for national stability. Many persons blame Congress, or the democratic form of government, or the organization of society based on private enterprise for the business collapse. These things are no more to blame for this collapse than they are to blame for the stalling of an automobile when the battery fails. If the battery fails, the thing to correct is the battery—not the gasoline, or the engine, or the grade of the road. If the exchange cog in our business machinery breaks, the thing to correct is that cog. The individual has two tasks. One is to forecast the future of prices and conduct his affairs accordingly. The other is to inform himself and help in guiding public opinion so that national progress can be made.

Using the information in this book to adjust your forecast and investment position should reduce the likelihood of significant loss. Trading disasters have had a profound impact on thousands of employees and entire communities. The failure of Long-Term Capital Management and financial firms in 2008 almost brought the global financial system to its knees. The 2008 Financial Crisis and the sharp economic slowdown that followed affected many businesses all over the world. These problems occurred when corporate officials let pride and overconfidence lead them into business practices that were not safe. Then, when problems developed, they were too slow to accept the action of prices for the assets they owned. We must study and respect prices because they are so important. Moving average crossovers are one of the best tools people can use to study prices. If more people followed the discipline of using these tools, there would be fewer trading disasters. It could also have the potential for reducing the pain individuals and society endure during economic recessions or bear markets.

7. Emotions and Investing

It is easier to know what to do than to do it

Soon after I (Dave) first heard about triathlons, I completed what is now known as an Olympic distance triathlon in 1984. After that, I thought, someday I would like to attempt what I thought would be the ultimate physical challenge—an Ironman triathlon. Many years later in 2000, I completed my first marathon in Vancouver. Once my youngest daughter had moved out of the house to attend university in 2006, I finished my first Ironman triathlon in Penticton, British Columbia. I completed the Big Sur International Marathon in California during 2007 to improve my running and then my second Ironman triathlon in Coeur d'Alene, Idaho in 2008.

It does not take much effort to sign up for an Ironman triathlon, or to buy goggles, a bike, and running shoes, and make a training schedule. It is many times more challenging to follow the schedule and use the gear to train for hours every day, for months, no matter what the weather is like or how one feels. Even though we may know what we need to do in a certain situation, it can be very hard to follow through with the right actions. Let me give you an example.

In 1995, I purchased a 21½ foot 1,500-kg (3,500 pound) boat over the Christmas holidays. The boat came without a trailer so I purchased one near my home and drove 300 kilometers to pick up the boat. Since the trailer was not set up to fit the exact dimensions of the boat, when the boat was placed on the trailer, the stern was farther back on the trailer than it should have been. Most of the weight of the boat was in the stern. When I was driving home on the highway at 110 kilometers per hour, the trailer began to sway back and forth because the boat was too far back on the trailer. Having a Professional Driver's Certificate from when I drove a concrete truck to help pay for my education, I knew that the best way to eliminate this problem was to accelerate. Stepping on the brakes would cause the trailer to sway even more, which could cause the truck to lose control. Accelerating would pull the trailer forward, which was supposed to stop the swaying. There was not much time to deliberate on what I should do and speeding up even more seemed illogical and dangerous. It took a lot of courage, but I put the gas pedal down to the floor and sped up. Sure enough, the trailer stopped fish-tailing. As soon as it did, I slammed on the brakes, slowed down to 95 kilometers an hour, said a prayer of thanks, and felt a big sense of relief.

In the same way, it is easy to understand that moving averages can be helpful. It does not take a rocket scientist to know that an investor should buy when a moving average crossover turns positive and sell when it turns negative. It is much more difficult to be disciplined enough to act on the signals in the heat of the moment. Why is it so hard to do what we know is right?

Human beings are amazing creatures. When we look back over time and think of the pyramids in Egypt, the ancient buildings in Rome, the beginning of air travel, color television signals passing through the air, and heart transplant operations, we can conclude that mankind has achieved great things. We are intelligent and have the capacity to accomplish more than we think is possible. Many of these accomplishments have come about as the result of acquiring knowledge and information. Of course, discipline and hard work were also major factors.

However, as we look back over the centuries, there is little, if any, evidence to show that mankind has made any progress when it comes to making better investment decisions. The 2011 European Debt Crisis, the 2008 Financial Crisis, the U.S. real estate bubble in 2007, and the bubble in technology stocks in 2000 are just recent examples showing us that the volume of information we consume often does not lead to better investment results.

Billionaire investor George Soros has said that markets are just as prone to go into boom/bust sequences and bubbles as into equilibrium. Investment bubbles are not just a North American phenomenon. The boom/bust sequence is not a recent development either. For example, a stock market and real estate bubble in Japan peaked close to 1990. At the time, the grounds of the Emperor's Imperial Palace in Tokyo were valued higher than all the land in California. The "lost decade" in Japan that followed has turned into the "lost decades."

Oil prices reached a bubble in 2008 as prices surged to US$147 per barrel in July. Five months later, oil prices had collapsed to just over $30. There was the famous U.S. stock market bubble in 1929. Stock prices declined by 90% within a few years, when the Great Depression ensued. As mentioned earlier, one of the more unusual investment bubbles occurred in Holland during the 17th century. Tulip bulbs became a fad in Holland in the early 1600s and eventually reached astronomical prices. According to the article "The Dutch Tulip Bubble of 1637" by Cynthia Wood, tulip traders were making as much as $61,710 (adjusted to 2006 U.S. dollars) a month before prices collapsed to one hundredth of their earlier value. There were likely many other unrecorded bubbles before 1637. What these examples show us is that while the volume and transmission of information has changed significantly over time, human nature has not. The human race has made many new discoveries and advances over the centuries, but the way we think and act seems to have not advanced at all.

The past shows that, when it comes to investments, many people do not act rationally and never have. Perhaps we never will, since we are emotional beings. Without emotions we would be robots. Without emotions, our hearts would not be warmed by the sweet smile of a young child. Listening to music would be no more enjoyable than looking at notes. We would not enjoy the touch of a person of the opposite sex. Emotions make us who we are and benefit us in many ways—except when we make decisions involving assets that trade on a market.

Legendary investor Warren Buffett has said, "To invest successfully over a lifetime does not require a stratospheric IQ, unusual business insight, or inside information. What is needed is a sound intellectual framework for decisions and the ability to keep emotions from corroding that framework." Good quality information is helpful for understanding what is happening with the economy, various investment sectors, and individual stocks. A sound decision-making process is also required. This awareness comes naturally to us. Most of the information we look at focuses on this. Because investing seems like a raw analytical exercise, we do not realize that emotions are a factor in our decision making. Therefore, very little emphasis is placed on managing our emotions. Famous baseball catcher, outfielder, and manager Yogi Berra said,

"Baseball is ninety percent mental. The other half is physical."

The same is true for investing. History shows that the emotional component of decision making seems to have been the major culprit causing investors to rush in to buy investments at ever higher and more ridiculous prices. From tulips in 1637 to U.S. real estate in 2006, individual investors, sophisticated professional investors, businesses, and individual families have suffered greatly by following their emotions and getting caught up in an investment fad. Getting caught up in a fad for a Slinky, Rubik's Cube, Cabbage Patch Doll, Lululemon clothing, or the latest Mercedes AMG sports car does not have the potential to cause much lasting financial harm to purchasers or their families. On the other hand, making a financial move into the latest investment trend with a major portion of one's life savings has the potential to result not only in financial ruin, but broken relationships, depression, and in the worst-case scenario, even suicide. The stories Dr. Janice Dorn writes about trading disasters are just a few examples of the large-scale destruction which results after emotions overrule sound intellectual frameworks for decisions. Therefore, the importance of recognizing how our emotions affect our investment decisions cannot be understated! When it comes to investing, our emotions are a much more important factor than we are aware of—whether we admit it or not.

Emotional drive is what enables a hockey team to go from losing five-to-one to winning the game. Emotions impact the most skilled and experienced surgeons so that they should not operate on their own family members. If we always acted rationally, there would be no crimes of passion. As mentioned earlier, people often line up before a store opens if goods are on sale at a significant discount. In contrast, investors tend to line up to buy when prices are high and sell when prices are low. If we acted rationally, most people would purchase investments when prices were cheap, not astronomical. Emotions impact even the most rational investor. The purpose of this chapter is to help individuals and professional money managers understand how market forces compel us to make the wrong decisions at the wrong time. With several devastating boom/bust sequences and bubbles having happened in just the last ten years, history shows, now more than ever, that we need help!

8. The Cycle of Market Emotions

"Since the beginning of time, man has been controlled largely by emotions—primarily, fear and greed. When a student of market action allows these emotions to influence his response, he loses many opportunities in the market. The student must at all times resist these emotions. Confidence and courage are required to overcome fear and greed. Courage is inborn. Confidence is gained by study, study, and more study."
John R. Hill, Commodity Research Institute

You are most likely reading this book because you have an interest in the financial markets. Some of you may decide to embark on a voyage to achieve success in the markets. As such, you become willing participants in what can be a Herculean struggle for survival (financial profits). This book is a rudder for you—a guide to help you stay the course and keep your head when so many around you seem to be losing theirs. At times, the journey will be smooth and seemingly uneventful. At other times, it may feel like you are in a tsunami where your very survival is threatened. You will see moves that leave you breathless and in awe; then, just as suddenly, the seas will be calm again. In a real tsunami, you would—at the first sign of danger—do everything possible to get to a place of safety. In the tsunami of the financial markets, some will live long and prosper. Others will survive in a vessel that has been damaged. Sadly, some will drift out into the vast ocean never to be seen again.

The opening quotation from John Hill addresses two important aspects of survival: inborn courage and learned confidence. He says that confidence is gained through study, study, and more study—but fails to tell us what or whom to study. Many believe that if they read enough books, join numerous newsletter services, follow the market guru "du jour," attend expensive seminars, or buy the even-more-expensive software, they will discover the Holy Grail of trading and investing. Most have been sorely disappointed to find that, after all the hype and hope, this Holy Grail remains elusive. Of course, it is important to read and study as much as possible about the markets you are trading in order to devise a trading strategy and trading plan. You cannot move forward without a plan, and you cannot make a plan without diligent study. Traders must be prepared to spend thousands of hours and many years studying charts and market movements, and this study must continue for as long as they are trading. But this is not enough.

> "Man is made or unmade by himself. By the right choice he ascends. As a being of power, intelligence and love, and the lord of his own thoughts, he holds the key to every situation."
> James Allen

What successful traders know is that true study means going within to discover their identity in the world of money. The markets have been their greatest teacher because the markets have told them who they truly are at the core of their being. I believe that trading and investing are at least 90% psychological. The single reason that most fail in the markets is that they do not take the time nor invest the money to understand their authentic being, how they think about making decisions and how they behave in an open adaptive system under conditions of uncertainty. After all is said and done and so much is written, promoted, marketed, and sold, the message is very simple: none of this works unless you know yourself. The Grail is within you.

Dave and I have worked diligently for many years to be in close touch with our emotions and the emotions of the millions of others who are trading with or against us. We do not believe that markets are totally random or totally rational. We have come to believe that technical analysis is, quite simply, an interpretation of emotions plotted on a grid. By studying charts and using specific indicators, we attempt to exploit these emotions to make money.

The sentiment roadmap in Figure 8.1 is a simple representation of the predictable cycle of human emotions. Understanding this cycle is one of your most important tools for navigating the ups, downs, booms, busts, calm, and chaos of the market ocean.

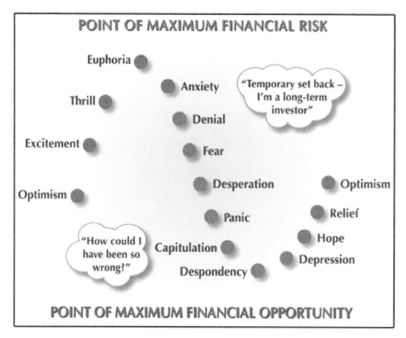

Figure 8.1: The cycle of market emotions. Produced by Janice Dorn, based on a concept from Westcore Funds/Denver Investment Advisors LLC, 1998

As markets begin to rise, optimism increases, excitement builds, and making money becomes thrilling. "Feel good" chemicals (dopamine, serotonin, endorphins, oxytocin, and others) flood through the brain. Over a period of time, investors in a bull market finally reach a level of adoration. The market is now almost impossible to resist, and you have a burning desire to get into it at any cost. It doesn't matter how much you pay because you believe that it won't ever stop going up and your position will be profitable. At this peak, lust and euphoria from the dopamine-drenched limbic brain overwhelm all rational thinking. All the news is wonderful and pundits are projecting higher and higher levels. You feel you can't lose and just have to participate. This is the point of maximal financial risk. Traders and investors who do not know themselves or understand the cycle of market emotions succumb to temptation. They buy. Then, the markets start to decline. Anxiety, denial, fear, desperation, and panic follow. There is a good deal of denial and rationalization on the way down. You may think it's just a temporary pull-back and that prices will go up again. Holding and hoping are common in the early stages of a decline. Various stages of anxiety, denial, and fear flood the brain of the trader who is now under the influence of large doses of the fictional narcotic called "hopium," and whose brain is doing everything possible to trick and put him or her off balance.

At some point, the pain becomes too great and denial is replaced by the reality that you are in a losing position. Eventually, panic is followed by capitulation, revulsion, and despondency. The market is now universally hated and looked on as a source of intense pain, suffering, and disease. The news flow is terrible, and talking heads begin to predict lower and lower prices. Everything seems to be falling apart. You may see headlines and magazine covers predicting imminent disaster. Ironically, it is at this point of extreme pain and revulsion that you are likely to find maximum financial opportunity. Most people have sold and felt immediate (albeit temporary) relief. Shortly thereafter, some begin to realize that the world is not coming to an end and that the markets are starting to turn up. This happened at the rise out of the 2009 lows when the markets began to climb what is called a "wall of worry." Hope turns into relief, which then leads to optimism, and then the cycle starts all over again.

The best traders and investors are constantly in touch with their feelings during this entire cycle. It is virtually impossible to pick a top or bottom in any market, so selling high and buying low is not an absolute science. It is a combination of art, science, and years of experience. Even though they are a proven formula for success, buying low and selling high are very difficult because our brains are not hardwired to do this. Successful traders and investors, especially those who have been through a number of market cycles, know that awareness of their emotions plus a behavioral discipline create a winning formula for success. Because of the way our brains work, selling into anxiety and denial is easier than selling at a peak. However, buying when there is depression and hope is something that most investors and traders can train themselves to do. Other chapters of this book provide specific tools to help investors and traders maintain behavioral discipline.

F. Scott Fitzgerald said, "Genius is the ability to put into effect what is in your mind." If you truly have an understanding of the cycle of market emotions, you will be in harmony with the market movements and not fight them constantly or put added stress on yourself. Don't be afraid to take profits and honor stop-losses at lower prices. Don't be greedy and think you have to catch the exact bottom or the exact top. As mentioned in the preface, it is virtually impossible to do this. Learn a lesson from one of the greatest investors of all time, the late Sir John Templeton, who said, "Bull markets are born on pessimism, grow on skepticism, mature on optimism, and die on euphoria."

> "Buy when others are despondently selling and sell when
> others are greedily buying."
> Joseph Mark Mobius (renowned global investor)

9. Emotional Management

"Emotional control is the most essential factor in playing the market. Never lose control of your emotions when the market moves against you. Don't get too confident over your wins or too despondent over your losses."
Jesse Livermore, Legendary Trader

One of the most difficult aspects of trading is emotional management. Year after year, we witness markets and economies that are news-driven, volatile, and filled with uncertainty. For many, it's a real emotional roller coaster. To say "don't get emotional" is pointless because everyone has emotions around money.

What can you do about your emotions in relationship to trading and investing? Of all the books and papers I have read or written about trading psychology, there is one aspect that stands out most clearly to me: the condition of living in the past. I believe that this is one of the most significant obstacles to trading success.

Figure 9.1: This illustration of an iceberg shows some of the emotions that surround money. Money and markets are highly charged and emotional topics. Traders and investors must learn to manage these emotions in order to be successful. Produced by Janice Dorn

The best traders move on and forget about a loss almost as soon they take it. They look at a loss as part of doing business and are confident in their trading plan and their ability to execute it. Of course, making money is important, but more important is finding a system of rules that will bring them more profits than losses. Making money in the markets is the by-product of executing consistently according to a defined trading plan. The best traders know how to take losses and not become depressed, angry, jealous, disgusted, or defeated. They also know how to take gains without gloating or boasting. They see only the trade they are about to enter, not the trade that just ended or the one that might be coming in the future. All past trades are out of sight and out of mind. All future trades are an illusion. Nobody knows what lies on the other side of the hard right edge of a chart!

Maintaining emotional composure is a difficult thing to do, but it must be done in order to move forward. If you are unable to detach from the past and the future, you will continue to be a victim of fear and greed. Fear doesn't form in a vacuum. It is a learned response to a particular event or probability. In the case of trading, when you have a trade that goes bad, regret and frustration can carry over into the next trade. Often, the fear is so consuming that you don't enter your next trade. Of course, Murphy's Law dictates that the trade you don't enter is the one you should have entered, and this compounds the existing emotional anguish.

Greed creates the opposite problem. After a couple of consecutive winning trades, the ego enlarges and invincible feelings overcome logic. This will ultimately lead you to trades that you normally would not have entered. Finding good trades is hard enough, while finding poor trades seems to get much easier after a couple of winners. Emotions cause perceptual distortion where you only see the part of the picture that your beliefs allow you to see. Instead, you need to know who you are in this present moment. You are the problem and you are the solution. Living in the past or the future does nothing but stir up emotions that negatively impact your trading and other aspects of your life. It is said that fear blinds us to opportunity and greed blinds us to danger. Make every effort to be fully present and you may be surprised at the outcome. When you are fully present, you are truly living exactly where life is happening. This allows you to experience every moment in the markets and life as precious and unique. It's the best way to defeat the enemy within you.

> "The ability to be in the present moment is a major
> component of mental wellness."
> Abraham Maslow

10. Trading Fear

"Fear is the main source of superstition, and one of the main sources of cruelty. To conquer fear is the beginning of wisdom."
Sir Bertrand Russell

Fear is, by and large, a misunderstood emotion. We owe our survival as a species to hardwired fear that has protected and kept us safe from physical threats for hundreds of thousands of years. But what about the litany of fears that plagues traders every day? Fear of losing, fear of watching profits disappear, fear of making mistakes, fear of missing out, fear of taking profits too soon—these are some of the many fears that paralyze and haunt us and create varying levels of anxiety (Figure 10.1). Perhaps the larger question is this: if there is so much fear and almost every trader feels fear, why do millions of people continue to trade? The answer lies in the way that fear is perceived.

For many, fear is a predator that is constantly lurking, sneaking up on them and ready to attack at any moment. In this state of mind, they are always running away from fear, crouching in a corner or looking for a safe place to hide. Fear blinds them to opportunity in much the same way that greed blinds them to danger.

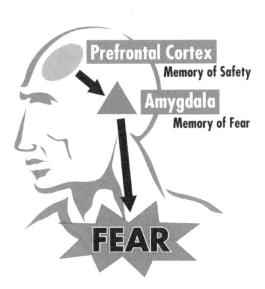

Figure 10.1: Fear of losing, fear of watching profits disappear, fear of making mistakes, fear of missing out, fear of taking profits too soon—these are some of the many fears that paralyze and haunt traders and investors and produce varying levels of anxiety. Produced by Janice Dorn

For others, fear is the prey. They move steadily and with discipline in the direction of the fear, always keeping it in front of them. As they approach the fear, they see it for what it really is—F.E.A.R: False Evidence Appearing Real. They see fear as something to go through in order to get what they desire—better trades, larger profits, or an enriched and more fulfilling life. For them, fear is not a brick wall, but a soft illusion. The more they approach the fear, the smaller it becomes, and the stronger and more powerful they become. They have a trading strategy and plan and are not afraid to execute it. They honor stop-losses and let profits run. They are not attached to the outcome of any one trade since they have mastered the ability to think in probabilities.

Lao-Tzu (Laozi), the founder of philosophical Taoism, wrote in *Tao Te Ching,* "There is no greater illusion than fear. Whoever can see through all fear will be safe." The remedy is to be a hunter and make fear your prey. Have the courage to look it in the face, see it for what it is, and chase it down. Allow fear to propel you forward, to motivate you and challenge you, rather than keeping you frozen and stuck. Facing the wind is a symbol of looking directly at something and of fighting greater odds. Visualize fear as the wind. Face it and then follow through with controlled, decisive, and smooth action. In this way, fear becomes an opening, not a closing, and you are one step closer to getting what you want from the markets.

"I must not fear. Fear is the mind-killer. Fear is the little-death that brings total obliteration. I will face my fear. I will permit it to pass over me and through me. And when it has gone past, I will turn the inner eye to see its path. Where fear has gone, there will be nothing. Only I will remain."
Frank Herbert, *Dune*

11. Trading Disasters by the Most Sophisticated Investors

"There's something happenin' here. What it is ain't exactly clear. There's a man with a gun over there. Tellin' me I got to beware. I think it's time we stop, children, what's that sound? Everybody look what's goin' down."
From *"For What It's Worth"* by Stephen Stills,
performed by Buffalo Springfield

Amid the non-stop commentary on business networks and the fear and greed of those who are watching every tick of the market, the big picture can be lost very easily. What really happened to the global markets over one weekend in January of 2008 when the U.S. markets were closed? How was it possible that the ES futures (the futures market for the S&P 500) tumbled some 68 points (the ES trades around the clock and is rarely down or up more than 10 points) at one point during the night?

These events sent shock waves through the global market community, and caused the U.S. Federal Reserve (the Fed) to do something stunning. Citing continuing concern about weakness in the economy and turmoil in the financial markets, the Fed slashed interest rates by a full 0.75%. This was the largest rate cut since 1987 and the first between regularly-scheduled meetings since the markets opened in 2001 following the attacks on the World Trade Center. A single trader lost some $7 billion by hiding accounts and overleveraging. It was, in part, the unwinding of these positions on Monday,

January 21, 2008, that sent the futures into a downward spiral and forced the Fed to act.

Here is some of the story as printed in www.businessweek.com on January 24, 2008, in a story by Carol Matlack entitled *"Soci?t? G?n?rale's* Fraud: What Now?"

> After a rogue trader cost the French bank $7.1 billion, many are left to wonder about the lucrative but risky equity-derivatives business. How could this possibly have happened? That was the question being asked in financial circles worldwide Jan. 24, after France's *Société Générale* (SOGN.PA), one of Europe's biggest banks and a global superstar in the booming derivatives-trading business, disclosed a staggering $7.1 billion loss from rogue trading by a single employee.

> The simple answer is this: One of the biggest frauds in financial-services history apparently was carried out by a 31-year-old trader in *Société Générale's* Paris headquarters, whom multiple news sources have identified as Jerome Kerviel.

According to *SocGen* representatives, Kerviel took unauthorized and fictitious directional positions totaling some 50 billion euros on European stock index futures. He also hid his losses by putting on fake hedges for index futures trades.

Carol Matlack continues,

> The fraud was discovered Jan. 20, 2008, a Sunday, which meant that *SocGen* had to start unwinding the positions on January 21, just as global equity markets were tanking on fears of a U.S. recession. "It was the worst possible time," said Janine Dow, senior director for financial institutions at the Fitch (LBCP.PA) ratings agency in Paris. *SocGen*, which also announced a nearly $3 billion 2007 loss related to U.S. mortgage-market woes, has had to seek a $5.5 billion capital increase and could even become takeover prey.

In October 2010, Kerviel was found guilty of forgery, breach of trust, and unauthorized computer use. He was sentenced to five years in prison (with two years suspended) and ordered to repay $6.3 billion. It is believed that Kerviel presently owes more money than anyone else in the world, and he has been called the most indebted person on the planet.

What is often lost in discussions of this sort about such huge losses of money is that the futures markets are zero-sum. That means for every winner there is a loser; the total gains of the winners are exactly equal to the total losses of the losers. When we read about huge "blowups" like *SocGen*, we need to keep in mind that people were on the other side of the trade and made huge amounts of money. Michael Lewis in *Liar's Poker* said, "Traders are masters of quick killing." The strong overtake, defeat, and often fatally injure the weak. It's the same in the wild, but money is not involved. In the markets, monies are the spoils of battle. Those with the best strategies and plans win by making the most money. Perhaps you now see why it is important to keep cool when others around you are losing their senses. Stop, breathe, ask yourself what is happening, and do not make silly moves that will surrender your hard-earned money to other traders. If there ever was a time to take charge of your limbic brain, it is right here and right now. Remember that your old brain will always make you feel greedy when you should feel fearful and vice versa.

> "There are two kinds of people that lose money: those that know nothing
> and those that know everything."
> Henry Kaufman, Economist

12. The Death of Denial

"The worst lies are the lies we tell ourselves. We live in denial of what we do, even what we think. We do this because we're afraid."
Richard Bach

Why do we run from the truth? What makes us close our eyes and bury our heads in the sand like ostriches, rather than face what appears to be a harsh reality? Why are we compelled to cling to dysfunctional relationships and losing stock positions in the midst of increasing drawdowns of our mental, emotional, physical, financial, and spiritual capital?

We act this way because we are driven by hope. We behave in a certain manner because we want to believe that, somehow, somewhere, sometime, things will get better. We refuse to cut losses in our personal lives and portfolios because it is an admission that we are wrong, that we can't make good decisions, and that we will have to say goodbye again. The final goodbye to someone or something for which we have yearned, lusted, and even made our own is painful. We cherish this hope as a comfort, believe that everything will be fine if we are more patient, if we hold on just a little bit longer and keep doing everything we can to make it right. Meanwhile every day, we are dying slowly inside.

As a psychiatrist and trading coach, I have the privilege of interacting with many people with a variety of presenting problems. These include bad jobs, unhappy or abusive relationships, memories of horrible childhoods, depression, self-destructive behaviors, addictions, compulsions, anxieties, phobias, and the devastating consequences of undisciplined and risky trading. It's always about what's wrong. After all, why seek help if things are wonderful? Why celebrate the positive aspects of life when there is so much misery and despair? Why bother to take personal responsibility when it is easier to remain in victim mode?

It is often easier to stay with the dysfunctional relationship or the losing market position because we "know" that everything is going to be fine if we just keep working on it. It will be OK. The person we love will change and the market position will turn around and be profitable. We forget about the fact that our lives are being ruined, that we can't eat, sleep, or exercise properly, and can't remember the last time we felt any semblance of serenity or joy. Just deny that the whole thing is happening and everything will, like some magic trick, turn out just fine. Won't it?

> "Denial ain't just a river in Egypt."
> Attributed to Mark Twain

Years ago, I bought many thousands of shares of a low-priced, four-letter stock because I became convinced that it was the best thing since sliced bread. I paid no attention to anything I read or heard because the stock was being touted by someone whose opinion I respected. It made no difference to me that the company had questionable management, massive debt, no revenues, and one of the ugliest charts on the planet. I had grown, fostered, and nourished a belief that this was going to be the big win for me. I truly believed that I would get in on the ground floor and then watch with delight as Wall Street finally noticed what a ground-breaking product this company had, and that the stock would start going up and up. Visions of a ten or twenty bagger infiltrated my brain and made themselves perfectly at home in my limbic system. I started having personal feelings about this four letter child.

I loved it, knew it was going to live up to every expectation I had about it, read every piece of news I could about it, told friends that this was the next biggest and best winner and that it was only a matter of time before everyone would see the beauty and power that I saw. My belief system was so skewed and distorted that I could not see the truth. I did not want to read or hear anything negative about the stock since I was now in love with it to the tune of tens of thousands of dollars. I owned it. It was my prize possession, and I felt the need to defend it against all naysayers. As with a marriage or new relationship, I didn't want to hear anything bad about it. My brain was filled with the neurochemistry of new love and attachment, so there was no need to disrupt it with reality. Just like every other new relationship, stocks are entered on hope.

Here is an example of some of the quasi-delusional thinking and denial of reality that took place in my brain over a period of two excruciatingly painful years:

> Oops! What is going on? Almost immediately after I bought the stock, it started to go down. This can't be happening. I don't want to believe that it is going down even though I see it right in front of me. There must be something wrong. OK. This is just a small, temporary correction and it will come back soon. Hmmm. I have a little loss here; maybe I made a mistake and should get out and watch it or read some more. Maybe I shouldn't do anything because I might read something posted by someone who was trying to talk the stock down and then I would be influenced to sell. I won't take any action at all. I am smart and educated and this company is the next big winner, so I'll hold on and it will come back. It keeps going down every day and I can't sell now because I will be taking too much of a loss, so I have to hold on. Anyway, I know that the minute I sell, it will turn around and start going up. It happens to me all the time. I just know it. It's the market, and everything is being sold, not just my beloved four-letter baby. I am a highly intelligent woman and I have made the right decision. I am not a loser and won't be a loser. I really want to win, and this stock is going to come through for me.

Figure 12.1: Denial of the reality of losing positions, both in the markets and in life, can cause mental, emotional, and physical distress that often leads to serious life-threatening illness. Produced by Janice Dorn

As soon as the market gets a bid, it will come back. Anyway, I have decided that I am not going to trade it. I will just stay in for the long haul since the story is developing, good news is supposed to be coming next month, they are going on the road to get sponsorship, and analysts will start recommending it. The stock chart now looks like death, but that doesn't matter because a lot of charts look like that and many have just turned themselves around into big winners. Maybe now that it's down 30% from where I bought it, I should buy more so that I can lower my cost basis. It wouldn't be that much money since the stock is cheap, and just think how much I will gain once Wall Street "gets it right." But my rule says never add to a losing position. Maybe I should break the rule, just this once. Let me think about it and sleep on it and see how it acts tomorrow. What a relief—it went up today by 10% and that's good news, so things are starting to improve. Too bad I didn't buy more yesterday because I would have had that extra cushion and lower cost basis. Oh well. Not to worry because things are really perking up now and I was right not to take the small loss and even more right not to take the large loss.

Now I am back at break-even and all I can say is "good for you for holding through." All that worry for months was worth it, and the market is now going to reward me for my excellent stock selection, patience, and loyalty. Now that I am at break-even, I no longer feel complacent, fearful, or despondent. In fact, I am now a little anxious because I have to figure out how to sell the stock when it really starts to take off. Do I take partial profits after it runs up another point or two, do I sell it all, or do I just hold on to it as I see it run up even further? What if I sell it all and it keeps going? Ugh. That would really be a bummer, especially when I have waited so long for the breakout. Yes! It looks like it's breaking out, so I could actually add to it since it is now a winner (well, sort of a winner because it's just a little over break-even). I know about buying break-outs because I read how so many people do it successfully, and this looks like the time to buy more. But I already have enough and I am starting to feel increasingly uneasy since it is just a little over break even. Interesting how I didn't experience this when the stock was losing and I was down so much (on paper, of course). In fact, when I had the losing position it was easier because I didn't have to do anything. I just sat and waited and knew it would come back. And it did. Now I am starting to get really scared because I have a teeny profit and maybe I should take it. But, what if I sell it and it keeps going up? I won't do anything. I will just watch it and see what happens tomorrow. I'm a winner on paper so it is OK now.

"There is the risk you cannot afford to take, and there is the risk you cannot afford not to take."
Peter Drucker, creator of Management by Objectives

But it wasn't OK. Far from it. The next week I sat in disbelief as the stock lost nearly 30% of its value. That was it. I simply could not take this roller coaster ride anymore. I was sick and tired of being sick and tired. I refused to endure one more minute of suffering. I could no longer sit in misery and despair, waiting for the market to throw me a bone so that I could get all excited and happy again. It was just simply too much torment and I was no longer taking responsibility. I was letting the markets dictate to me how I would feel that day. I was allowing the markets to exploit every aspect of my personality that would cause me to be weak, tricked, and unbalanced. I had to get my head out of the sand, get out of denial, and sell the position.

After two years of mental machinations and emotions that covered the entire gamut of any "feelings" chart, tens of thousands of dollars vanished into the market abyss. I bought with hopes and dreams and sold with despair and defeat. I ran into the other room and screamed into a pillow. Suddenly, I felt a sense of utter calm and tranquility. I was free from some two years of daily suffering, and the agony of thinking I knew something when it was really about how much I did not know. I was no longer a prisoner of brain scramble, endless torment, and depletion of personal energy. By taking action I stripped through the denial and magical thinking. I took personal responsibility, empowered myself, and gained courage. Yes, I have scars and wounds which are reminders of hard fought times and lessons learned. It is idiocy to hold and hope, and bravery to admit you are wrong and get out before it's just gone too far. This experience is etched in my brain, and I vow to never forget it so I don't repeat it.

I committed a large number of trading blunders and drove myself into a state of almost complete mental, emotional, physical, and spiritual draw-down. I lost money. I held on because I could not get myself out of denial. It was only when the denial lifted that I felt both courageous and free. I faced the truth and got out of hope and fear. Through this brutal experience I learned lessons that I like to share with others if they want to listen. I know what it feels like to lose, because I have been there. I know what courage it takes to play this game, to get rid of false evidence and false distinctions, to stop playing ostrich, and to deal with the absolute truth of a situation.

In the markets, as in life, the only way to grow and preserve yourself is to get rid of what is not working for you. It doesn't matter if it's your relationship, your house, your job, or your position in the markets. If you do not have the courage to cut your losses, they will fester and take you down with them. To see and know in your heart what is right and not to do it is complete lack of courage.

To be courageous is to do, in the face of seemingly overwhelming obstacles, what must be done. Courage is getting out of denial, admitting you made a mistake and taking personal responsibility. Courage is freeing yourself from the shackles of lies, hopes, dreams, and white picket fences that are built on shifting sands. Courage is listening to the voice inside of you, and following your heart, which never lies to you. Only in knowing what is false does one come closer to the truth. Courage is the eternal and heroic struggle to find and face your authentic self, look it squarely in the eyes, and know that you are now truly becoming the person you want to be.

"Many of you spend your entire life running from the mistaken belief that you cannot bear the pain. But you have already borne the pain. What you have not done is feel and see everything you are beyond that pain."
Khalil Gibran, Lebanese artist and poet

13. Nobody Knows Anything: Overconfidence

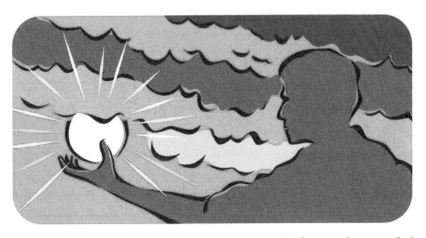

Figure 13.1: Confidence can be a wonderful trait for traders and investors. Overconfidence may lead to major errors. Produced by Janice Dorn

"And in a sense, whether it's derivatives or securitized mortgages or all those other financial instruments, each one has its own peculiar characteristics and risks, but all of them have this common thread: People who think they are really smart, think they can place a really big bet and borrow lots and lots of money to enhance their bet, discover they weren't as smart as they thought they were."
David Wessel, Economics Editor of *The Wall Street Journal* and
author of *In FED We Trust: Ben Bernanke's War on the Great Panic*

Once upon a time (in 1994 to be exact) a secretive hedge fund called Long-Term Capital Management (LTCM) was formed. From 1994 to 1997, the fund nearly tripled the wealth of those who invested in it. Then, between early 1998 and September 1998, the LTCM portfolio dropped from $100 billion to $600 million. On September 13, 1998, to avoid a potential market crash, the Federal Reserve Bank of New York organized a rescue package under which a consortium of leading investment and commercial banks injected $3.5 billion into LCTM and took over its management in exchange for 90% of its equity. The failure of LTCM is a cautionary tale about hubris, overconfidence, and the limits of modern financial theory.

LTCM seemed destined for enormous success. It was founded by John Meriwether, famed bond trader from Salomon Brothers who was a pioneer of fixed income arbitrage, and among the first to bring quantitative finance to Wall Street. He appeared to be the Mr. Spock of trading—cool, calculating, totally rational, and intellectually brilliant. In *Liar's Poker*, Michael Lewis describes Meriwether as a master of Liar's Poker, a game using serial numbers on one-dollar or one-hundred-dollar bills. It is also a metaphor for the culture within Salomon Brothers and other big banks when there are huge risk-taking opportunities with immediate payoffs and a clear distinction between the winners and the losers. Meriwether's team included Nobel-Prize-winning economists Myron Scholes and Robert Merton. He also brought in some of the best traders from Salomon Brothers. The impressive credentials of the genius team of LTCM convinced 80 investor clients to put up the minimum investment of $10 million each. This brought the total equity in LTCM to $1.3 billion. In 1994, this was a significant amount of money for a start-up hedge fund. The auspicious team then proceeded to build trading models based on the assumption that markets were logical and would always tend toward equilibrium. It appears that they were convinced they could not fail.

From 1994 to 1997, LTCM performed very well, and its funds under management had grown to $7 billion. Its team made huge financial bets with very large leverage. In his book *Inventing Money: The Story of Long-Term Capital Management and the Legends Behind It*, Nicholas Dunbar describes how

LTCM ignored two underlying assumptions behind the market models they used. These assumptions were that (a) markets are always liquid, meaning that an asset can always be sold at a reasonable price, and that (b) markets tend toward equilibrium, where "mispricings" are corrected. What it failed to take into consideration was that during market panic, liquidity dries up as investors move their money to safer investments. While market equilibrium may be true in the long run, there can be "mispricings" that persist for long enough periods of time to cause losses of many millions or even billions of dollars.

It would appear that Meriwether was completely confident about his market opinions. Dunbar described him as "Wall Street's most aggressive warrior king." In an article in *Le Monde diplomatique*, November 1998, Ibrahim Warde writes, "Asked whether he (Meriwether) believed in efficient markets, Meriwether replied 'I MAKE them efficient.'" It is said that if he believed the market would go in a certain direction and it went against him, he would not change his opinion. Often, he would increase the size of his position. If his mathematical models showed a "mispricing," he remained confident that the value would return to "fair value" over time, so he kept his position or added to it. As a result, LTCM was massively over-leveraged. It is reported that $50 was borrowed for every $1 invested. It is believed that in 1998 the LTCM portfolio amounted to well over $200 billion (borrowing capacity in terms of leverage) while net asset value was around $4.8 billion. Its swaps position was estimated to be approximately $1.25 trillion in notional value.

Indeed, the genius team was spreading itself across thin ice and skating very fast to avoid cracking the ice and falling into the freezing water below. They failed and fell hard. During three months in 1998, LTCM lost 90% of its assets under management and was unable to meet the $1.3 trillion margin call on many thousands of outstanding positions. One dollar invested in LTCM was now worth about 25 cents. LTCM's collapse came close to causing a total meltdown of the global financial system. The amounts were huge enough to send the entire global financial community into terror and to cause new rules to be written.

In the massive media coverage surrounding this event, much emphasis was on the psychological underpinnings of LTCM's demise. After several years of astounding success, the logical, rational, quantitative Nobel-Prize-winning geniuses had become infected. The virus was a combination of pride, arrogance, defiance, and hubris. I call this the Limbic Brain Virus. These giants of finance were unable to get their trading brains out of the Neanderthal cave. Absolute conviction that their quantitative models were right led to one of the most tragic incidents in market history.

Mr. Meriwether had seen three decades of market gyrations, recessions, and credit contractions. Yet, it appears that he was still a victim of his limbic brain. I have never met Mr. Meriwether and so this is not a personal assessment. It's a guess. He is but one example of how genius can truly fail when it is overconfident and floundering in the hazy, polluted, and bloated detritus of hubris and pride. Through all of market history, there have been countless examples of pride leading to financial destruction. Inexplicably, the hubris returns over and over again as if shapeshifting. Overconfidence doesn't appear to die. It just fades away for a while, and returns in another incarnation.

Let's look at another great moment in trading infamy as it relates to a guru who may have caused many of his investors to shed tears based on losing positions in natural gas. In September 2006, Amaranth Advisors LLC collapsed after losing roughly US$5 billion in a single week on trades in natural gas futures. The failure was the largest hedge fund collapse in history. Trader Brian Hunter placed huge bets on natural gas (NG) futures; the total number of his contracts is estimated to have been in the tens of thousands. Hunter was trading billions of dollars' worth of natural gas using leverage. A change of just one penny in the price of natural gas would have meant $1 million or more in profit or loss for his positions. When prices went in the complete opposite direction from what Hunter predicted, the results were catastrophic for Amaranth, resulting in a loss of $6 billion.

Amaranth suddenly had to inform investors that its $9 billion portfolio had experienced losses exceeding 65%. The fund suspended redemptions in the fall of 2006, then hired a liquidator only days later.

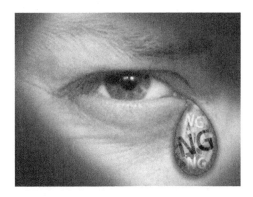

Figure 13.2: A teardrop of natural gas. The failure of Amaranth Advisors LLC while trading natural gas futures (NG) was the largest hedge fund collapse in history to date. Produced by Janice Dorn

If even a tiny teardrop for the natural gas fiasco was shed, it was likely short-lived. In 2007, Hunter started up a new hedge fund and people scrambled to get in. According to one estimate, Hunter raised $800 million in start-up capital, after putting up US$1.7 million of his own funds. That made sense to Christopher Holt, a Toronto-based finance consultant and investment manager, who made this comment for a Reuters article by Svea Herbst-Bayliss, "A number of people who invested with Hunter in the past may be very eager to get in again. As ironic as it sounds, these people would have had the chance to hear Hunter's explanation of what went wrong the last time and be assured that it won't happen again. The guys who come back from the dead actually have a pretty high success rate."

The concepts of pride and overconfidence have important implications for all investors and traders. A number of studies have shown that human beings are almost universally irrational about money. The explanation lies in the human brain and its one quadrillion neural connections. For two million years, *Homo sapiens* have survived by engaging in herding behavior. They have either fought or fled (the fight-or-flight reaction) at the first sign of impending danger. These traits do not lend themselves well to successful trading. In contrast to the two million years of *Homo sapiens* history, modern finance theory has existed for only about forty years. When placed on a twenty-four-hour scale, that's less than two seconds! In and out of the markets, human beings make a litany of errors. Many of these are due to what are called cognitive biases. These include, but are not limited to, bandwagon effect, confirmation bias, in-group bias, and anchoring. Detailed discussion of each cognitive bias is beyond the scope of this book but presents a fascinating study for anyone interested in the way that our brains prevent us from behaving in a rational manner.

Generally speaking, confidence is a fabulous trait. It underpins motivation, persistence, energy, and optimism and allows us to accomplish things that we otherwise might not have undertaken. Confidence is not a bad thing. It helps free us from the analysis paralysis that comes from listening to or watching "round the clock" financial infotainment networks as they parade their steady stream of experts. A multibillion-dollar industry is built around books, tapes, seminars, webinars, and gurus who inspire people to be confident and keep pushing forward through all obstacles. Unfortunately, most of this "expert advice" does not work. It might work temporarily, but rarely produces long-term change in an individual. If it did, we would not have a situation where at least one in three people in the United States takes at least one mood-altering substance each day. The total costs of drug abuse and addiction due to use of tobacco, alcohol, and illegal drugs are estimated at $524 billion a year. Illicit drug use alone accounts for costs of $181 billion annually in health care, productivity loss, crime, incarceration, and drug enforcement. At the time of this writing, there is an epidemic of prescription opioid abuse, and new, "legal high" designer drugs are flooding into Europe and the United States. Perhaps the self-help gurus will have to push even harder and raise their book and seminar prices more to get people to follow them to an enriched and fulfilling life with unbounded happiness, because what they are doing now does not appear to be working.

In his book *Stock Market Wizards: Interviews with America's Top Stock Traders,* Jack Schwager writes, "One of the most strikingly evident traits of all the market wizards is their high level of confidence." Schwager continues, "… but the more interviews I do with market wizard types, the more I become convinced that confidence is an inherent trait shared by these traders, as much a contributing factor to their success as a consequence of it. An honest self-appraisal in respect to confidence may be one of the best predictors of a trader's prospect for success in the markets."

Confidence is not really the main problem for traders and investors. Rather, it's overconfidence that causes trouble. As a nation, the United States is deeply overconfident, sometimes to the point of being delusional. All a person has to do is watch the auditions for television competitions such as *American Idol* or *America's Got Talent* to see examples of unfortunate and misguided overconfidence in action. Over 82% of people say that they are in the top 30% of safe drivers, and doctors consistently overestimate their ability to diagnose certain diseases (something to think about if you're wondering whether to get a second opinion). Mutual fund managers, analysts, and business executives at a conference were asked to write down how much money they would have at retirement and how much the average person in the room would have. The figures were $5 million and $2.6 million, respectively. The professor who asked the question said that, regardless of the audience, the ratio was always approximately 2:1. This is an example of overconfidence in action.

Somewhat ironically, it turns out that the more difficult the question or task (such as predicting the future of a company or the price of a stock), the greater the degree of overconfidence. Perhaps more surprising than the degree of overconfidence itself is that overconfidence does not seem to decline with time. One would think that people might learn to become more realistic about their capabilities, especially in an area where results can be calculated. They don't. Part of the explanation is that we often and conveniently "forget" failures and tend to focus on the future, not the past or the present. Neurobehaviorally, people are prone to remember failures quite differently from successes. They are inclined to attribute success to knowledge or skill and failure to bad luck. As a result, the brain plays tricks by telling a person that the outcome will be different next time. The trade that went bad resulted from circumstances beyond his or her control and had nothing to do with the prediction. As with so many experiences in life, there always seems to be something or someone else to blame when things don't work out as predicted or planned.

Overconfidence in financial decision making can be detrimental to the health of our portfolios in several ways. The first is overtrading. The groundbreaking work of Brad Barber and Terrance Odean from the University of California showed that investors who switch to online trading suffer significantly lower returns and concluded that "trigger-happy investors are prone to shooting themselves in the foot." The second is inflated estimates of the ability to pick stocks. Most managers believe that they are above-average stock pickers even when there is little evidence to support this belief. Barber and Odean also showed that, after trading costs (and before taxes), the average investor underperformed the broad market by approximately two percent a year.

The third way that overconfidence hinders portfolio performance is in attempting to time the market. Barber and Odean reported that investors tend to trade in and out of mutual funds at the worst possible times because they are chasing performance. From 1984 to 1995, the average stock mutual fund showed a yearly gain of around 12.3%, while the average investor in a stock mutual fund gained around 6.3%. That is, during this period, the average mutual fund investor would have made nearly twice as much money by simply buying and holding—and an even higher percentage if taxes are figured in. (This is not an argument for or against the buy-and-hold philosophy because there are many times when active trading is preferred.)

In a summary of their paper entitled "The Behavior of Individual Investors," Barber and Odean write,

> We provide an overview of research on the stock trading behavior of individual investors. This research documents that individual investors (1) underperform standard benchmarks (e.g., a low cost index fund), (2) sell winning investments while holding losing investments (the 'disposition effect'), (3) are heavily influenced by limited attention and past return performance in their purchase decisions, (4) engage in naïve reinforcement learning by repeating past behaviors that coincided with pleasure while avoiding past behaviors that generated pain, and (5) tend to hold undiversified stock portfolios.

These behaviors deleteriously affect the financial well-being of individual investors.

What are some simple steps traders and investors can take to begin the process of overcoming overconfidence? The first is to get over yourself and to admit and accept that you must be authentic about who you really are in the world of money. This is not an easy task. You must also begin to accept that overconfidence is a form of self-sabotage and take steps to understand why you are making the same mistakes over and over again but expecting different results. As part of this process, it is important to learn about and make peace with your trading and investing personality and the cognitive biases that hinder you from succeeding.

No matter how many technical or fundamental indicators, programs, calculators, or newsletters you use, it won't matter if you don't know who you are and continue to execute poorly. All of the answers to trading success lie within you. As difficult as this may be to accept, the Holy Grail of trading and investing is radical honesty with yourself and how your brain functions under conditions of uncertainty. Benjamin Graham, sometimes called the Father of Value Investing, said, "The investor's chief problem—and even his worst enemy—is likely to be himself."

One of the best and most disciplined ways to get a handle on overconfidence is to keep a rigorously honest trade journal. In order to get from where you are to where you want to be as a trader or investor, it is necessary to look at your mistakes and your successes and learn from them. There are many simple formats for a trade journal, and taking the time to enter each trade will produce a document that provides a great guidepost for discovery.

It is important to realize that trading success is about learning at least one new thing every day. This way you put yourself onto a learning curve and keep your mind sharp. You will begin to see things you never saw before and realize that you are getting to where you want to be. It's a voyage with no end in sight, so prepare to enjoy it as you move forward. Study lessons from market history, including the great failures and successes of others. Learn as you go that there are no substitutes for humility and gratitude and that you don't know what you don't know and often don't know that you don't know. Learn to be comfortable with uncertainty and stay firmly in the realm of probability.

Take total personal responsibility for every trade. Analyze it, dissect it, and learn from it. Look inward, not outward, for the reasons that you succeeded or failed in each trade. In this process, learn the truth about yourself. Stay open, positive, and confident, but say "goodbye" to overconfidence before your equity curve says "goodbye" to you.

The examples of trading fiascos such as *SocGen*, LTCM and Amaranth show that it does not matter if an investor has extensive experience or power, has a Nobel Prize, or has been entrusted with millions of dollars. Every human being has the potential to allow his or her emotions to take over, and as a result, make costly and destructive mistakes. Refusal to accept this may be the first step to falling down a slippery slope.

"Vanity is a mortgage that must be deducted from the value of a man."
Otto von Bismarck (1815-1898)

14. Extreme Volatility in Oil Prices Causes Bear Markets

Oil prices and interest rates are some of the most important factors impacting stock prices and the global economy. Changes in interest rates affect those who have money or those who are in a position where they have enough wealth to borrow money. On the other hand, changes in oil prices impact almost everyone on the globe. Since most goods have to be transported, and sources of transportation use fuel, oil prices affect everyone, from those on welfare in developed countries to AIDS orphans in Africa. Oil prices also impact almost every business in the world. Therefore, the significance of changes in oil prices cannot be understated.

History seems to show that the actual price of oil is not the most important factor when it comes to investing. What seems to matter most is how much and how fast the price of oil increases. Since 2008, Dave Harder's Investment Updates have referred to Leeb's Law for oil prices. In 2004, investment experts Stephen and Donna Leeb wrote a book entitled *The Oil Factor: Protect Yourself—and Profit—from the Coming Energy Crisis.* Based on historical evidence, they postulated that investors should sell stocks when oil prices rise more than 80% in a twelve-month time frame, and buy back stocks when the year-over-year change falls to 20% or less. A chart from his book showing the percentage change of oil prices over a rolling twelve-month time period is provided in Figure 14.1.

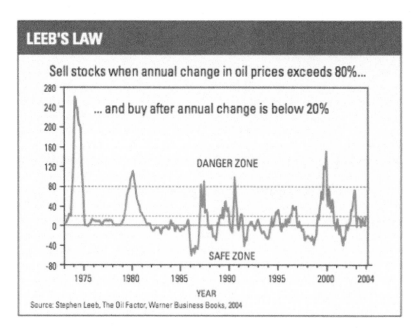

Figure 14.1: Chart from Stephen and Donna Leeb, *The Oil Factor: Protect Yourself and Profit from the Coming Energy Crisis*, Warner Business Books, 2004

The first time oil prices met those criteria was in January 1974. By that time the S&P 500 Index was already down by 20%, and the Canadian TSX index was down 9% from a record high. Nevertheless, both market averages fell another 30% after January 1974 in a bear market very similar to the 2008 decline. The chart in Figure 14.2 shows the S&P 500 Index from 1971 to 1975. The arrow pointing straight down shows when oil prices were up 80% over the previous twelve months. The diagonal arrow shows the decline in stock prices which followed that sell signal.

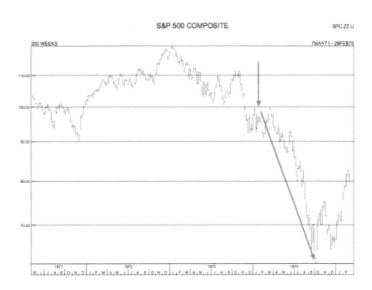

Figure 14.2: S&P 500 1971-1975. Source: Thomson Reuters

The second time oil prices advanced more than 80% within twelve months was in January 1980 (see red arrow pointing down). A few weeks later, the S&P 500 started a sell-off of 17.1%, which did not cross the 20% threshold. However, by March 1980, the TSX had declined more than 20%. The S&P rose close to 40% after the 17.1% correction in the spring of 1980 and finally peaked almost a year after that buy signal. Then the S&P 500 Index finally declined more than 20%. See the chart in Figure 14.3 for the S&P 500 from 1979 to 1983.

Figure 14.3: S&P 500 1979-1983. Bear market for the S&P 500 after oil prices increased more than 80% in 12 months on January 1980. Source: Thomson Reuters

The requirements for Leeb's Law were met for the third time when a cluster of signals occurred in 1987. The first signal occurred in January. Another two signals were given soon after this in July and August 1987. Stock prices rose more than 30% from the start of 1987 until the peak on August 23, 1987. After Labor Day, stock prices started declining, culminating in the Crash of 1987. By October 20, 1987, the Dow Jones Industrial Average had declined 40% from its peak in the space of only two months, as demonstrated on the chart in Figure 14.4. It is important to realize that a big rise in oil prices still had a major impact on equity markets even though the price of oil peaked at US$22.76 a barrel in 1987, well below the previous record high of $38.30 recorded at the peak in 1981.

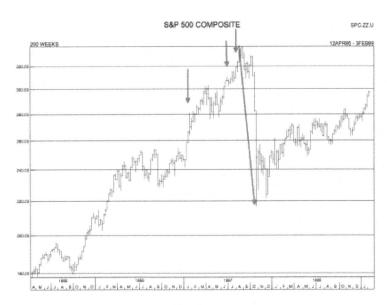

Figure 14.4: S&P 500 1985-1988. Source: Thomson Reuters

Oil prices spiked again after Iraq invaded Kuwait in August 1990. In this case, stock prices had already fallen 20% and hit the lows by the time oil prices had increased by 80% over 12 months. See the chart in Figure 14.5.

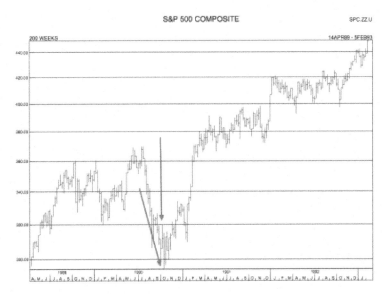

Figure 14.5: S&P 500 1989-1992. Source: Thomson Reuters

Nine years later, oil prices also rose by more than 80% during one year as of July and August 1999, and again as of January 2000. Stock prices continued to advance until September 2000 when the "tech wreck" began. It is important to note that the high for oil prices in 2000 was $37.80, slightly below the all-time high of $38.34 attained in April 1981. The events of 1987, 1990, and 2000 show that oil prices do not have to rise to new highs to cause a problem—they just have to rise 80% within any twelve-month period, as Leeb suggests. See the chart in Figure 14.6 for this period.

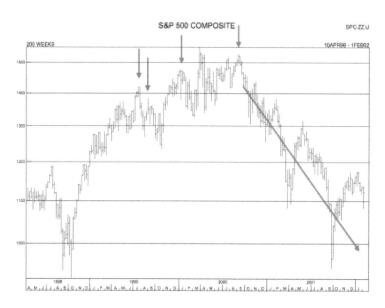

Figure 14.6: S&P 500 1998-2001. Source: Thomson Reuters

In April 2008, several months before the Financial Crisis hit, the rise in oil prices again met Stephen Leeb's Law. The S&P 500 reached a recovery high one month after April, on May 23, 2008, and the S&P/TSX hit an all-time high two months later on June 6, 2008. See the chart in Figure 14.7, which includes the decline during the Financial Crisis.

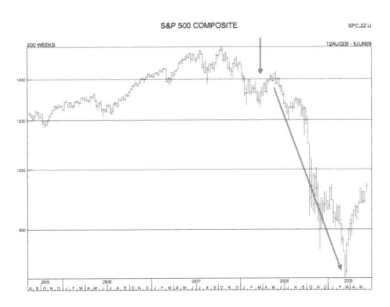

Figure 14.7: S&P 500 2006-2009. Source: Thomson Reuters

Most recently, oil prices were up more than 80% in twelve months in November 2009, as reported in Dave Harder's November 23, 2009, Investment Update. Stock markets rallied and corrected less than 20% in the summer of 2010. Then markets rallied to new recovery highs and peaked on May 2, 2011, seventeen months after the Leeb's Law sell signal occurred in November 2009. From the intra-day high on May 2, 2011, to the intra-day low on October 4, 2011, during the European Debt Crisis, the S&P fell 21.6%. Even though there was a long delay, Leeb's Law was accurate once again. See the chart of the S&P 500 from 2008 to 2012 in Figure 14.8.

Figure 14.8: S&P 500 2008-2012. Source: Thomson Reuters

Many business historians say that the 1981-1982 bear market and recession was caused by record high interest rates, that the 1987 crash was caused
by the advent of program trading which caused stocks to become overvalued, that the 2000-2003 bear market and recession was caused by a bubble
in technology stocks, and that the 2008 bear market and Financial Crisis was
caused by irresponsible lending practices. While these explanations may be
true, oil prices, nevertheless, experienced major price increases before every
one of these bear markets and/or recessions. Is that only a coincidence?
Possibly. Does that mean that actions like this can be ignored? At your peril!

In the past, the longest that the S&P 500 has advanced after a sell signal
without a bear market has been seventeen months in 2011. The next longest
advance continued fourteen months after oil prices triggered a Leeb's Law
buy signal in July 1999. It took just less than a year to fulfill Leeb's Law after
oil prices rose more than 80% in February 1980. Other stock market declines
of 20% occurred soon after the signal or before the signal was issued.

Stephen Leeb's Law also gives buy signals for stocks. He has found that,
after rising as much as 80% in the previous year, stocks often turn up again
when the increase in oil prices is reduced to only 20% in a twelve-month

period. However, that premise does not seem to be nearly as accurate as the sell signals using the 80% rule. Rather than buying when the rise in oil prices has been reduced to 20%, I have found that it is better to buy when the long-term moving average crossovers for the S&P 500 and the Canadian S&P/TSX have turned positive after a decline of 20% or more in the S&P 500.

As stated at the beginning of this chapter, oil prices have a major impact on almost everyone and everything on the planet. Consequently, it makes sense that a sharp rise in oil prices would affect world economies and world stock markets. Since 1974, the S&P 500 has dropped 20% or more before, during, or after every occasion when oil prices have increased by 80% or more. The only decline of 20% or more in the last forty years without an 80% rise in oil prices was the 1998 Clinton Impeachment/Russian Default/Long-Term Capital bear market. That decline only lasted a few months.

Years after a bear market, some investors and business leaders worry and remain too cautious because they do not want to take the chance of being blindsided by another unexpected crisis or market decline. This happens because very few take the time to analyze what really causes a serious bear market.

Contrary to popular thought, an unexpected crisis, on its own, rarely derails a bull market for the longer term.

As mentioned earlier, the 20% decline in the S&P 500 during the summer of 1998 caused by the Clinton Impeachment process, the failure of the Long-Term Capital Hedge Fund, and the Russian debt default was not preceded by an 80% rise in oil prices. However, the S&P 500 was back at an all-time high by the end of 1998, so those events did not impact the longer-term decline for very long.

The 2008 Financial Crisis was preceded by an 80% rise in oil prices as of April 2008. The 20% decline in the S&P 500 that happened in the summer of 2011 during the European Debt Crisis and the U.S. Debt Ceiling Crisis was preceded by an 80% rise in oil prices as of November 2009. In November 2009, crude oil prices traded at the $70 level, less than half of the record high price recorded in 2008. What really creates havoc with consumers, businesses and countries that import a lot of oil, is extreme upside volatility in oil prices from any level. Huge price increases in oil are like a major global tax increase, forcibly extracting money from individuals and businesses, making it difficult to plan for the future.

After the 2011 market decline, the S&P 500 Index formed a double bottom after October 4, 2011. After that, the long-term moving average crossover indicators turned positive for the S&P 500 and the Canadian S&P/TSX Index on January 23, 2012. Consequently, as of January 23, 2012, the impact of the November 2009 spike in oil prices had been eliminated. Even though it seemed like Cyprus and Greece were going to default on their government debt in May 2012, the S&P 500 only experienced a normal 10% correction in May 2012 before continuing to rise again, as opposed to the 20% decline in 2011.

There were a number of worrisome times after May 2012 when the U.S. reached its debt ceiling, when there was concern the U.S. would reach the "fiscal cliff," and when the U.S. government entered a shutdown on October 1, 2013. Nevertheless, market corrections were only minor and short in duration. Not only were market corrections of no real consequence in 2012 and 2013, but U.S. market averages recorded one of the best years in more than a decade during 2013. In 2013, the S&P 500 rose 29.6%, the strongest gain since 1997. The Dow Jones Industrial Average added 26.5% in 2013, the best year since 1995.

What was the major difference between 2011 and the period from 2012 to 2014? After November 2009, a huge rise in oil prices forecast a bear market in equities within 18 months. After the 2011 20% decline, a double bottom in the S&P 500, and improved momentum as of January 23, 2012, the risk of a severe decline was eliminated. The one other major factor that causes bear markets, an inverted U.S. yield curve (which is discussed in the following chapter), had not existed since 2006. Consequently, as of January 23, 2012, the risk for North American equity markets was as low as it ever gets.

After markets are strong for many years, investors wonder when the bull market will end. Experts point out high levels of optimism, a large number of Initial Public Offerings, heavy insider selling, high levels of margin debt, the duration of a bull market before previous bear markets, and a whole host of other negative variables. However, history shows that every longer-lasting bear market since 1970 has been preceded by a major spike in oil prices. Other negative factors or crises only had longer-term ramifications when oil prices jumped by 80%. Therefore, if investors could only look at one factor as a warning sign of a serious bear market, it would be volatility in oil prices.

The table in Figure 14.9 is a helpful checklist prepared by François Trahan, Michael Kantrowitz, CFA, and Emily Needell, CFA, from Cornerstone Macro LP. This checklist shows the variables that were present before or during declines of 15% or more in the S&P 500 since 1972. This checklist also shows that a sharp rise in oil prices was the most common factor for serious corrections. Factor 9 shows that an International Crisis occurred during only four of the twelve major corrections. It is also helpful to notice that markets experienced a major correction seven out of twelve times when valuations were cheap.

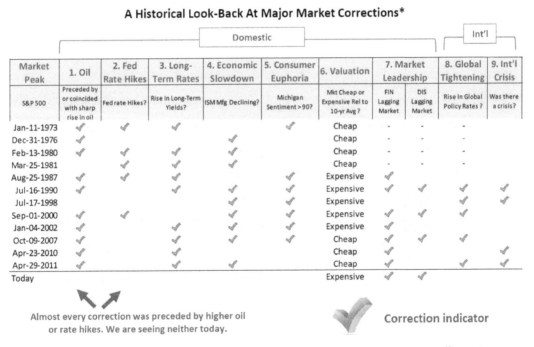

A Historical Look-Back At Major Market Corrections*

Market Peak / S&P 500	1. Oil / Preceded by or coincided with sharp rise in oil	2. Fed Rate Hikes / Fed rate Hikes?	3. Long-Term Rates / Rise In Long-Term Yields?	4. Economic Slowdown / ISM Mfg Declining?	5. Consumer Euphoria / Michigan Sentiment >90?	6. Valuation / Mkt Cheap or Expensive Rel to 10-yr Avg?	7. Market Leadership FIN Lagging Market	7. Market Leadership DIS Lagging Market	8. Global Tightening / Rise In Global Policy Rates?	9. Int'l Crisis / Was there a crisis?
Jan-11-1973	✓	✓	✓		✓	Cheap	-	-	-	
Dec-31-1976	✓			✓		Cheap	-	-	-	
Feb-13-1980	✓	✓	✓	✓		Cheap	-	-	-	
Mar-25-1981		✓	✓	✓		Cheap	-	-	-	
Aug-25-1987	✓	✓	✓		✓	Expensive	✓			
Jul-16-1990	✓		✓	✓	✓	Expensive	✓	✓	✓	✓
Jul-17-1998				✓	✓	Expensive			✓	✓
Sep-01-2000	✓	✓		✓	✓	Expensive	✓	✓	✓	
Jan-04-2002	✓		✓	✓	✓	Expensive	✓			
Oct-09-2007	✓		✓	✓	✓	Cheap	✓	✓	✓	
Apr-23-2010	✓		✓			Cheap	✓			✓
Apr-29-2011	✓		✓	✓		Cheap	✓		✓	✓
Today						Expensive	✓	✓		

Almost every correction was preceded by higher oil or rate hikes. We are seeing neither today.

✓ Correction indicator

Figure 14.9: Economics, Policy and Strategy, Cornerstone Macro LP, April 8, 2014.

Investors spend much of their time and energy focusing on an endless stream of statistics such as corporate earnings, economic growth, budget deficits, unemployment levels, elections, political issues, potential military conflicts, etc. As human beings, we are interested in these developments. Sometimes they are important to the economy and us. However, raw historical information shows there are really only two factors that are the most important to monitor in order avoid a serious market decline. The most important and most common factor is an extreme rise in oil prices. The second most significant and common factor is U.S. interest rates and bond yields.

If oil prices have not risen more than 80% in a twelve-month period and the U.S. yield curve is not inverted, that is when investors and business leaders should be taking the most risk they are comfortable with. According to history, it is not rational to hold unusually high levels of cash out of fear that a crisis will suddenly knock markets and the global economy down for many months. Waiting for an abundance of good news or an absence of worrisome signs is often counterproductive. Looking back, we can see that a crisis has only created trouble for stock markets when a big rise in oil prices has already had a negative impact on economies around the world.

It is as if a spike in oil prices is always the straw that breaks the back of the market and economy. It is the common denominator in almost every major market correction. In some ways, global economies and markets are like the human body. We are exposed to viruses and diseases all the time. If people are healthy, rested, and well nourished they are unlikely to become ill from a virus. However, if a person is tired, not eating properly, and is under stress, he or she is much more susceptible to becoming ill.

A sharp rise in oil prices and/or an inverted yield curve in the United States has the effect of "weakening the immune system" of global economies and markets. That is when longer-term issues or an unexpected event can act like a virus to knock healthy economies and markets "flat on their backs." Taking over a competitor at a high price, starting to develop a huge real estate property, adding a major addition to a factory, and borrowing heavily to invest or speculate could be devastating if they are done after oil prices have spiked higher and the yield curve has inverted. When oil prices rise sharply, government leaders should also prepare for a possible slowdown in the economy and not enact measures on the assumption that economic growth will continue at the current pace.

There are times to be cautious and there are times to be aggressive. There are always a host of factors that cause anxiety and uncertainty. History shows the volatility of oil prices is one of the easiest and best factors to monitor in order to provide us with the confidence to take on more risk or to reduce risk at the appropriate time. Investors, business owners, and government officials should take advantage of this simple, reliable indicator to make well-informed, prudent decisions.

History shows there can be a time lag of up to eighteen months or so until stock prices fall, after oil prices have risen by 80% or more in a twelve-month time frame. Nevertheless, few indicators are so simple, and so reliable, for giving notice that a severe decline is forthcoming. Since stock markets can sometimes experience a strong rise for a long time after a sell signal, short-term and long-term moving average crossovers can be used for timing tools to move into cash after stock markets peak and a Leeb's Law sell signal is in effect. As with all other indicators, it still takes discipline and experience to put one's faith in advance warning tools like this. It may be very simple, but doing so is not quite as easy as it sounds. Even so, this discipline is worth striving for.

After a Leeb's Law sell signal, investors are forewarned that a decline of 20% or more should occur within eighteen months. There are very few tools that provide investors with this type of significant, reliable information. However, we must remember that a sell signal has been triggered as the following weeks, months, and quarters pass.

As human beings, we often think we are smarter than we really are. I recently flew in a twelve-passenger helicopter from Vancouver Harbour across Georgia Strait and the Gulf Islands to Victoria, B.C. Even though the helicopter pilot is highly trained, very experienced, and flies the half-hour flight many times in a day, he still has a simple checklist mounted on the dashboard so he does not forget anything.

My office is in Abbotsford, B.C., Canada, a city of 130,000 people located 60 kilometers, or 40 miles, east of Vancouver. When I attend the annual

Abbotsford International Air Show and look at the military aircraft on display, the pitot tube (which measures airspeed) and other parts of the plane have protective covers with red flags attached to them. Even though the flight crew and the pilot know procedures backwards and forwards, it is still possible for them to forget to do a most basic task (like removing the protective covers) that they have done many times before. The tragic hang-gliding fatality mentioned earlier in the book is an example of that. Consequently, like attaching red flags to protective covers on a military aircraft, it is important to prepare a simple, visible reminder that cannot be ignored to act as a constant reminder of the risks ahead—such as placing a red flag on one's desk. The chapter "It Is Time for a Revolutionary Change in Portfolio Management" will provide information on how to incorporate this information into an investment strategy.

15. A Point of Interest

For the past twenty-five years, my wonderful wife of thirty-three years, Marianne, has volunteered for an organization that provides help to single mothers and their young children. In 2004, a five-year-old girl called Catalina came to live with our family for a year so her mother could deal with some issues. Catalina went back to live with her mother again after that year but she had become part of our family. (My wife and I have three married daughters and four grandchildren.)

Catalina wanted to improve her snowboarding. One beautiful January day, I took her to a local ski hill to teach her. The ski hill is at an elevation of 1,500 meters, or 5,000 feet. The temperature in the valley floor was close to the freezing level, so we naturally wore our ski jackets, gloves, and ski pants as we made our way from our vehicle to the chairlift. We all know that temperature falls as altitude increases. However, by noon it was so warm that we could not bear to wear our gloves and jackets any longer, and I took them back to our vehicle. There had been an unusual temperature inversion, and we were experiencing California weather in the middle of winter. The scientific fact that temperature declines with higher altitude had been "suspended" for a while.

A temperature inversion is a deviation which occurs when the temperature increases with height. It was a real treat to ski in only ski pants and a T-shirt in January. When the day was over and I stopped to buy gas for my SUV on the valley floor, it was so cold I had to put my ski jacket on!

Similar circumstances can occur with interest rates. Long-term interest rates are usually higher than short-term interest rates. Consequently, the yield (interest rate) on a ten-year Canadian or U.S. government bond is usually two percent higher than the yield on a one-year bond. The extent of the difference in rates over various lengths of time is called the yield curve.

Just like temperature inversions, interest rates can also undergo an abnormal change. Sometimes, the yield on short-term bonds will rise to the point where they are actually higher than long-term bonds. This usually happens when the economy has been so strong that officials at the Federal Reserve become concerned that inflation may rise. When concerns about inflation mount, the Federal Reserve will often increase short-term interest rates to try to slow the economy down by "taking the punch bowl away from the party." As this happens, the yield on shorter government bond prices will also move higher. When the yield on a one-year bond increases to the point where it is higher than the yield on a ten-year bond, the yield curve changes from being a normal yield curve to being an inverted yield curve.

An inverted yield curve has significant ramifications. Individuals and businesses often service debt. When short-term interest rates rise, individuals have less money to spend and the costs for businesses increase. This dynamic can reduce sales and lower corporate profits for companies in many sectors of the economy. Moreover, banks make profits by borrowing money at low short-term rates and lending it out to customers at higher long-term interest rates. When short-term interest rates increase to the point that they are higher than long-term rates, banks cannot make money on new lending, so profits decline. This in turn curtails lending and is negative for the economy. Consequently, an inverted yield curve is a red flag for business owners, warning them that there will likely be a slowdown in the economy, if not an outright recession.

In 1996, Federal Reserve Bank economists Arturo Estrella and Frederic S. Mishkin published a report in *Current Issues in Economics and Finance*, entitled "The Yield Curve as a Predictor of U.S. Recessions." Out of twenty-six indicators that were examined, they discovered that the basic yield curve was the best indicator to use for predicting a recession. They wrote, "The yield curve—specifically the spread between interest rates on the ten-year Treasury note and the three-month Treasury Bill—is a valuable forecasting tool. It is simple to use and it significantly outperforms other financial and macroeconomic indicators in predicting recessions two to six quarters ahead."

The table in Figure 15.1 shows that a recession has followed an inverted yield curve every time since 1970. On average, the recession has started twelve months after the yield curve inverted. However, the time lag between an inverted yield curve and the start of a recession has varied from as short as six months to as long as seventeen months.

Event	Date of Inversion Start	Date of the Recession Start	Time from Inversion to Recession Start	Duration of Inversion	Time from Disinversion to Recession End	Duration of Recession	Max Inversion
	⇕	⇕	Months ⇕	Months ⇕	Months ⇕	Months ⇕	Basis Points ⇕
1970 Recession	Dec-68	Jan-70	13	15	8	11	−52
1974 Recession	Jun-73	Dec-73	6	18	3	16	−159
1980 Recession	Nov-78	Feb-80	15	18	2	6	−328
1981-1982 Recession	Oct-80	Aug-81	10	12	13	16	−351
1990 Recession	Jun-89	Aug-90	14	7	14	8	−16
2001 Recession	Jul-00	Apr-01	9	7	9	8	−70
2008-2009 Recession	Aug-06	Jan-08	17	10	24	18	−51
Average since 1969			12	12	10	12	−147
Std Dev since 1969			3.83	4.72	7.50	4.78	138.96

Figure 15.1: Yield curve chart, courtesy of *Wikipedia*

Lower interest rates eventually follow a period when the yield curve has inverted. Since lower profits and a slower economy are negative for stock prices, severe bear markets have often also followed this type of inverted period. In the report "The Yield Curve," John Mauldin, president of Millennium Wave Advisors LLC, warned, "The stock market drops an average of 43% before and during a recession. That is an ugly number. But it is a very real number. Much of the drop happens prior to a recession."

However, it is hard for investors to know how to react when the yield curve inverts, since markets can sometimes continue to rise substantially for a year or more after it happens. Since markets can keep rising and the outlook seems promising, investors are tempted to think the inversion will not have much of an impact this time. I have learned this is a dangerous assumption!

In the same article (written on December 31, 2005), John Mauldin commented about what happened after the yield curve inverted in July 2000. He noted, "But most observers suggested we ignore full-blown yield curve inversions as well. I think it was something like 50 out of 50 blue chip economists failed to predict the last recession even a few months out. They ignored the yield curve, all finding out reasons why 'this time it's different.'" The conditions during every cycle and inverted yield curve are never exactly the same. Nevertheless, the consequences of an inverted yield curve do not seem to vary much. The charts in Figures 15.2 to 15.8 show how the S&P 500 has reacted when the U.S. yield curve has inverted since 1968. The red arrows point to the date when the U.S. yield curve inverted.

Figure 15.2: The yield curve inverted in December 1968, one month after the S&P 500 peaked. The arrow points to the time when the yield curve inverted. From the high, the S&P 500 Index fell 36.1% over 19 months. Source: Thomson Reuters

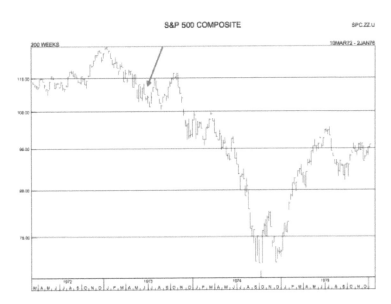

Figure 15.3: The U.S. yield curve inverted again in June 1973. By this time, the S&P 500 had already declined 13.3% from the peak. Even so, the S&P fell a total of 48.2% from the high over a 21-month period. Source: Thomson Reuters

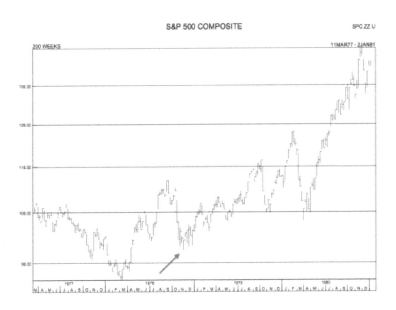

Figure 15.4: The yield curve inverted in November 1978 when the S&P 500 had just completed a rather severe 17.1% correction. In this case, markets actually rose for another 15 months before falling 17.1% in February and March 1980. A bear market decline of 20% or more did not follow in this case. Source: Thomson Reuters

Figure 15.5: While an official bear market did not occur after the 1978 yield curve inversion, the U.S. yield curve inverted again in October 1980. This time, the S&P 500 peaked a month later on November 28, 1980, and then fell 27.1% over the following 20 months. Source: Thomson Reuters

Figure 15.6: The yield curve did not invert before the 1987 Stock Market Crash. However, it did so in June 1989. The S&P 500 peaked more than a year later on July 20, 1990, and then fell 19.9% in three months as the United States prepared to attack Iraq. Source: Thomson Reuters

Figure 15.7: The U.S. yield curve also inverted in July 2000. Although the NASDAQ was already well below the March 2000 peak, other North American market averages started one of the longest bear markets in a generation in September 2000. The S&P 500 fell a total of 47.1% over a 25-month period. Source: Thomson Reuters

Figure 15.8: The most recent U.S. yield curve inversion occurred in August 2006. U.S. markets continued to advance until October 2007. Then the S&P 500 fell 56.7% over 16 months during the Financial Crisis. On average, a major decline in the S&P 500 began 5.4 months after the U.S. yield curve inverted. However, the time frame

for a stock market decline to begin after the yield curve inverted varied from negative six months (1973) to fifteen months (1980). Source: Thomson Reuters

So, what should an investor do when the yield curve in the United States inverts? This is another scenario where long-term moving average crossovers can be extremely helpful. If the long-term moving average crossovers turn negative after the yield curve is inverted, the risk of a stock market decline of 20% or more is much higher than if the yield curve has not inverted. It is also common for oil prices to rise 80% or more within eighteen months or so of an inverted yield curve. (A very strong economy, which requires the Federal Reserve to raise interest rates, often causes oil prices to rise as well.) These two developments are the best warning signs of a recession and a bear market. If these conditions do not exist, the likelihood of the U.S. economy moving into a recession is very low. The major problem with these clear indicators is that markets and the economy can sometimes continue to be very strong for so long after they occur that we tend to ignore them as months, and perhaps even a year, pass. Therefore, reducing equity exposure as soon as the yield curve inverts can be counterproductive. Rather, investors should seriously consider reducing equity exposure when the long-term moving average crossovers turn negative after the yield curve has inverted in the United States.

Reducing equity exposure if the S&P 500 falls more than 15% from the high point of the year when the yield curve has inverted also enables investors to capture much of the upside when markets are strong while limiting losses to 15%. For example, if the S&P rises 25% in the twelve months after the yield curve inverts (this can happen when optimism is high after the economy and markets have been strong for several years) and then falls 20%, an investor can still have earned a profit of 10% for the year after selling out when markets dropped 15%. Having a "circuit breaker" in place to limit losses at a time when the risk has increased significantly can reduce investor stress and anxiety. This practice can be better than parking money in cash for a year as soon as the yield curve inverts and then watching stock prices soar. Sitting on the sidelines for a long time during a bull market can tempt investors to buy at the wrong time. When the long-term moving average crossovers turn positive for the S&P 500 and the S&P/TSX again, the investor who reduced equity exposure can add to equity positions once more.

There is another indicator that can be used to confirm that higher interest rates and/or oil prices are having a negative impact. The Conference Board Leading Economic Index (LEI) includes various indicators that usually start to deteriorate before the economy does. This indicator does not provide signals that are as clear as an 80% rise in oil prices or an inverted yield curve. Even so, when the value of the Index starts to decline when oil prices and interest rates rise to danger levels, this decline can be useful to confirm that the risk of a recession and bear market is increasing. See the chart of this Index in Figure 15.9.

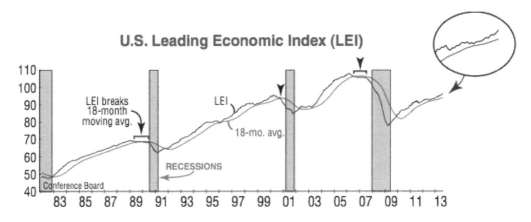

Figure 15.9: The Conference Board Leading Economic Index for the U.S. Axis title: (2004=100). Recession information provided by NBER

In summary, business owners, real estate developers, equity investors, and fixed income/bond investors must be in a heightened state of alertness when an inverted yield curve occurs. This inversion means that there is a high probability of a recession and a severe market decline. It takes incredible discipline to accept these potentially negative ramifications when it seems like consumer confidence, investment optimism, and economic activity have continued to improve month after month, quarter after quarter, as if nothing has changed. The situation in 2000 verifies that even top ranked economists have trouble managing this type of situation. The next time the U.S. yield curve inverts, we will all be tempted to think "it will be different this time." History suggests it will not be.

When I let my garden hose run to fill up the hot tub or the swimming pool, I put a colorful band of some sort around my wrist so that I do not forget to turn it off at the right time. Before I did this, I sometimes became distracted by other things and ended up creating a problem when water overflowed. In the same way, it is helpful to have an obvious reminder on a window, computer screen, door, day-timer, etc., when the yield curve is inverted so that we do not become complacent as the economy and markets enter what history has shown to be a very real "danger zone." A method for using this data is included in the chapter "It Is Time for a Revolutionary Change in Portfolio Management."

16. It's All Relative

There is a popular investment saying that "a rising tide lifts all boats." This assumption is generally true. When bond, commodity, real estate, and stock market prices go up, most individual assets will indeed follow along and rise in price as well. However, while a rising tide will raise all boats in a marina by exactly the same height, individual bonds, commodities, real estate properties, stocks, and global equity markets can advance or decline at completely different rates than the overall market.

For example, residential real estate prices in the U.S. held up fairly well in the late 1980s when over-lending for commercial real estate caused the Savings and Loan Crisis. The bubble in Japanese stock prices burst in 1989 after the Nikkei 225 Index peaked at 38,957. Prices initially collapsed and remained in a downtrend for more than a decade while other global markets soared. I was in Thailand in May 1998, ten months after the Thai baht collapsed. This collapse started the events that produced the Asian Crisis. I was invited to speak at a conference in Bangkok where business leaders told me how the value of their companies had dropped by 90%. This drop had occurred as U.S. and other global equity markets and economies kept improving for another two years. These Thai business leaders must have felt like they were on another planet.

At times, the trends of various market sectors can also move in opposite directions. As technology stocks and stock markets experienced their last meteoric advance from late 1998 to March 2000, the U.S. index of banking stocks fell significantly. Then, even though there is seldom a "place to hide" in a bear market, the price of financial stocks actually performed well during the 2000-2003 bear market when almost every sector lost value.

Years later, the price of almost every stock was hammered during the Financial Crisis of 2008. Most stocks made a good recovery by 2011. Then, after March 2011, U.S. stocks outperformed most global stock markets. Since I am in Canada, and resource prices seemed to be in a long-term uptrend, I assumed that it would continue to be prudent to hold overweight positions in Canada, as I had since 2002. From December 31, 2002, to December 31, 2012, the Canadian S&P/TSX rose 9.22% per year while the S&P 500 only increased by 2.26% per year (in Canadian dollars). Foreign equities, as measured by the MSCI EAFE Index, advanced 3.33% (in Canadian dollars). Because the 16- to 18-year growth phases for real assets started in 1999, it also seemed likely that gold bullion and resource companies should continue to outperform as they did in the late 1970s. Even though the European Central Bank and the Federal Reserve were printing massive amounts of money, the value of real assets and the S&P/TSX were lower at the end of 2013 than they were in the spring of 2011. This happened as the Dow Jones Industrial Average and the S&P 500 recovered to record highs. Most global market averages could not keep up with U.S. markets as they began to outperform Canadian and other global equities for the first time in twelve years.

A very high-profile example of how variable the returns in individual stocks can be is the price trend of Apple Inc. shares. The shares of Apple peaked at a price of just over $700 in the fall of 2012 and traded in the $450 range in March 2013, a loss of more than 35%. This happened as U.S. stock market averages were in an uptrend, even reaching new all-time highs!

The Reverend Dr. Samuel Johnson (1696-1772) said, "Nothing focuses a mind like a hanging." Challenging times in markets focus the minds of investors and portfolio managers. One never stops learning. Following the trend of moving average crossovers is the highest priority. However, the situation from 2011 to 2013 illustrated that in making investment decisions it is not good enough to just follow the long-term trend. The long-term moving average crossovers turned positive for most global markets by February 2012, but U.S. markets were much stronger than Canadian markets.

This example reveals the value of using an additional, reliable tool that can point out which sectors and individual positions have the potential of earning the highest return with the least amount of risk. It should be an indicator that also takes emotions out of the decision-making process. Since the price of an asset takes into account all of the variables investors are considering, this tool, like moving average crossovers, must be based on the price of an investment.

When it comes to investing, the first priority is to follow the trend. The second highest priority is investing in assets or investments that exhibit the best relative strength.

Relative strength information is very basic. It does not focus on the actual price, but on performance compared to the overall market. For example, relative strength data for the S&P 500 Index will simply compare how all of the 500 stocks in the Index have performed compared to the S&P 500 over a given period of time. The stocks that decline the least when the S&P 500 Index loses value are likely to be the shares that will rise the most when markets advance. The stocks that rise the most when the S&P 500 advances are likely to continue to be the best performers on the downside until the outperformance ends.

Global equity markets which are the first to rise from the lows and which appreciate the most are likely to stay in the uptrend the longest and produce the highest return. For example, it was very noticeable that the S&P 500 peaked on October 11, 2007, while the Canadian S&P/TSX peaked eight months later on June 6, 2008. This indicated that the S&P/TSX Index had more strength than the S&P 500. When stock prices were pulverized during the Financial Crisis, the S&P/TSX Index fell 50.6% from the intraday high to the intraday low, while the S&P 500 dropped 57.5%.

In the spring of 2013, the Emerging Markets were the first global sector to turn negative according to the long-term moving average crossovers I use. This happened as the Japanese Nikkei 225 soared. It is important to be aware of this movement, especially given the extraordinary monetary stimulus the

Bank of Japan was providing. With the Japanese Yen in a free fall, it is harder for goods in other countries to compete with Japanese products. With the Nikkei 225 down more than 60% from where it was in 1989, using the long-term moving average crossover indicators as a buy and sell indicator for Japanese equities might be very profitable.

Of course, like any other market indicator, relative strength information is not perfect. No asset will outperform forever, so there will always be changes in relative strength over time. When a stock, sector, or global market shifts from a position of relative strength to relative weakness and vice versa, the data will lag behind. Therefore, the data may not be helpful during these transition phases. However, in many cases, periods of outperformance or underperformance can last for many quarters or even many years so the information is useful much of the time.

It has been said that, similar to Isaac Newton's law of motion, a market trend stays in motion until it stops. Using relative strength rankings is a very good way to determine which individual assets, sectors, or global markets have the potential to produce better returns in an uptrend. They may also decline less than others during a correction or bear market. Relative strength data is simple mathematical information, so there is no chance of emotions influencing its results.

When looking to buy, an investor is like a paraglider, looking for the area against the mountainside with the strongest lift.

Figure 16.1: Hang glider in Harrison Mills, B.C. Photo by Dave Harder

A friend and colleague said that planning to sell short is like "looking for the wettest paper bag to throw a rock into." Another analogy for selling short would be a skier searching for the double black diamond runs with the steepest slope.

Figure 16.2: Signs at the Whistler Blackcomb ski resort in Whistler, B.C., giving directions to the Mathews Traverse easy ski run and the "Whistler Bowl to Shale Slope" most challenging double black diamond run. Ski runs are rated in terms of difficulty and slope. Green is the easiest, blue is intermediate, and black is difficult. Double black diamond runs are the most challenging since the slope is so steep a skier can have difficulty coming to a stop if he or she falls. Photo by Dave Harder

Figure 16.3: Picture at the top of the Horseshoe ski run at the Whistler Blackcomb ski resort in Whistler, B.C. Double black diamond ski runs are for expert skiers only. Short selling is only for expert investors and traders. Photo by Dave Harder

Roger W. Babson stated, "The question of when to buy is far more important than what to buy." That may well be true. However, even though it may not be the highest priority, knowing what to buy still ranks as an important factor if one is trying to maximize returns with the least amount of risk. I have learned that relative strength information seems to be the best way of knowing what to buy, so I have been incorporating it into my strategy.

Relative strength information can also alert investors that it may be time to sell. Jesse Livermore wrote, "It takes buying to move the market up, but when buying dries up, stocks will fall of their own weight." When the price of a stock or sector falls more than that of others for no reason even when all seems to be well, it can be a very good indicator that the buying is drying up. As mentioned previously, it is not always important to understand why the price is moving. Often that will be revealed much later. The most important thing for an investor to do is to accept what the money is doing and then act accordingly.

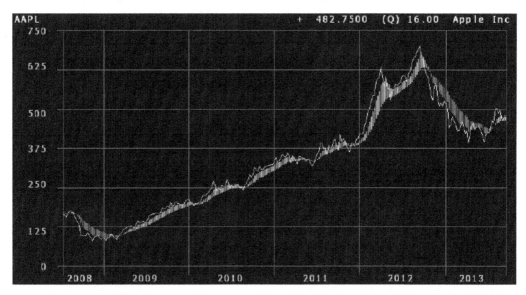

Figure 16.4: The long-term moving average crossover for Apple Inc. Data for charts compiled by Thomson Reuters

Figure 16.4 shows that the long-term moving average crossover turned negative for Apple Inc. at $629.71 in October 2012, well below the peak of $705 in September 2012.The share price continued to fall into 2013, even as many other U.S. stocks were advancing enough to enable the S&P 500 and DJIA to reach all-time highs. Quite a number of analysts and experts were undeterred. They kept exclaiming how Apple Inc. had over $120 billion in cash, was a world-leading brand, and was working on an Apple TV product. However, Apple shares had simply reached a peak in popularity and money was being withdrawn. Poor relative strength indicated weakness in the share price. That, together with the long-term moving average crossover turning negative, provided all the evidence investors required to realize that all was not well at Apple.

An analyst recommended buying Apple in March 2013, and asked me for feedback regarding his recommendation. I responded with a copy of the long-term moving average crossover chart together with a comment that the momentum and relative strength data did not support a buy recommendation. He replied, saying he realized the "technicals" did not look good, but the fundamentals were supportive. However, the long-term moving average crossovers are not mere schematic drawings or diagrams. They are clear indicators vividly showing those who care to take note that money is either moving in or out of an investment. His behavior was like that of someone who is taking off on a runway by looking at the weather forecast instead of the windsock.

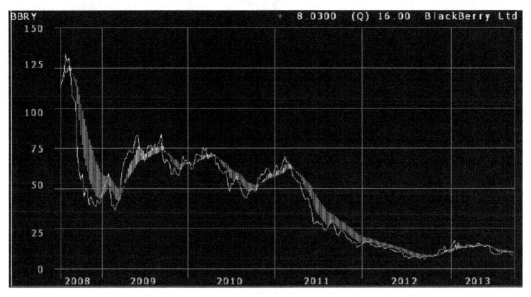

Figure 16.5: Long-term moving average crossover for Research In Motion, now called BlackBerry. Data for charts compiled by Thomson Reuters

The action of Research In Motion/BlackBerry shares from 2010 to early 2013 is a perfect example of what happens when a stock displays relative weakness and then relative strength. RIMM (RIM.TO) was weaker than the S&P 500 and the S&P/TSX in 2010. After early 2011, the share price collapsed, starting a long downtrend, even as analysts continued to issue buy recommendations on the stock due to its "attractive valuation." RIM was a very popular investment for Canadians at the time, as Apple has been for Americans. Investors should not have made any investments in RIM until the long-term moving average crossovers turned positive. Relative strength also needed to improve in order to provide verification that the compulsion to sell was being replaced by a desire to buy the shares again. This happened in November 2012. When global equity markets were correcting in November 2012, RIM shares actually started rising. This was like a traffic light turning from red to green. While it seemed like all the media attention was focusing on the decline in Apple Inc. shares, RIM was displaying its first important instance of relative strength in years. This was a positive sign. For additional confirmation, the long-term moving average crossover turned positive for RIM on November 16, 2012, at a price of $9.20. A week after that, several Canadian and U.S. analysts recommended buying the stock. While Apple shares continued to fall after November 2012, RIM shares increased 63% from $9.20 to $15.00 in the spring of 2013.

However, the long-term moving average crossover turned negative for RIM on June 28, 2013, at a price of $10.46. As of the summer of 2014, the future of BlackBerry is uncertain. Will the company be sold and split up into parts? Will the founders of BlackBerry purchase the company and rebuild it the way Steve Jobs rebuilt Apple Inc.? No one knows. Using long-term moving average crossovers together with relative strength data can guide investors as the company evolves.

History was also being repeated as the price of Apple shares collapsed in the absence of bad news during the fall of 2012. When a company becomes the most valuable company in the world, as Apple Inc. did on August 20, 2012, it can be a sign that the share price and the company's products have reached a peak in popularity. This happened decades ago, in the 1970s, with companies such as General Motors and IBM. I first witnessed what happens when a company becomes the biggest company in the world when Microsoft reached that milestone with a value of $616.34 billion in December 1999. The share price of Microsoft peaked shortly after and lost half of its value in the following fifteen months. It turned out the high value of Microsoft was also an indication that the entire technology sector was too popular, since most other technology stocks suffered as well.

In 2008, PetroChina Co. Ltd was the biggest company in the world, followed by Exxon Mobil Corporation. Sure enough, oil stocks and oil prices followed the actions of General Motors, IBM, and Microsoft years earlier, by nosediving from all-time highs by the end of 2008.

In August 2012, Apple Inc. replaced Exxon as the most valuable company in the world. When the share price of Apple reached $665 on August 20,

2012, the total value of all Apple Inc. shares ($623 billion) finally surpassed Microsoft's record of $618.9 billion set in 1999. History suggested the price could fall sharply in the months ahead. Therefore, when the share price fell from just over $700 to the $600 level, it had history and relative strength against it. When the price fell to $629.71 on October 6, 2012, the long-term moving average crossovers turned negative as well. Analysts seemed to ignore these three important factors. At the end of March 2013, the relative strength of Apple shares ranked close to the bottom 10% of all the companies in the NASDAQ 100. The outlook for Apple should be more promising when the longer-term trend and relative strength improve, as they did on August 6, 2013. Relative strength information can be another very useful arrow in an investor's quiver.

Exxon Mobil took the top spot away from Apple in 2012. That may not bode well for energy companies and oil prices. Time will tell. Many portfolio managers were optimistic that the energy sector would perform well in 2014. Simple relative strength information will have helped investors confirm or deny that as the year progresses. It may also help to alert investors when trends change as they may be doing in Japanese equity markets.

Remember, it's all relative!

17. The Pervasive Impact of Long-Term Cycles

"If some lose their whole fortunes, they will drag many more down with them...believe me that the whole system of credit and finance which is carried on here at Rome in the Forum, is inextricably bound up with the revenues of the Asiatic province. If those revenues are destroyed, our whole system of credit will come down with a crash."
Cicero, 66 B.C. (Translation by W.W. Fowler, 1909)

This comment from more than 2,000 years ago is eerily similar to what many are thinking after the Financial Crisis. Economies and equity markets go through various cycles. Even though North American equity markets have experienced distinct phases of growth and consolidation over the last century, this important factor seems to be mostly ignored. These are the responses I get when I bring up the topic of long economic and market cycles: "In our modern-day society, the world is so interconnected that cycles do not exist anymore." "We are so sophisticated and knowledgeable now, that to think economies and markets follow cycles is like believing in a horoscope." "This is a waste of time; let's go on to another topic." The majority of people may not accept the fact that there are cycles, yet an understanding of how cycles work helps to put many things that are happening into perspective. Physician Oliver Wendell Holmes, one of the best writers of the 19th century, said, "A page of history is worth a volume of logic."

Winston Churchill declared, "The farther backward you can look, the farther forward you are likely to see."

If history is so important for investing, let us look back to see what we can learn about economic and market cycles. Generally speaking, most people are optimistic and driven to improve the living conditions of themselves and their families. However, long periods of economic optimism and success can lead to overconfidence. If profits are high, enterprising individuals believe that producing more goods should only increase growth and earnings. Leaders at financial institutions also become more confident and eager to reap profits, so they lower lending standards and encourage their customers to borrow more. This causes a flurry of real estate development, business expansion, corporate takeovers, and buyouts. However, over time, too much production, higher prices, and higher stock valuations cause problems. Central banks typically "take away the punch bowl from the party" by raising interest rates. Eventually, higher costs and an overabundance of supply reduce sales and profits. These factors can even create losses until the supply is reduced enough to match the demand once again.

When the economy responds by slowing down and asset values fall, financial institutions raise lending standards and curb lending. These actions often make a bad situation worse, leading to boom-and-bust cycles. When central bankers finally feel that the excesses from the previous boom have been removed, they usually lower interest rates in an attempt to stimulate borrowing and economic growth. Over a period of many months, the cycle of increasing production typically begins all over again. As a result, throughout history, economic, business, and investment cycles have been as constant as the passage of time.

For example, if a man cut and split two cords of firewood in a summer two hundred years ago, it might have been enough to keep his family warm throughout the winter. If he could cut and split four cords, he might have had enough for two winters in case he could not for some reason do this task the next summer. If he could split six cords, perhaps he could keep four and sell two. If there was a shortage of firewood he could make a lot of money selling the two cords. If he did make a lot of money selling the extra wood, others would likely follow and do the same. As more and more people split extra firewood to sell, all of a sudden there would be more wood than people needed after splitting their own. Then prices would fall and it would not make sense for individuals to go to all the work of making extra firewood the next summer. Consequently, by the following winter, prices might stabilize as demand matched the supply. The summer after that, it would seem more attractive to produce extra firewood again. Once there was a market for extra firewood, supply and demand would produce normal cyclical volatility. The same cycle still holds true today for basic crops, livestock, commodities, and other goods. In his book *Panics and Crashes and How You Can Make Money Out Of Them*, author Harry Schultz wrote that a typical business cycle consists of seven phases. First is the shortage of a product. The second stage is the development of a concept to address the shortage. The third stage is the profitable production of the product. During the fourth stage, over-production and over-supply lead to losses. Losses are experienced in the fifth stage. Cutbacks in production characterize the sixth stage. In the seventh and final stage, the cutbacks result in a shortage, enabling the whole cycle to start over again.

Readers may accept the fact that there are business cycles, but are there really also economic and market cycles? If so, are they of any consequence? See the history of the S&P 500 Index from its inception in the early 1920s to September 2013, as shown in Figure 17.1, and come to your own conclusion.

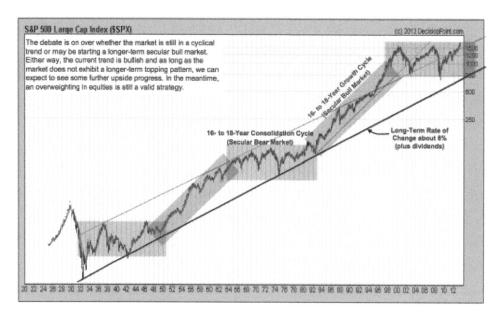

Figure 17.1: Chart prepared by Decisionpoint.com and Bob Dickey, Technical Analyst, March 2013

It does not take long for someone with an open mind to observe that there have been very clear cycles where markets rise sharply for 16 to 18 years and then consolidate for 16 to 18 years. When stocks (financial assets) consolidate, commodities (real assets) rise—as was the case from 1966 to 1982. When financial assets perform well, real assets consolidate, as was the case from 1982 to 2000. For example, gold and oil prices had massive increases during the 1970s and peaked in 1980 and 1981 respectively. During the 1970s, gold bullion values rose from US$40 per ounce to US$850, while oil prices rose from the single digits to over US$35 per barrel. After gold peaked in January 1980 and oil prices hit an all-time high in April 1981, their prices entered an 18-year consolidation/correction phase until gold bottomed at $250 in 1999, and oil bottomed at $10 in 1998. Then gold bullion prices increased from $250 in 1999 to $1900 per ounce in 2011. Oil prices multiplied from $10 in 1998 to more than $100 per barrel in 2012 after reaching a high of $147 in 2008.

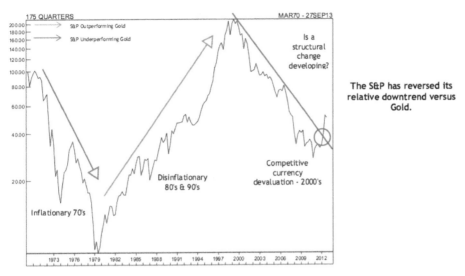

Figure 17.2: Gold (a real asset) outperformed the S&P 500 in the 1970s when stocks (financial assets) were in a consolidation phase. From 1981 to 2000, the trends reversed and the S&P outperformed gold when stocks were in a growth phase. From 2000 to 2013, gold outperformed the S&P 500 as real assets were in a growth phase and financial assets were in a consolidation phase. Since early 2012, the S&P 500 has outperformed gold. This reversal may mark the end of the boom in resources and the start of a new 16- to 18-year growth phase for equities. More time is required to confirm if this is the case. Chart produced by Robert Sluymer, Thomson Reuters

The S&P 500 Index made almost no progress from 1966 to 1982, and then rose nearly fourteen times in value from 1982 to 2000. Since gold and oil bottomed just before 2000, the S&P 500 Index has made little progress for the last thirteen years. The earth has seasons. Planets move in cycles. Markets also have cycles. Economic cycles of boom and bust are still commonplace. The facts are almost impossible to refute. These long-term cycles have such a significant impact on so many things that investors must understand them, just as a farmer must understand seasons.

If you doubt the pervasive, powerful patterns of cycles, consider this: in 1998, seventeen years after the resource bubble burst in 1981, Russia could not pay the wages of government workers and was on the verge of defaulting on the bonds it had sold. In the meantime, the U.S. economy had been doing so well during the 1980s and 1990s that the U.S. government announced it was going to stop issuing 30-year bonds on October 31, 2001, because it expected to be debt free in the very near future. In 2000, the economists and policy analysts at the U.S. Congressional Budget Office (CBO) projected government surpluses that would eliminate the debt of $3.5 trillion in a decade. As it turned out, government debt ballooned to $9 trillion by 2010 and sat at more than $16 trillion in 2013. The chart in Figure 17.3 shows the CBO forecasts in blue. Random Walk forecasts (using current data and probabilities to create a forecast) are in gray. This example once again demonstrates how expert forecasts are unreliable, no matter how intelligent experts are or how much information they can access. A 2012 study by Federal Reserve Board of St. Louis economists Kevin Kliesen and Daniel Thornton, entitled "How Good are the Government's Deficit and Debt Projections and Should We Care?" pointed out that Random Walk forecasts turned out to be more accurate than those made by the CBO.

One-Year Deficit Projection Errors as a Percent of GDP: CBO and Random Walk Projections

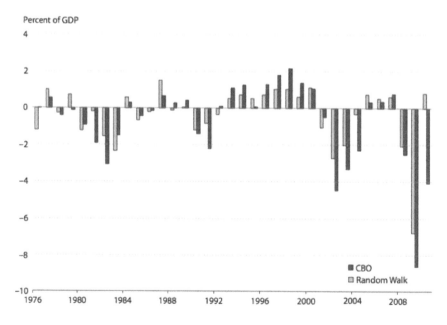

Figure 17.3: Chart produced with permission by Kliesen, Kevin L. and Thornton, Daniel L. "How Good Are the Government's Deficit and Debt Projections and Should We Care?" Federal Reserve Bank of St. Louis *Review*, January/February 2012, 94(1), 21-39

In 2014, fourteen years into another uptrend in the resource cycle, Russia is almost debt free, whereas the United States has been forced to increase its debt ceiling. In late 2012, U.S. politicians had to grapple with the Fiscal Cliff scenario. In 2013, it seemed as though the U.S. was in such a deep hole that it would never recover. It is very important for investors to understand the significant impact of cycles. It is also important to remember that tough times do eventually lead to good times, no matter how unlikely it may seem.

A decade after the resource boom went bust in 1982, the debt levels in Canada were the worst of any country in the G7 except Italy. Income taxes were increased, government spending was cut, and a value-added tax (the Goods and Services Tax - GST) was introduced. The Canadian economy slowed while it went through this stage. However, by 2005, Canada was reaping the benefits of those actions. In 2013, Toronto replaced Chicago as the fourth largest city in North America. As a result of the austerity measures implemented in the 1990s, Canada is now respected as one of the strongest economies in the West, with a healthy financial position and lower tax rates than many other countries.

In 2014, the U.S. and Europe find themselves in the condition that Canada was in around 1990. Government spending will have to be reduced. Benefits may be trimmed, prisons closed, pension payments cut back, and retirement ages increased. The U.S. military may also be asked to reduce expenditures. Marijuana may be legalized to earn tax revenues. Major cities like Detroit have declared bankruptcy just as New York City did in 1975. Taxes will probably have to be increased in the U.S., and the "brain drain" may reverse as Canadians who moved to the U.S. for higher paying jobs in the 1990s come home again. Ten years from now, the United States as a whole, including American cities now in dire straits, may be rejuvenated, while resource towns such as Tumbler Ridge in British Columbia and Fort McMurray in Alberta may have been transformed into ghost towns.

What is surprising is that the media rarely, if ever, mention the influence of the 16-year cycle. This lack does not mean it does not exist.

While market cycles are like economic seasons caused by overconfidence and pessimism, many treat them as voodoo science. It seems as though many are so focused on the short term that they cannot bring themselves to accept the significance of a 16-year cycle that can last a fifth of one's lifetime. This is not unusual. Earlier chapters show that human beings are not as rational as they think. Individuals involved in business and markets are often perceived as being very rational since business is all about the numbers. However, history shows that many in business and markets get carried away in trends just as often as ordinary citizens do.

On May 3, 2013, Becky Quick from CNBC interviewed Berkshire Vice Chairman Charlie Munger. Charlie Munger is almost 90 years old so he has seen many bank failures. He stated,

> You can't trust bankers to govern themselves. A banker who is allowed to borrow money at X and lend it out at X plus Y will just go crazy and do too much of it if the civilization doesn't have rules that prevent it. What happened in Cyprus was very similar to what happened in Iceland; it was stark raving mad in both cases. And the bankers, they'd be doing even more if the thing hadn't blown up. I do not think you can trust bankers to control themselves. They're like heroin addicts.

Since I began my investment career in 1981, I have also witnessed major bank failures in the United States, Europe, and Japan. At no time was this more evident than after the Financial Crisis when many of the biggest, strongest banks around the globe fell in stature. Fortunately, prudent regulations, discipline, and sound management enabled Canadian financial institutions to rank as some of the strongest in the world in 2013. The Canadian banks accomplished this status by growing carefully instead of growing quickly. There are very competent bankers everywhere. However, there have been many more failures of major financial institutions than can reasonably have been expected. While ordinary corporate failures result in losses, bank failures also have a profound impact on consumer and investor confidence. Excessive lending during good times often leads to the failure of large financial institutions during recessions. This is a major reason why 16- to 18-year economic cycles occur.

Sixteen, seventeen, or eighteen years is a very long time in this day and age. If a person gets an MBA at age twenty-four and manages a business for sixteen years, he or she will be forty years old. This person could be at the halfway point of his or her entire career if he or she expects to work for thirty years. If this individual's career began in a U.S. manufacturing business or investment firm when a consolidation period of the cycle started in 1930, 1966, or 2000, he or she would think that running a business is tough slugging, wondering if good times would ever come back. In contrast, if an individual began to manage a gold mine or an oil company in 1930, 1966, or 2000, he or she would experience boom times for close to sixteen years.

On the other hand, if someone had begun an investment or business career in 1950 or 1982, after sixteen years they would have thought that boom times would never end. But someone who ran an oil company or gold mine after 1950 or 1982 might have been close to depression by the time 1966 or 2000 rolled around.

Earlier, the authors compared the way markets function to the way fashions change. Long-term market cycles and economic cycles are also similar to long-term fashion cycles. For example, horn-rimmed glasses were in style during the late 1950s and early 1960s. After that they seemed ugly, so nobody wanted to be seen wearing them. In 2014, they are quite popular again. Fashions for men's ties moved from wide ties in the 1970s to narrow ones in the 1990s and then back to an in-between size in recent years.

From the 1960s to 2000, young men (and male basketball players) wore short shorts and knee-high socks. During the 1960s and 1970s, older men who wore shorts down to the knees were viewed by the younger crowd as being out of style. Since 2000, it has become fashionable for males (and male basketball players) to wear long baggy shorts and short socks. I can just imagine what it will be like twenty years from now when a new generation might switch to wearing short shorts again. Then the new generation will probably scorn their fathers for wearing the long baggy shorts that are so commonplace in 2014.

My wife and I took our three daughters on a nine-week trip across Canada in 1995. At Algonquin Provincial Park in Ontario, my daughters bought me a purple T-shirt with a mountain scene. I enjoyed wearing this comfortable shirt. However, when I wore the shirt to work outside fifteen years later, my daughters said I should not wear it anymore because that color was no longer fashionable. Long-term market cycles are similar. Gold and other commodities were in high demand in the 1970s, and then it was like the tap was turned off from 1981 to 2000. Technology and Internet stocks were hot in the 1990s. After 2000, no one wanted them. However, just as things that were in style a long time eventually come back, gold and commodities soared again after 2002. Technology stocks could start to perform very well again before 2020. Most people can relate an interesting story about things that have gone in and out of style. It appears to be easy for people to recognize long-term cycles in clothing styles. Long-term cycles are just as common in markets and economies. However, for some reason, individuals and the media do not seem to recognize them. As a result, they miss out on a factor that impacts many things and situations around us.

The current consolidation cycle for stocks and boom time for commodities is very similar to the 1970s in many ways. Former U.S. President Jimmy Carter (1977-1981) wrote a book in 2010 entitled *White House Diary*. On September 29, 2010, *USA Today* published an article written by Carter, who stated that he had received many responses from people citing the similarities between the 1970s and now. He writes, "Thirty-five years ago, the American people were eager for fundamental changes after the embarrassment and lies of Watergate and the Vietnam War, the assassinations of Martin Luther King Jr. and the Kennedy brothers, and revelations that the CIA and top leaders had been involved in criminal acts, including murder. As a Georgia farmer, I was considered by many to have no association with these stains on our national character."

In the same way, one of the reasons President Obama has been so popular is that he is not connected to the business establishment, which is considered responsible for environmental damage and the Financial Crisis. Today, the Tea Party movement is a reaction to the desire for "fundamental change" due to the irresponsible actions of government and business leaders that led to the Financial Crisis and monumental debt.

While Jimmy Carter was a man of integrity, Americans were embarrassed and humiliated when, on his watch, Iran took sixty-six U.S. citizens and diplomats hostage on November 4, 1979. The 2012 movie *Argo* was based on this true story. The mighty U.S. was not able to free most of the hostages for 444 days. An attempt by the military to free them only made things worse when planes and helicopters involved in the rescue crashed and burned. Eventually, the hostages were released when the U.S. paid Iran a ransom, not in U.S. dollars, but in gold. Sound familiar? When gold was close to its peak in early 2012, India announced it was paying Iran for its oil with gold bullion.

The American people were embarrassed and humiliated in the 1970s, while Canadians were feeling good since commodity prices were booming. (The negative sentiment of Americans at that time can be sensed when one is watching television reruns of *All in the Family*, which was produced in the 1970s.) During the 1980s and 1990s, Americans became proud and self-confident, while Canadians experienced soaring government deficits, rising unemployment, and a weak currency. By 2000, superb stock gains in previous years resulted in many Americans proclaiming a buy, hold, and prosper strategy for stocks. In recent years, one did not have to spend much time south of the 49th parallel in order to observe that Americans now feel the way Canadians did in the 1990s. The buy, hold, and prosper mentality for stocks has morphed into the buy, hold, and suffer strategy.

In 2013, Canada was respected around the world and Canadians felt proud again. This respect was confirmed in November 2012, when the British government announced that in 2013, Mark Carney, the Governor of the Bank of Canada, was going to become the first non-native of England to lead the Bank of England in its 318-year history.

On the other hand, many Americans feel that the U.S. will never again be the nation of strength and prosperity that it was in 2000. We must remember that the United States rebounded from the era of the 1970s to become an even more powerful nation with great pride in the 1980s and 1990s. The history of cycles suggests that this could well happen again—but not until 2014 to 2016.

In 1979, the cover of a *Business Week* magazine declared the death of equities. One of the best bull markets in history began when investors least expected it, in 1982. The buy, hold, and prosper strategy will probably start to work very well again in 2016 or so, just when most investors are likely to give up on stocks, as they did at the end of the 1970s.

Americans must keep these cycles in mind and not become too discouraged. The following list of the similarities between the 1970s and the past decade illustrates how influential these cycles are:

1970-1980	2000-2010
Americans are angry and frustrated.	Americans are angry and frustrated.
Gold, silver, and oil prices soar.	Gold and oil prices surge to new record highs.
The Canadian dollar trades at par or higher.	The Canadian dollar rises 50% to trade at par.
New York City declares bankruptcy.	California's debt is ranked lower than Vietnam's.
The U.S. struggles in the Vietnam War.	Little progress is made in the Afghanistan conflict.
The 1974 recession hits the U.S. hard, but Canada, Russia, South America, and the Middle East thrive.	The Financial Crisis rocks America and Europe.
The DJIA falls 45% during the 1973-1974 Bear Market.	The DJIA falls 54% during the Financial Crisis.
The S&P 500 and DJIA make little progress.	The S&P 500 and DJIA are lower than they were in 2000.
The TSX soars at the end of the 1970s.	The TSX outperforms U.S. markets after 2000.
Agricultural commodity prices soar.	Agricultural commodity prices reach record highs.

| High inflation causes cash to lose value. | Inflation at 2% is higher than interest rates so cash loses value. |

Figure 17.4: Comparison of 1970-1980 and 2000-2010 in Canada and the U.S.

As time goes on, more similarities emerge between the period from 1966 to 1982 and the current consolidation period from 2000 to 2016/2018. Since Canada is more of a resource-based economy than the United States, the Canadian economy usually performs better than its U.S. counterpart during the consolidation phase of a 16- to 18-year cycle. Australia, Brazil, the Middle East, and Russia are usually strong at the same time. The Canadian economy and other resource-based countries often suffer when lower resource prices produce conditions for U.S. industrial companies to do well. Consequently, it is very interesting to observe that the U.S. seems to be following the path that Canada did in the 1980s and 1990s.

After the resource boom went bust in 1981, the Canadian dollar dropped as low as US$0.62. In 2002, some referred to the Canadian dollar as the North American peso. Canada was the undisputed underdog in North America.

In 2014, it seems as if we are seeing the exact opposite. Canada is in very good financial shape while U.S. debt is soaring. Canada is being lauded around the world for its responsible financial management while Occupy Wall Street campaigns spread across the U.S. in 2012. Real estate prices have fallen in the U.S. while Canadian real estate prices have risen to the point where they are on average more than 80% higher than the average price in America. Taxes and costs for government services are rising in the U.S. Homeland Security has been a drag on the U.S. economy, costing billions of dollars. In the 1980s and 1990s, resources and Western Canada were in a slump, while manufacturing in Ontario and the United States' economy were flying high. Now Ontario and the U.S. are in a slump, while resources and western Canada are strong. It seems as though Canada and the United States are on opposite alternating cycles.

In the late 1960s and throughout the 1970s, the U.S. suffered through the Vietnam War, the Nixon Impeachment, rising oil prices, and government intervention with wage and price controls. During that time Canada benefited from a boom in commodity prices. From the start of 1966 to the end of 1980, the U.S. DJIA Index made next to no progress, while the TSX rose 173%. (Most of the rise in the TSX occurred in the final three years of that period, from 1977 to 1981.) Then, from 1981 to 2000, the TSX rose only 393% while the DJIA rose 1,019%. From 2001 to the end of 2012, the S&P/TSX rose 39% while the DJIA only increased 21%. (The figures above do not include dividends.) From December 31, 2000, to the end of 2012, the Canadian dollar increased by 51% against the U.S. dollar, from US$.6671 to US$1.0080. If American investors had invested in the Canadian S&P/TSX Index from December 31, 2000, to December 31, 2012, they would have earned a total return of 90% compared to only 21% in the DJIA. What a contrast to the 1980s and 1990s!

If these cycles continue to repeat themselves, the Canadian economy and stock market could outperform their U.S. counterparts for several more years, until 2016/2018. Significant gains usually occur in the final stages of a market or economic cycle. This pattern suggests that resource and commodity prices might have their final advance of this 16-year cycle in the years after 2012. However, no cycle plays out exactly the same, so investors must observe what the money is actually doing to determine when these long-term cycles are changing. Figure 17.2 showed that the growth cycle for commodities may have already come to an end after peaking in 2011, having lasted only thirteen or so years.

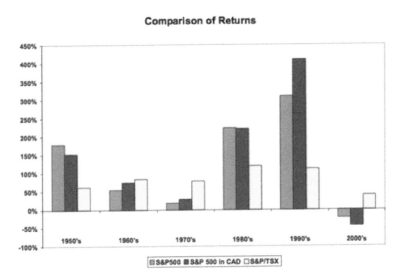

Figure 17.5: Table produced by Matt Barasch, Feb 21, 2012

In Figure 17.5, note how well the S&P 500 performed in the 1950s, 1980s, and 1990s. When resource and commodity prices were strong during the 1960s, 1970s, and 2000s, the S&P/TSX outperformed the S&P 500 in U.S. dollars and Canadian dollars.

The impact of the 16- to 18-year cycle on Canada and the U.S. has been so profound that it has even impacted Canada's national game of ice hockey and the National Hockey League in both the U.S. and Canada. While young people in the U.S. were protesting against the messy Vietnam War in the early 1970s (remember that young men could receive an envelope in the mail any day forcing them to join the U.S. military in order to fight in Vietnam, as opposed to voluntary enlistment now), there was widespread optimism in Canada. During those years, resource prices were strong, and the Canadian dollar was worth more than the U.S. dollar. One of the ways this optimism manifested itself was the addition of three new Canadian hockey teams to the NHL. Canada wanted to send its sons to the NHL instead of to war. Consequently, the Vancouver Canucks joined the NHL in 1970, the Winnipeg Jets entered in 1972, and the Québec Nordiques, during 1979.

However, by the mid-1990s, the long-drawn-out decline in resource prices made it difficult for the Canadian economy to grow. There were also concerns about Québec separation. Lower ticket sales, and the fact that NHL players are paid in U.S. dollars while the value of the Loonie (the name of a one-dollar Canadian coin) fell sharply, had a very negative impact on most Canadian NHL teams. Conditions were so bad that the Québec Nordiques had to be relocated to Colorado in 1995 to become the Avalanche. No one could be found to take over the ownership of the beleaguered Winnipeg Jets in 1996, so they were moved to Phoenix and became the Coyotes. The Canucks struggled to meet their payroll for many years until the value of the Loonie finally improved after 2002.

In 2014 the tables are turned. Many of the newer U.S. NHL hockey teams which were started during the U.S. boom years a decade ago are struggling to survive. In the meantime, Canadian teams are doing so well that almost every game for every team has been sold out for years. Winnipeg has built a new stadium since hockey fans there had been desperate to bring their old Winnipeg Jets team back. In the midst of the 2011 Stanley Cup Playoffs, the NHL approved the sale of the Atlanta Thrashers to a group from Winnipeg who planned to relocate the team to their city, subject to selling 13,000 season tickets. The team owners wanted season ticket holders to commit for five years. While the people in Atlanta do not want to spend money on hockey tickets during hard times, the fans in Winnipeg shocked almost everyone by snapping up all 13,000 season tickets in only two minutes, with only another fifteen minutes required to process the orders! There could not be clearer evidence of the powerful financial and psychological impact that the 16-year resource cycle has had on Canada and the United States.

Other pieces of evidence are also very interesting. The Canucks played in General Motors Place in Vancouver until it was renamed Rogers Arena after GM's troubles in 2009. (Rogers Communications is a large Canadian firm.) In the 2011 Stanley Cup Playoffs, the Vancouver Canucks were playing the Boston Bruins. The arena in Boston used to be called the Fleet Center when FleetBoston Financial sponsored it. However, in 2005, the Toronto Dominion Bank from Canada gained control of the naming rights after it purchased FleetBoston Financial. Now the arena is called the TD Garden.

In 2013, the U.S. was out of favor and Canada was in favor. Until the cycle changes in a few years, that is.

Since the consolidation phase for stocks began in 2000 and should last for approximately sixteen years, it could continue until 2015 or even 2018. Therefore, commodity prices may advance for another three to six years. On the other hand, the cycle could change earlier than usual, meaning a new growth phase for stocks and consolidation phase for commodities might already be underway.

As mentioned earlier, gold rose from $35.00 in 1970 to $850 in 1980 (x 24). Oil prices rose from $2.92 a barrel in 1965 to $38.34 in 1981 (x 13). From the 1998 lows, oil prices rose for ten years to a peak of $147 in July 2008 (x 14). Gold bullion prices rose to a high of $1,895 in September 2011, almost seven times the value of the low in 1999. Can gold prices move higher from here?

The lowest long-term gain for oil or gold since the 1960s was times 13 for oil in 1981. Thirteen times the low gold price of $253 equals $3,289. The largest gain was times 24 for gold in 1980. If that increase occurred again, gold prices would rise to $6,072 per ounce. We must be aware that past performance is no guarantee of future results. On the other hand, history often repeats itself.

Analysts have looked at asset bubbles over the last century, studying the long-term price patterns before and after bubbles for the Dow Jones Industrial Average in 1929, gold in 1980, the Tokyo Stock Market (Nikkei) in 1989, the NASDAQ in 2000, and oil in 2008. The blue line in Figure 17.6 shows the pattern of prices when all these bubbles are combined. The black line shows how the price of gold has followed this typical bubble pattern from 1999 to May 2013. The horizontal axis is months and the vertical axis is the value. It shows that for a major asset, prices increased tenfold over 120 months (ten years) in an average bubble. It will be interesting to see if gold will spike to new highs or if gold prices will be dead in the water for another sixteen years or so. From the spring of 2013 to early 2014, the long-term moving average crossovers remained negative for the yellow metal. The relative strength for gold is also weak compared to the S&P 500 and the S&P/

TSX. Long-term moving average crossovers together with relative strength data will help investors to allocate their capital to the assets that have the best potential for appreciation. Those who adore gold may be disappointed that gold prices did not skyrocket higher after 2011. However, since it seems as though gold did not enter a bubble stage in the last ten years, gold prices may perform better in this consolidation phase than they did after 1980.

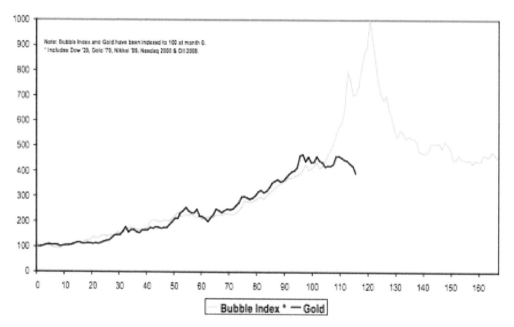

Figure 17.6: Chart prepared by Haver Analytics and Kien Lim, May 2013

The passage of time is also important when we look at the pattern of stock market cycles. We can compare the pattern for North American markets since 2000 with the previous resource cycle uptrend that ended in 1982. North American markets experienced a 50% bear market during the middle of the 16-year cycle in 1973 and 1974, just like they did in 2008.

Figure 17.7: Charts courtesy of MSN.com by Bob Dickey, March 2013

After the bear market ended in December 1974, stock prices recovered much of their losses for almost three years (33 months to be exact) until late 1977. December 2011 is 33 months after the bottom of the bear market caused by the Financial Crisis. At the 33-month time frame after the 1974 bear market bottom, commodity prices and stock prices really started to spike higher, especially in Canada. In 1978, the TSX rose 23.6%. This rise was eclipsed by a 38.4% gain in 1979 and capped with a 25.1% gain in 1980. Then the resource cycle and bull market came to an end. By the end of 1980 the TSX was 72% higher than the previous all-time high in 1973.

During the same period, the S&P 500 eked out a 1.1% gain in 1978, rose 12.3% in 1979, and 25.8% in 1980. By the end of 1980, the S&P 500 was only 13% higher than the previous record high compared to 72% higher for the TSX. Investors may want to overweight Canada and other resource-rich nations if resource prices are strong. The bull market in resource stocks during the 1970s, the bull market in technology stocks in the 1990s, and the rise in U.S. real estate prices during the 2000s show us that the biggest gains usually occur during the final stages of the uptrend during the long-term cycle. Prices often rise much longer and higher than expected. We could be in the final stage of the 2000-to-2016/2018 cycle.

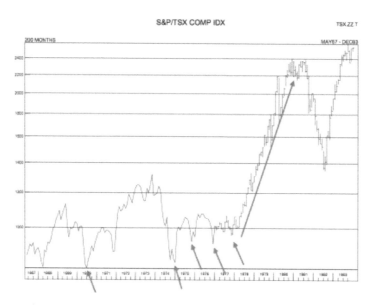

Figure 17.8: S&P/TSX Composite Index 1967-1983. Source: Thomson Reuters

The TSX Index had many strong rallies during the 1970s. The strongest, which began in 1977, produced a gain of 140% over three years in the later stage of the 16-year cycle. The TSX tripled from the 1974 low. The 1974 low can be equated to the 2009 low in terms of the 16-year cycle. (Arrows mark their beginnings.) The chart of the DJIA in Figure 17.9 shows that it did not manage to move to higher highs at all during this time frame.

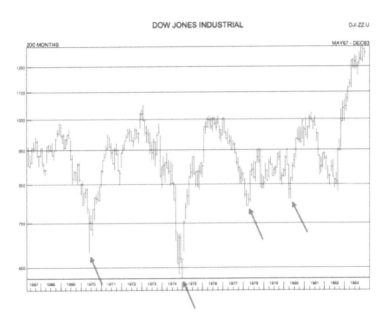

Figure 17.9: Dow Jones Industrial Average 1967-1983. Source: Thomson Reuters

The DJIA and S&P 500 also experienced some powerful rallies during the 1970s but were not able to move much above the 1966 highs until the 16-year cycle ended. Then the resource bubble burst in 1981 as a severe recession began. Figure 17.8 shows that the TSX was able to rise more than 100% above the previous all-time record highs. The current resource cycle seems to be following a different path than it did in the 1970s. If there is not a major improvement in commodity prices soon, it may be a sign that the resource boom is over.

The S&P 500 Index peaked in 2000. However, gold and oil prices bottomed at least a year earlier. Therefore, 2013 could be fourteen years into the 16- to 18-year cycle. During the previous consolidation phase, gold peaked in the spring of 1980 and oil peaked in 1981. We must remember that the time frames for cycles are not precise or exact. They last for approximately 16 to 18 years, not precisely 16.0 years. Moving average crossovers can help investors determine when these long-term trends reach their climax and change direction. The technology bubble burst after it seemed as if everyone was talking about all the Internet stocks he or she was buying. The resource cycle should be close to an end when the newspaper boy is talking about the penny mining stock that is the latest fad. When television shows and magazines crop up about resource companies and panning for gold, they should be a sign that the trend is close to an end. If people are quitting their jobs to day trade penny mining stocks, it will also be a sign that the trend is near the end. That is what happened in North America in 1999 and in China in 2007. There was a shortage of hotel maids in some big Chinese cities in 2007 because they could make more money by investing than they could by working for a living. Those stories circulated just before stock market prices collapsed in China in early 2008.

Some suggest that the demand for natural resources to accommodate the phenomenal migration of people from the country to the city in China, India, and third world countries will keep commodity prices high for decades. Jim Rogers has been telling this story for years. He has been right. However, if resource stock and commodity prices participate in a parabolic rise, they will get ahead of themselves and collapse just as they did in the 1980s. Keep in mind that the demand for oil increased by 28% from 1980 to 2000 while oil prices generally drifted from over $35 per barrel in 1981 down to $10 in 2000. (Some believe oil companies manipulate prices. If so, they have been failing miserably.) The use of the Internet, technology, and smartphones has grown exponentially since 2000, yet the NASDAQ and most technology stocks are still well below the 2000 highs.

Investors must ensure that they do not get caught up in the optimistic thinking behind investment fads. Recall the lessons of history and try to remain objective while you participate in the trends. Use the disciplined approach of moving average crossovers to guide investment decisions. Equity and precious metal markets could produce gains in the years ahead. However, before this 16- to 18-year cycle ends, they could undergo one last severe correction before the next 16- to 18-year uptrend in financial assets begins. From the 1981 peak to the 1982 bear market lows, the S&P 500 and TSX Index both lost close to 40%. Then, when the new long-term uptrend began in August 1982, these market averages rose close to 100% in one year! That is extreme volatility. If that type of volatility happens at the end of this 16-year cycle, investors will certainly require a disciplined approach to manage risk during a final bear market and to benefit from the powerful rally that should initiate the start of a new 16-year growth cycle. On the other hand, the transition to a new 16-year cycle might be so different this time that we will not realize it has occurred until after the fact.

Cycles suggest that U.S. and European economic growth could be lower than normal until this cycle ends. Thereafter, leaders with characteristics like Paul Volcker (who was one of President Obama's economic advisors), Ronald Reagan, Margaret Thatcher, or Paul Martin are likely to emerge. After 1980, U.S. Federal Reserve Chairman Paul Volcker and President Ronald Reagan came into a fight like cowboys with guns blazing. They killed the inflationary psychology that was pushing interest rates higher and higher. The Iron Lady, Margaret Thatcher, made difficult decisions to get the British economy on a sound footing in the 1980s. Canadian Finance Minister Paul Martin enacted policies to reduce Canadian government debt and get the country on a path to prosperity in the 1990s.

Since this current cycle is due to end sometime between 2016 and 2018, it could be that Americans are becoming ready to accept strong medicine and a radical change to reduce government debt. The Fiscal Cliff discussions in late 2012 may have been the strong medicine the U.S. needed. The history of cycles suggests that America should be ready for a new type of leader around 2016. The changes Americans have experienced since 2000 seem to be bringing them to the point where they are more willing to accept this medicine.

The following example illustrates how a particular mindset can change due to shifting circumstances. My Search and Rescue team was called to rescue a paraglider pilot in September 2012. Paragliders were originally designed to be large enough to enable a pilot to soar for hours and even gain altitude if he or she could find an updraft near a mountain. Most paraglider pilots wore protective gear and sturdy boots. However, a new "minimalist" approach has led to the production of smaller paragliders that only enable a pilot to glide downward. Some of these pilots prefer to feel free, so they only wear street clothes and running shoes instead of more protective apparel.

Just before dusk on September 22, 2012, two "minimalist" paragliders decided to jump off the top of Mt. Cheam in Chilliwack, B.C. (elevation

2,100 meters or 6,913 feet) and glide to the valley floor below, wearing no protective gear or extra clothing. They took off, knowing that the top 1,000 meters (3,000 feet) of the mountain was socked in with clouds. One of the paragliders landed safely, but the other was taken off course by an updraft in the clouds and crashed into the rocky side of a mountain at the 1,500-meter (5,000-foot) level, breaking his ankle so severely that it was almost severed. It was dark by the time our team arrived at the scene with our equipment. There was no road or trail access to this steep area. The RCMP and the private helicopters we usually use are not authorized to fly at night, so a small crew of rescuers was sent to hike along a dangerous ridge to the slide area; in addition, a large Cormorant helicopter, which can fly by night and in clouds, was summoned from 442 Squadron on Vancouver Island. We were concerned that the injured young man might bleed to death. However, paramedics on site informed us that if a leg is severed well below the knee, blood vessels and veins will constrict and almost stop the bleeding. The human body is amazing!

We were able to communicate with the injured paraglider via a walkie-talkie he had with him. Had he been rescued soon after crashing, his primary concern would most likely have been anticipating the pain he would experience when his ankle was being packaged for the stretcher. As it turned out, the helicopter arrived close to 11 p.m. and was not able to find him since he was in the clouds. The paraglider did not know if he would survive the night and neither did we, but nothing else could be done until daylight. We asked him to turn off his walkie-talkie, put it in his shirt to save the battery power, and to contact us at 6 a.m. The hikers had to turn back at 2 a.m. when cliffs surrounded them. It was a tense situation with a life on the line.

In the morning, the paraglider was still alive and had checked in. When daylight appeared, the Cormorant was able to fly above the clouds into sunlight and then back down the cliff face, lower two rescue technicians and a stretcher, and fly away. In the space of fifteen hours, the paraglider had gone from not having a care in the world to lying motionless in the rocks with no food and water throughout a cool night, not knowing if he would lose his foot or even survive. I am sure that when the SAR technicians finally reached him, the least of his concerns was the pain his ankle might cause him during the rescue.

His priorities had changed drastically. There was only one overriding concern—to get off this mountain and into safety, no matter how painful the experience might be. The Cormorant returned, lifted him and rescuers into the helicopter, and flew to the Abbotsford International Airport, from where he was flown by air ambulance to the Royal Columbian Hospital in New Westminster, B.C. He did survive!

A SAR tech and flight engineer look out the Cormorant's rescue door as they approach the scene of Saturday's paraglider crash in Chilliwack. (RCAF/19 Wing Comox)

Figure 17.10: A Search and Rescue Technician and a Flight Engineer at the rescue door of a Cormorant helicopter on approach to the scene of a crashed paraglider, Department of National Defense, 2012. Reproduced with the permission of the Minister of Public Works and Government Services Canada, 2013

The American people have gone through a similar change in mindset over the last thirteen years. In 2000, the U.S. was so successful that it was expected to be debt free in 2002. Americans had few serious cares or concerns. However, all of a sudden the 2001-2003 recession, the 2001 terrorist attacks, the collapse of real estate prices, the Financial Crisis, and slow growth changed everything. In 2007, many Americans would have been totally opposed to the implementation of tax increases to improve the situation for the long term. In 2012, after years of enduring skyrocketing annual budget deficits and a Debt Ceiling Crisis, priorities seemed to have begun to change. More and more Americans are becoming willing to accept spending cuts if they will improve the overall financial health of their country. This type of shift is what typically happens near the end of long-term 16-year cycles to get the economy and markets back into the growth phase. This is what happened in Canada in the 1990s and is what should transpire in the U.S. as it approaches the final years of the consolidation cycle.

To help us envision the type of action we might see in the future, it is worthwhile to consider how Reagan and Volcker killed the inflationary demon in the 1980s. As the price of fuel and living costs increased in the 1970s, Canadian and U.S. workers kept demanding higher and higher wages to keep pace with the rising prices. This was a time when many workers believed their employers were exploiting them. At the time, many individuals (especially university students) thought that socialism was a better alternative than capitalism. Therefore, corporations were regarded as "evil" (this view is once more becoming prevalent) and unions were increasing in strength and numbers. The U.S. Federal Reserve increased interest rates from 6% in the early 1970s to 10% by 1980. However, it seemed like the Fed was always behind rising costs, since inflation kept rising more than interest rates. In early 1980, the Fed increased rates from 10% to 14% within a few weeks in an attempt to eliminate the inflationary psychology. The economy and markets suffered, so rates were lowered shortly thereafter. Unfortunately, as the year progressed, it became clear that all attempts to curb the destabilizing trend of rampant inflation had failed.

Then in 1980, Republican leader Ronald Reagan was elected as the U.S. President, replacing President Carter, who was a Democrat. In 1981, U.S. air traffic controllers were just another one of the many groups that went on strike thinking that they were indispensable and underpaid. At that point, President Reagan and his advisors showed true leadership and a willingness to think outside the box. After the air traffic controllers announced strike action, President Reagan demanded they return to work within forty-eight hours. When only 1,300 of the nearly 13,000 workers returned, Reagan promptly fired 11,345 who refused to comply and banned them from the civil service for life. The union was decertified soon after. This action is now described as one of the most important events in late twentieth century labor history. Talk about sending a message!

Meanwhile, Fed Chairman Paul Volcker increased interest rates to above 15% in 1981 and kept them there. The U.S. Prime Rate peaked at 20% in June 1981. In late September 1981, the Bank of Canada announced that the rate for the new series of Canada Savings Bonds would be 19.5%. Even so, many experts were forecasting that rates were going to move well above 20% in the future. The picture below is a scanned copy of the CSB brochure I have kept in my files all these years. Some things are just too unique to be thrown away.

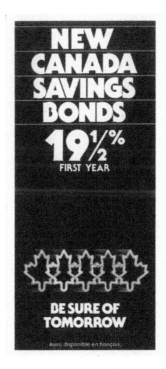

Figure 17.11: 1981 Canada Savings Bonds brochure. With permission from the Bank of Canada

By keeping interest rates at historically high levels until the summer of 1982, Paul Volcker used financial "waterboarding" to bring investors, borrowers, businesses, and workers to their knees. (I recall the belief at the time that we would never see interest rates below 10% again.) By then, North

American economies were in a severe recession with very high unemployment. Countless U.S. businesses were declaring bankruptcy every week. However, this bold, unpopular action by leaders with a vision for the longer-term good of the nation eliminated high levels of inflation. Their actions paved the way for lower interest rates and two decades of prosperity. In 1993, President Bill Clinton eliminated the ban on the air traffic controllers who had lost their jobs. As mentioned before, by 2000 the U.S. government was close to being debt free. A similar type of leadership will be required to take meaningful action to reduce U.S. and European government debt. If this happens, there could be some very good years ahead in global economies and markets, followed by one more final bear market and recession in four years or so. After that, individuals and pension funds should once again be able to fund their retirement plans with returns from investment portfolios.

Long-term cycles have a profound impact. If readers understand this, they can make sense of what is going on. Americans could then have hope that they will eventually get their government debt under control and regain their pride. Meanwhile, Canadians in the resource industry might be able to make hay in the next few years while the sun shines. However, they should be prepared for a very long period of much lower prices in the future. Those who own high-priced homes in resource towns like Fort McMurray, Alberta, could see their values fall by up to 80% or so if oil prices collapse as in 1981. The writers know people who have never recovered from the losses incurred after 1981 when interest rates rose to 20% and real estate prices collapsed along with commodity prices. In the U.S., up to 500 businesses were declaring bankruptcy every week in 1982.

The coming years should eventually provide opportunities to make big profits by shorting commodities and resource stocks. However, many ordinary young people and families who are working hard to make an honest living in the resource industry may lose their homes if they are not prepared for what is likely to happen. We sincerely hope that the information in this chapter will help at least some individuals to plan ahead and be prepared to avoid the pain and suffering likely to occur when the bloom falls off the resource rose.

The year 1982 was a difficult time to start a career in the resource sector, while it was the perfect time to start a career in the investment/finance industry. In contrast, the early 2000s was a very good time to start a career in the resource sector. Those who started a career in the finance/investment industry in 2000 have either lost their jobs or have experienced extreme anxiety for many of the following years. Conversely, those who start a career in the resource industry in 2016 to 2018 may experience cutbacks, layoffs, and challenging times. Ordinary workers who presently own real estate in areas relying on the resource sector could see the value of their homes plummet over the next decade. I have learned a very important truth regarding resources or commodities. When it relates to investing:

It is best to presume that there is not a shortage of anything.

Higher commodity prices eventually make it possible to bring on more production, resulting in lower prices. Thus, investors should be very careful to not use the words "peak oil" or "they are not making any more of it" as a rationale for making an investment.

Those who start a career in the industrial or financial sector in the near future will likely have the wind at their back and the best opportunity to be successful for the next sixteen years. Understanding the role of long-term cycles can help people to make prudent decisions for purchasing a home, starting a career, or planning for retirement.

An awareness of long-term cycles can prepare people for major shifts that do not occur very often in a lifetime. We must remember that it is very difficult to predict the future. Therefore, trying to predict exactly when long-term cycles will change is risky. It is more prudent to be approximately right instead of precisely wrong. However, investors must realize that even though gold or oil investments have provided excellent results over the past thirteen years, they may not necessarily repeat the same performance over the following thirteen years. That fact that equity markets made little progress from 2000 to 2013 does not mean that long periods of tremendous gains are gone forever. Americans should recognize that there have been many other periods when it has seemed as if the United States would never return to previous levels of global superiority.

Investors must understand cycles in order to be psychologically prepared for major market and economic shifts. This understanding will enable investors to change their investment strategies when the long-term moving average crossovers indicate a change in the long-term trends. In the coming years, investors in the commodity and resource sectors must pay special attention to the very long-term moving average crossovers for commodities like copper, crude oil, gold bullion, natural gas, silver bullion, potash, and uranium, since they can have very long periods of over- and underperformance. Currencies that are influenced by commodity prices can also be affected by this.

18. The Shortcomings of Prominent Investment Methods

There are many ways of analyzing investments and creating investment disciplines. This chapter explains why the authors believe using moving average crossovers together with warning signals from a sharp increase in oil prices is one of the best disciplines for investors to use.

Previous chapters have shown that the process we use for making most other good decisions does not work when it comes to making investment decisions. This is not because markets are rigged or "controlled" but because of the way human behavior affects markets. Over the last century, professional investors have tried to develop methods of investing which remove emotions from the decision-making process. Many of the various investment disciplines have been successful to some degree. However, none of them seem able to account for how markets will behave, since no one can predict human behavior. Nonetheless, investors keep trying to invent better investment strategies by developing more complicated systems or new products designed by "financial engineers." Here is an evaluation of the shortcomings of the most popular investment strategies that have been developed to date.

Acquiring and analyzing investment information such as cash flow, earnings, price-earnings ratios, book value, dividend yields, and the business model of a company (called fundamental research) should work well, but that is not always the case. If a good understanding of the economy, market sectors, and individual companies was the key to making profitable investment decisions, very few would have suffered losses from the collapse in technology stocks after 2000. If the volume of information was critical to investment success, few would have been caught in the 2008/2009 bear market. Great losses have occurred during the last decade even though more information than ever before in history has been available to ordinary and professional investors.

In 2008, Minyanville published a comment about fundamental investing written by Vinny Catalano. He quoted billionaire hedge fund manager Paul Tudor Jones, who remarked,

> Why work when Mr. Market can do it for you? These days, there are many more deep intellectuals in the business, and that, coupled with the explosion of information on the Internet, creates the illusion that there is an explanation for everything and that the primary task is simply to find that explanation.

> Today there are young women and men graduating from college who have a tremendous work ethic, but they get lost trying to understand the logic behind a whole variety of market moves. While I'm a staunch advocate of higher education, there is no training—classroom or otherwise—that can prepare for trading the last third of a move, whether it's the end of a bull market or the end of a bear market. There is typically no logic to it; irrationality reigns supreme, and no class can teach what to do during that brief, but volatile reign.

Minyanville concluded,

> As we can see from…Tudor Jones' comments, the reasons for the rise and fall of stocks goes far beyond pure fundamentals alone.

> The bottom line to the bottoming process is that fundamentals are not, never were, and never will be the sole answer for why stocks gyrate as they do at the end of a move, be it bubble or panic.

As mentioned earlier, if fundamental analysis was a profitable process, there would not have been so many financial losses during the first decade of the new millennium. Fundamental analysis did not seem to be beneficial for those who made this analysis their profession either. While expert advice can be beneficial for many things, history shows that very few, if any, of those regarded as economic and market experts were able to guide investors to make profitable decisions from 2000 to 2003. There were almost no warnings about potential calamity from any of the major investment/research firms during 2008.

People are always writing books about and issuing forecasts of economic disaster. They do so because forecasts of disaster sell. Due to human nature, we are attracted to predictions of impending disaster. Our basic instinct and first priority is to protect our loved ones and ourselves from danger. Improving our financial situation is a much lower and less urgent priority. Writers and the media know this tendency and take full advantage of it. Television and media headlines try to include worrisome forecasts that will attract our attention.

For example, imagine you are walking through a department store where there are televisions for sale. If you hear a news broadcaster say, "stock prices fell sharply today," you will be more likely to stop and listen than if the broadcaster had said, "stock prices moved higher today." This reaction is why the media often try to concentrate on or emphasize the negative, as opposed to the positive.

However, often a few respected experts do accurately predict a bear market. Since this accuracy is so unusual, they often gain fame and notoriety. Unfortunately, in almost every case I can recall, an expert who accurately forecasts a bear market once usually only does it once. The late Joe Granville became a guru for accurately predicting the 1981-1982 bear market. Elaine Garzarelli became famous in 1987 for turning bearish just before the 1987 crash. Ravi Batra was on the talk show circuit after the 1987 crash because he had just written his book *The Great Depression of 1990*. Do you remember the great depression of 1990?

Robert Prechter (who practices the Elliott Wave Theory of technical analysis) also became well known after the 1987 crash. Before and after the 1987 crash, he predicted that the Dow Jones Industrial Average would fall from its peak of 2700 all the way down to 400. The DJIA bottomed near the 1700 level and has never returned to that level again. American economist Nouriel Roubini gained notoriety in 2008 for correctly forecasting the Financial Crisis. It is a natural reaction for us to listen to experts who have accurately warned of bear markets in the past. Unfortunately, history shows that most experts who make one excellent call for a serious decline rarely follow with another one. Market peaks are very difficult to forecast. In almost every instance, experts who accurately predict a serious decline turn out to be one-hit wonders. It also seems as though they remain bearish for far too long after a bear market is over. Fear sells. Every expert knows this reality, and some try to take advantage of our basic instincts in order to enrich themselves at the expense of investors.

Unfortunately, the long record of booms, busts, bubbles, manias, and high-profile trading disasters confirms that even the most sophisticated, experienced investors can make colossal mistakes. These mistakes can be serious enough to destroy a lifetime of savings, family relationships, careers, and even large companies built over more than one hundred years. Recent events in the U.S. and Europe illustrate that overconfidence and greed by the leaders of many of the world's biggest financial firms even have the potential to bring the entire global financial system to its knees.

Big swings in stock prices during the early 1900s, together with recollections of the 1929 crash, prompted leaders in the investment industry to work towards developing sound, objective investment disciplines that took the emotions out of investing. The shortcomings of fundamental research during the 1920s drove people such as the economist and professional investor Benjamin Graham to develop a method that would outperform the markets by investing in stocks trading at attractive valuations. This strategy is called value investing. History shows that value investing can provide attractive returns over the long term, since it steers investors away from stocks where over-optimism has caused the price to rise more than is justified. Some of the biggest market losses occur when stock prices rise too high and then fall precipitously. Value investing has the potential to keep investors in safer stocks when markets move into a bubble phase and push stock prices to ridiculous levels. However, when markets fall hard, almost all stocks go down, even the undervalued ones. The undervalued stocks may decline less than the overvalued stocks, but usually they still suffer. Remember the saying, "When the tide goes out, all the boats go down."

Sometimes stock prices fall significantly and become undervalued, but continue to lose even more value. This type of situation is where value investing falls short. In a February 15, 2012, report about sentiment and value investing, former RBC Chief Institutional Strategist Myles Zyblock stated, "For example, our work shows that changes in perception account for about two-thirds of a market's return on a six-month time horizon, and that even under the conditions of attractive value, bearish sentiment can drive prices lower and vice versa."

This scenario is what happened during the Financial Crisis from September 2008 to March 2009. Warren Buffett follows the investment methods taught by value investor Benjamin Graham. Buffett invested $5 billion in Goldman Sachs on September 24, 2008. On that day, the price of Goldman Sachs common shares closed at US$133. That was an attractive price compared to the peak price of $250 in 2007. However, two months later, on November 21, 2008, the price bottomed at $47.41, a 64% discount to the September 24, 2008, price. The share price remained below $80 for more than two months, so there would have been plenty of time to make a purchase at a much lower price.

To be clear, Mr. Buffett purchased preferred shares, which paid a high dividend, instead of the common shares. Nevertheless, in all likelihood, he could have arranged a much more attractive deal for his shareholders had he waited for a sign of a market low instead of "trying to catch a falling knife." Had he waited several months to buy, he could have invested his $5 billion at a much better value. Moreover, he could have saved himself and all the investors in his fund five months of anxiety had he kept his $5 billion in cash during the market turmoil that engulfed global markets during that period.

Mr. Buffett is one of the best investors—and no investor ever bats 1,000. This example is not a criticism of Mr. Buffett, just an illustration of a shortcoming of value investing. The arrow on the daily price chart of Goldman Sachs (Figure 18.1) from May 2008 to April 2009 shows when Mr. Buffett decided to invest $5 billion in preferred shares of the company at $133.

Figure 18.1: Goldman Sachs Group Inc. May 2008-April 2009. Source: Thomson Reuters

Other value investors followed in Mr. Buffett's footsteps and invested more and more as prices declined. Blue chip stocks like Bank of America shares closed at $33.07 on September 24, 2008, before going into a nose dive, only to bottom at a low of $2.53 five months later. At the end of 2012 they were still worth only $11.61. Citigroup peaked at $273.50 and closed at $189.60 on September 24, 2008, on a trajectory to less than $10 a share at the 2009 bottom. By December 31, 2012, its shares had only recovered to $52.09. However, stocks that traded at attractive valuations in September 2008 traded at very attractive valuations in October 2008, and at extremely attractive valuations in November 2008. By the end of February 2009, prices were incredibly attractive. A saying goes, "Don't look for a gold nugget in front of a bulldozer." The same principle can hold true for buying value stocks.

During the 2000-2003 bear market and the Financial Crisis, the strategy of buying stocks when they appeared to represent good value only resulted in bigger losses, as markets resembled an escalator on the downside. Those who added leverage got themselves into a very dangerous position. Some were forced to sell out at prices significantly below the purchase price just a month or two after buying. Value investing is a good system, but it has its shortcomings, especially when markets fall sharply. Markets do fall sharply—bear markets are much more violent than bull markets. Individual investors, professional investors, and money managers should have a system that they can rely on all the time, especially during the worst market conditions. Fundamental research does not work very well. Value investing can provide attractive returns over the long term much of the time, but it does not offer much guidance during times of extreme market volatility, as attested by value investor Jeremy Grantham. See his comments below from Part 2 of the First Quarter 2011 edition of the *GMO Newsletter*:

> A word about being too early in investing: if you are a value manager, you buy cheap assets. If you are very 'experienced,' a euphemism for having suffered many setbacks, you try hard to reserve your big bets for when assets are very cheap. But even then, unless you are incredibly lucky, you will run into extraordinarily cheap, even bizarrely cheap assets from time to time, and when that happens you will have owned them for quite a time already and will be dripping in red ink. If the market were feeling kind, it would become obviously misvalued in some area and then, after you had taken a moderate position, it would move back to normal. That would be very pleasant and easy to manage.
>
> But my career, like most of yours, has been filled with an unusual number of real outliers. That certainly makes for excitement, but it also delivers real pain for even a disciplined value manager. Following is a snapshot of some of those outliers. In 1974, the U.S. market fell to seven times earnings and

the U.S. value/growth spread hit what looked like a 3-sigma (700-year) event. U.S. small caps fell to their largest discount in history, yet by 1984 U.S. small caps sold at a premium for the first time ever. By 1989, the Japanese market peaked at 65 times earnings, having never been over 25 times before that cycle! In 1994, emerging market debt yielded 14 points above U.S. Treasuries, and by 2007 had fallen to a record low of below 2 points. By 1999, the S&P was famously at 35 times peak earnings; in 2000, the value/growth spread equaled its incredible record of 1974 (that I, at the time, would have almost bet my life against ever happening again). Equally improbable, in 2000, the U.S. small/large spread beat its 1974 record and emerging market equities had a 12 percentage point gap over the S&P 500 on our 10-year forecast (+10.8 versus -1.1%). Further, as the S&P 500 peaked in unattractiveness, the yield on the new TIPS (U.S. Government Inflation Protected Bonds) peaked in attractiveness at over 4.3% yield and REIT yields peaked at 9.5%. Truly bizarre. By 2007, the whole world was reveling in a risk-taking orgy and U.S. housing had experienced its first-ever nationwide bubble, which also reached a 3-sigma, 1-in-700-year level (still missed, naturally, by 'The Ben Bernank').

Perhaps something was changing in the asset world to have caused so many outliers in the past 35 years. Who knows? The result, though, for value players, or at least those who wanted to do more than just tickle the problem, was overpriced markets that frightened them out and then, like the bunny with the drum, just kept going and going.

While value investing has its devoted followers, some portfolio managers used to maintain that growth investing would produce returns that outperformed the markets. T. Rowe Price is regarded as the father of growth investing. He started his own firm in 1937, around the same time that Benjamin Graham developed his principles for value investing.

T. Rowe Price believed that a company which was in a growth industry and exhibited signs that it could continue to grow through different cycles produced high returns for the shareholder. He also stressed that one should only invest in a company if it was trading at a reasonable price. His investment philosophy is known as GARP—Growth at a Reasonable Price. The ability to invest in companies that are growing the most in sales and revenue can produce very attractive returns as long as the markets are in a rising trend. Over the last century, the U.S. markets have had 16- to18-year periods of a powerful uptrend, followed by 16- to 18-year periods of making little or no progress. Consequently, growth investing became very popular during the 1990s. That was when the technology boom drove many stocks higher within the powerful 18-year uptrend from 1982 to 2000. During the 1990s, the motto for some GARP investors became growth at any price instead of growth at a reasonable price. That philosophy was only successful for a few years. History shows that growth investing usually only works well when the economy and equity markets are strong. Therefore, after the 16- to 18-year cycle shifted to the consolidation phase in 2000, the shortcomings of an investment discipline based on growth were made obvious to all. The significant impact of the 16- to 18-year cycle was discussed earlier.

As computing power improved, investment experts began to use technology as a research tool. Now they could mine historical investment data for valuable insights, something that was very time-consuming to do before. Investopedia defines Quantitative Analysis as "a business or financial analysis technique that seeks to understand behavior by using complex mathematical and statistical modeling, measurement and research. By assigning a numerical value to variables, quantitative analysts try to replicate reality mathematically." Many portfolio managers rely on using information such as the stock price in relation to cash flow, record of dividend increases, and ratios such as prices to sales in order to determine if a stock should be purchased.

Financial analyst James P. O'Shaughnessy is regarded as the pioneer of quantitative analysis. He has written several books, including *What Works on*

Wall Street: A Guide to the Best-Performing Investment Strategies of All Time, which made the bestseller list in the late 1990s. In 2005, I had the pleasure of having dinner with Mr. O'Shaughnessy and hearing about his research firsthand. He looked back at forty-five years of U.S. financial statistics to find common characteristics in companies whose share price outperformed the market over the long term. *Barron's* has called him a "world beater" and a "statistical guru." The investment funds he managed performed well, especially during the declining years of 2001 and 2002. However, that period was not a normal bear market. Financial stocks, which comprise a major portion of U.S. and Canadian market averages, rose nicely in 2001 and 2002 while most other stocks declined. This development occurred because financial stocks declined from 1998 to 2000 as money shifted out of "old fashioned brick and mortar companies" and into Internet companies.

Financial stocks bottomed in the spring of 2000 when the NASDAQ peaked, and recovered during the following years. Mr. O'Shaughnessy's discipline astutely took advantage of that situation. However, when the Financial Crisis drove stocks into a bear market, almost all stocks fell and O'Shaughnessy's portfolios did not perform well relative to the S&P 500 Index. In 2008 and 2009, his approach indicated that the shares of U.S. financial firms were attractive investments. By March 2009, the shares of some of the largest, most respected U.S. financial firms such as Citigroup and Bank of America were relegated to the realm of penny stocks when their share price dropped below the $5 level. What worked on Wall Street from 1950 to 2007 did not work that well in 2008 and 2009. However, his strategies have performed well again after 2009, producing excellent results over the longer term.

Wikipedia's article on quantitative analysts states that major financial firms "such as AQR or Barclays, rely almost exclusively on quantitative strategies while others, such as PIMCO, Blackrock or Citadel, use a mix of quantitative and fundamental methods. (PIMCO is the world's largest bond manager with almost $2 trillion under management.) Virtually all large asset managers and hedge funds rely to some degree on quantitative methods."

Many machines, bridges, and pipelines work perfectly well until they are subjected to great stress or high pressure. Stress tests are used to reveal the maximum capacity under peak conditions. They often reveal weakness that is not known or anticipated. Mechanical engineers use stress tests all the time to make sure bridges, airplanes, beams, and buildings can withstand the tolerances for which they are designed. However, it is more challenging to put financial models through a real life stress test.

Many of the "financial engineers" who designed the quantitative models failed to design them well enough to withstand the turmoil markets face from time to time. Although it may be hard to believe, in some cases they used selective information to make their models look better than they actually were. Wikipedia goes on to say, "In the aftermath of the financial crisis, there surfaced the recognition that quantitative valuation methods were generally too narrow in their approach. Through working with a large pool of some of the world's most talented quantitative analysts, economists and mathematicians from the financial industry and academia, transparency continues to be improved, leading to constant improvement." In other words, quantitative analysis also failed to "understand" market behavior (which is human behavior) when it was put to the test of real, long-term market conditions.

Chris Brightman, from Research Affiliates in Newport Beach, California, commented on quantitative systems in the August 2011 *Fundamentals* newsletter:

> Paradoxically, quantitative risk management was part of the problem. While risk models are useful tools for measuring risk, using models to tightly control risk is misguided and dangerous. Because no model is, or ever can be, a complete description of the complex system that is a market, all risk models fail to capture some risk. By eliminating all of the risks measured by models, the quants transferred the risk in their funds into the areas their models could not measure and they did not understand.

Quant strategies produce remarkable profits in the early stages. But inevitably, the process becomes unstable and often ends with violent illiquidity events, such as the stock market crash of 1987, the Long-Term Capital Management-induced crisis in September 1998, and the quant meltdown in August 2007. The largest losses in those episodes were suffered by the most recent investors who were attracted by dazzling early performance records. Instead of consistent profits, the latter investors were stuck with shocking losses realized during fund liquidation as investors fled from the imploding strategies.

Quantitative analysis is a valiant attempt to remove human emotions from security selection and portfolio management, but it also has serious short-comings. Is it any wonder that we experience financial crises when so many of the world's largest and most powerful financial firms rely on a system that does not function as it is supposed to when the going gets rough? It seems as though no matter how hard we try, we just cannot provide a formula for how investors will react from time to time.

Along with fundamental analysis, value investing, and growth at a reasonable price investing, quantitative analysis is also a good methodology for normal market conditions. However, markets do not always act in a normal fashion. Sometimes they can act in a totally unpredictable manner. That is when most investment disciplines eventually fail, just when investors and portfolio managers need them the most!

In order to enhance the raw mathematical data of quantitative investing, some experts decided to look at subjective attributes of a company. This strategy is called qualitative analysis. According to *Webster's New World Finance and Investment Dictionary (2003)*, "Credit and securities analysts use qualitative analysis to examine general industry trends, analyze the effectiveness of management, determine whether new products or services are being adopted by the market, and determine how the behavior of the overall economy is likely to affect a company's financial performance. Qualitative analysis is a more refined form of fundamental analysis and has the same shortcomings as fundamental investing." Investopedia goes on to say, "Although quantitative analysis is a powerful tool for evaluating investments, it rarely tells a complete story without the help of its opposite—qualitative analysis."

In the last century, humankind has designed and built sophisticated vehicles, airplanes, ships, bridges, towers, dams, and buildings that, with a few exceptions, have been able to withstand all that nature has brought to bear. We can now understand and predict how materials will react under extreme conditions. While humans often respond to certain situations in similar ways, we still cannot create a formula for human reactions, and probably never will. The words of Paul Tudor Jones, mentioned in the beginning of the chapter, bear repeating: "There is no training—classroom or otherwise—that can prepare for trading the last third of a move, whether it's the end of a bull market or the end of a bear market. There is typically no logic to it; irrationality reigns supreme, and no class can teach what to do during that brief, volatile reign." I would add that the investment disciplines described thus far do not teach us what to do during those times either. Technical analysis looks at historical market data and attempts to identify trading patterns based on how investors have acted in the past. However, these patterns can be open to many interpretations. Nevertheless, there are some positive features of technical analysis which will be mentioned later on.

The principles of investing in value stocks and growth stocks at a reasonable price were created in the 1930s. Qualitative analysis was developed in the 1950s. The growth of computing power and instant data over the Internet in the 1990s made quantitative analysis ubiquitous. There is much potential money to be made by finding a good system for trading in stocks, options, commodities, currencies, and derivatives. As a result, investment firms have recently taken quantitative analysis and technology to the next level.

19. The Power of One:
1% Is Still One Out of One Hundred

The most recent investment/trading strategy to be embraced by financial firms is based on mathematical models. Mathematical models have been employed for long-term investment strategies, risk management purposes, pricing models for derivatives and credit default swaps, debt ratings, and high frequency trading activities. It has been reported that by 2010, 70% of all daily trading on the New York Stock Exchange was directed by high frequency trading firms (HFT) that take advantage of short-term price discrepancies. In most cases positions may be held for only seconds, and no positions are held by the end of each trading day. High frequency trading has been blamed for the May 6, 2010 Flash Crash, when U.S. stocks fell close to 10% in a matter of minutes before recovering. The minor short-term repercussions of HFT pale in comparison with the damage caused by trading systems based on arithmetic algorithms in 2008.

The losses which brought Lehman Brothers and U.S. insurance giant AIG to their knees came from the rapid devaluation of credit default swaps (CDS) and collateralized debt obligations (CDO). These were a major cause of the 2008 Financial Crisis. Credit default swaps are basically insurance policies against the default of debt. It is estimated that this unregulated market grew to over $50 trillion by 2008. The price of these credit default swaps was determined entirely by mathematical formulas that turned out to be faulty. Austin Murphy, Professor of Finance at Oakland University, wrote "An Analysis of the Financial Crisis of 2008: Causes and Solutions." He concluded, "Close financial analysis indicates that theoretical modeling based on unrealistic assumptions led to serious problems in mispricing in the massive unregulated market for credit default swaps that exploded upon catalytic rises in residential mortgage defaults." Maybe that is why PIMCO's Bill Gross said, at the 2012 Barron's Roundtable, that credit default swaps are "extensions of gambling."

Wikipedia describes a collateralized debt obligation as "a promise to pay cash flow to investors in a prescribed sequence, based on how much cash flow the CDO collects from the pool of bonds or assets it owns." CDOs were split into different risk classes or tranches. If there was not enough income collected to pay all of the investors, the lower-risk classes would be the first to suffer. The lending frenzy in the U.S. around 2006 escalated to the point where people with no income were encouraged to borrow money to invest in real estate. It looked as if they were eligible to borrow as long as they had a pulse.

At various points, a large number of mortgages, which varied from low-risk to high-risk, were put in a package to be sold to investors. (Another term for this was an asset-backed security.) By pooling good quality and lower quality mortgages, those who made the original loans thought the package as a whole should be reasonably safe. Don Coxe, former Chief Strategist of BMO Harris Bank in Chicago (who grew up in my home town), wrote that this approach was analogous to a restaurant getting rid of sewage by putting a tablespoon of it into every bowl of soup. Money management firms and pension plans were clamoring for more and more CDOs because they offered higher rates of return than other bonds. The bond ratings agencies enabled this façade to mushroom by giving most CDOs high credit ratings. Of course, when the music stopped, losses were substantially more than the bond ratings implied.

Before the Financial Crisis, the company I work for was under pressure to offer asset-backed commercial paper (ABCP) to its clients. At the time, the senior trader at the bond desk had decades of experience and knew the difference between good quality debt and higher risk paper. She did something unusual. She scrutinized the fine print in an objective manner and refused to let crowd behavior influence her judgment. As a result of her analysis, she advised the senior management not to offer any ABCP products to the firm's clients.

However, the young MBA graduates with red suspenders saw that there were a lot of underwriting fees to be made from putting ABCPs together and selling them. As mentioned earlier, institutional investors were buying these products *en masse* from competing firms. The financial institution seemed to be missing out on revenue and was losing clients because "old fashioned" thinking did not comprehend the benefits of this new way of selling debt. Fortunately, the firm I work for put the interests of clients first, as it always attempts to do. It did miss out on a lot of revenue and profits before 2007. However, when the prices of "rock solid" Canadian ABCP assets collapsed in 2007, well before the Financial Crisis, individual investors and institutions in Canada paid the price.

In the end, an agreement was reached to combine all the outstanding ABCP debt into a $32 billion bankruptcy and repackaging deal. One of Canada's largest pension plans, the *Caisse de dépôt et placement du Québec,* with assets of over $170 billion, was the biggest loser. The institution I work for made a sacrifice when it refrained from selling ABCP products to its clients. However, it was rewarded when the business and reputation of the bank improved as clients returned to rely on the advice of experts who did not adjust their standards according to the popularity of a product. In 2012, this firm was named the safest bank in North America and the tenth safest bank in the world by Global Finance.

Experienced officials at Goldman Sachs in New York also realized that the orgy of mortgage debt and home buying was going to end badly. However, Goldman Sachs continued to market and sell CDOs to institutional clients who wanted to buy them. At the same time, the firm positioned itself to profit when it all unraveled. Goldman Sachs profited from continuing to sell CDOs for a few years, but the damage to its reputation and the ensuing litigation by regulators has dealt a major blow to the iconic firm that will impair it for many years. A December 14, 2011, *Bloomberg* article states, "Goldman Sachs

Group Inc. (GS), the fifth-biggest bank by assets, has lost at least 38 partners in 2011, as the firm heads toward the end of its worst year for profit and share performance since 2008." There is a lesson here. The temptation to focus on short-term gains instead of doing what you know is right can be very costly! Even the world's most knowledgeable and experienced corporate executives can succumb to that temptation. Emotions are very powerful, even in the highest echelons of the "rational" business world.

In reference to mathematical models, Professor Austin Murphy goes on to say, "Many practitioners today apply pure mathematical theories to evaluate credit risk and estimate credit risk premiums to be required." Rajan, Seru, and Vig (2008) have provided an analysis of the very large forecasting errors that result from the application of such models that fit "hard" historical data extremely well but ignore human judgment or "soft information." The models of such "quants" who have wielded so much influence over modern banking are, according to some analysts, "worse than useless." The result has been catastrophic for many institutions religiously adhering to them. For instance, one major insurer of debt via credit default swaps (AIG) placed "blind faith in financial risk models;" and their small elite staff of modelers, who initially generated large income for the firm for a few years, later produced decimating losses. (Morgenson, 2008)

Prior to 2007, many experts believed the United States had only experienced declines in regional real estate prices, not nationally. Since the U.S. had seemingly never before experienced nationwide falling real estate prices, the executives at AIG believed this would never happen. The financial "engineers" developed their models on this basis. However, U.S. real estate prices had actually suffered a nationwide decline during the 1930s Depression. AIG insured more credit default swaps than it could ever hope to cover if real estate prices fell across the whole country. This strategy was based on the premise that this type of decline would never happen. Is it justifiable to not include information about the past just because one has not experienced a particular situation? Were the executives, directors, and mathematicians really not aware of the 1930s U.S. real estate experience? Or did they succumb to greed and ignore this information so that they could justify using excessive leverage? In any case, we know that those who ignore history are destined to repeat it. The long-lasting collapse in U.S. real estate prices shows this reality.

How the selective use of market data made it past so many experienced and knowledgeable investment executives boggles the mind. Perhaps it is just another example of how greed and the prospect of short-term returns cloud the judgment of so many who are responsible to manage risk. In some cases, risk managers brought concerns to senior executives, but they were ignored.

The rising popularity of mathematical investment systems revealed another major weakness throughout the investment industry—an ignorance of market history. There frequently seems to be a lack of acknowledgement of or respect for what has happened in the past. The failure to include data in many mathematical formulas about unusual price movements in the past was a factor in global markets repeating some of the worst downturns in history.

> "You can shave a man's face many times, but
> you can only slit his throat once."

Although this proverb applies to many situations in life, it does not seem to be applicable when we look at how often investment models have failed due to a lack of historical perspective.

Debt rating agencies such as Standard and Poor's, Fitch, and Moody's, rely extensively on mathematical models when evaluating debt securities. As is all too obvious, these ratings agencies seem to lower the ratings on bonds well after bad news has exposed issues and prices have fallen accordingly. Pavilion Global Markets Chartered Market Technician James McKeough has remarked, "Bond ratings are reduced after the horse has left the barn, county and state." In his book *The Black Swan: The Impact of the Highly Improbable*, Nassim Nicholas Taleb claims that the value of financial products cannot be determined by the basic models experts are using. Much of such work seems meaningless at best and dangerously misleading at worst.

Professor Murphy states that another problem with mathematical models is that "…existing mathematical credit risk models have a tendency to underestimate the likelihood of sudden large events." The impact of "sudden large events" is greater due to the fact that they are unexpected. How can mathematical tools, or any form of analysis, hope to factor in the significant impact of major, sudden, unexpected events? It does not take a rocket scientist to determine that doing so is impossible. Yet, somehow, the regulatory and corporate leaders believed that they could.

The investment community was so blind to the influence of sentiment on market action that it embraced the Efficient Market Hypothesis for decades. Is it any wonder that the financial community also embraced the latest fad of mathematical models and committed billions of dollars to them without testing them over a complete market cycle? When new airplanes are built, they are tested extensively on the ground and then in the air by test pilots. It seems that those in the financial industry did not have the patience to test their models in real life before employing them. In addition, no one in authority was ensuring that they take this wise precaution.

Portfolio managers also relied on mathematical formulas to make investments based on probabilities. These models were supposed to be accurate 99% of the time. It turns out that what happened in the other 1% of cases was catastrophic, since everyone who was using the same models made the same mistakes. Would a reasonable person fly in an airplane from Los Angeles to Australia if the plane was only going to function normally 99 times out of 100? Would you cross a bridge where one car out of one hundred might crash and burn? Would you deposit money into your bank account if it disappeared one percent of the time? Again, it is difficult to fathom why so many senior executives and portfolio managers would risk billions of dollars based on a discipline that would fail in such a short period of time. The record shows that this strategy not only failed, it failed in a spectacular way. However, this kind of failure is not unusual for new investment models. Georg Wilhelm Friedrich Hegel (1770-1831) wrote,

"We learn from history that we learn nothing from history."

The advent of program trading in the 1980s encouraged portfolio managers to invest more than they normally would. They did so by purchasing portfolio insurance derivatives to protect them from losses. This strategy was called program trading. Buying in excess caused stock prices to go up to very overvalued levels by the summer of 1987. When selling ensued, the writers of the derivatives were forced to sell. It all ended with the Crash of 1987, when the Dow Jones Industrial Average lost 20% in one day on October 19, 1987—a day that is still seared into my memory.

Money managers also rely on mathematical tools for probabilities of return. The Capital Markets' Chief Institutional Strategist at the firm I work for wrote, "If you believe bell curve math is helpful in explaining the return distribution for financial markets (we don't), this 4.8% sell-off (on August 4, 2011) was a 4 sigma event based on daily data back to 1928. A 4 sigma event is one that should not happen more than once since the ice age ended. Yet, this is the 84th worst daily sell-off in our sample that includes 20,990 days."

The Dow Jones Industrial Average fell 13.47% on Black Monday, October 28, 1929, and 11.73% on Tuesday, October 29, 1929, which is referred to as Black Tuesday. I remember when the S&P 500 fell only 3.1% out of the blue on July 7, 1986, and 4.8% on September 11, 1986. Those first, early days of unusual downside volatility led up to the Crash of 1987, when the S&P 500 fell 20.47% on October 19, 1987.

This evidence suggests there is something very wrong with bell curve math if it assumes that a 4.8% one day sell-off like the one which occurred on August 4, 2011, should not happen more than once since the ice age ended.

Perhaps the designers only used the last twenty years of data, which would have omitted the data from 1986 and 1987. In any case, this failure seems to have been just another example of investment professionals using an untested system that does not take into account what has happened, not just in the distant past, but also in the relatively recent past. Looking back, one can see that investment systems using mathematical models were of no help during the Financial Crisis when U.S. market averages dropped as much as 50% in a matter of months. Talking about sophisticated money management systems, hedge fund manager David Einhorn stated (in David Orrell's book *Economyths*) that they give users "a false sense of security...like an airbag that works all the time, except when you have a car accident." An article from the well-respected *Economist* magazine also describes how trusted models failed.

Figure 19.1: The *Economist* Newspaper Ltd, London (Jan 2009). Illustration by S. Kambayashi

In the January 27, 2012, *Coxe Strategy Journal*, Don Coxe (former Chief Strategist at Chicago's Harris Bank) wrote,

> It seems the CAPM (Capital Asset Pricing Model) is about to join the Black-Scholes-based risk models that disembow-eled Long-Term Capital Management and the models used to confect the toxic debt that caused the crash. On the evidence, investors relying on conventional financial models should treat them with HazMat care. Now that reliance on the CAPM has caused two financial crises, investors should run—not walk—away from the model.

What should they run toward? What will be the next model that will captivate everybody's attention and lead to the next crash?

In conclusion, we leave you with a statement from Wharton management professor Sidney G. Winter, who was named a Fellow of the American Econometric Society in 1987: "As computers have grown more powerful, academics have come to rely on mathematical models to figure how various economic forces will interact. But many of those models simply dispense with certain variables that stand in the way of clear conclusions. Commonly missing are hard-to-measure factors such as human psychology and people's expectation of the future." This deficiency is not only characteristic of mathematical models; it is a common thread in all the various forms of analysis discussed thus far.

If most of what they rely on to make investment decisions does not seem to work, what are investors to do? Investors and portfolio managers need to use tools that reflect human psychology as an integral part of their investment process. They need to run to an investment system that shows what investors are actually doing with their money. This strategy is more helpful than following models that are forecasting what the money should do.

20. Trends Can Sometimes Last Much Longer than We Expect

"Faced with the choice between changing one's mind and proving there is no need to do so, most people get busy on the proof."
John Kenneth Galbraith

Before every Super Bowl game begins, the team from the American Football Conference (AFC) and the team from the National Football Conference (NFC) participate in a coin toss to see which team will start the contest by kicking the ball. We all know that the odds of winning or losing a coin toss are 50%. What are the odds that the NFC, for instance, could win several coin tosses in a row? How many wins in a row would be most unusual? How many wins in a row would be almost impossible?

Until 2012, the NFC had won fourteen coin tosses in a row! The odds of that ever happening are 16,000 to 1, yet we experienced it in our lifetime. Almost no one would have reasonably expected that the NFC could have such a long winning streak, but it occurred nonetheless.

Planets move with precision throughout the universe, the laws of physics remain the same, and seasons continue with regularity. However, forest fires, floods, and drought occur when the forces of nature cause extreme weather patterns that last much longer than usual. Eventually, however, weather patterns change and environmental conditions return to normal.

Like the weather and coin tosses, market trends can also exist for much longer than can reasonably be expected. Market conditions often return to the norm as well. However, that process can sometimes take years or even decades! Winning a coin toss fourteen times in a row is an amusing trivia item that would not have much of an impact on anyone. In contrast, when one takes the wrong side in an investment position that defies the odds, it can result in untold losses. Investors sometimes use axioms such as "what goes up must come down" to justify a purchase or sale. Yet one does not have to look very hard to find examples that prove how costly it can be to base an investment on a well-regarded but faulty premise.

The late economist Herbert Stein, a former senior fellow at the American Enterprise Institute, said, "That which cannot go on forever won't." This has often been rephrased as, "That which cannot continue won't." Every year the odds increased that the NFC would lose the coin toss because winning it could not continue forever. The value of markets and assets cannot go up or down forever either. However, sometimes they can continue to rise or fall for much longer than anyone can envision, even in his or her wildest dreams. This is why the assumption that a market trend will reverse, or will always return to equilibrium, is most dangerous! For example, it is taking more than forty years for long-term North American interest rates to return to the average rate (calculated over the last 200 years) of slightly over 5% for 30-year U.S. government bonds. In late 2011, the Chief Economist for the IMF, Olivier Blanchard, said, "…post the 2008-2009 crisis, the world economy is pregnant with multiple equilibria—self-fulfilling outcomes of pessimism or optimism, with major macroeconomic implications." When the global financial system can collapse at any time, what is an equilibrium?

One of the most profound statements about investing was written by economist John Maynard Keynes decades ago: "The market can stay irrational longer than you can stay solvent." That is so true. Crowd behavior and herd mentality can sometimes enable price trends to carry on much longer and move prices to greater extremes than anyone reasonably expects. Previous chapters explained how investors and portfolio managers purchased stocks during the Financial Crisis, thinking they were bargains after prices declined

20%. When prices fell 30% they bought more with giddy enthusiasm. After prices fell 40% they bought more, certain that the bottom had been reached. When prices collapsed to a decline of 50%, the losses from all the purchases were so great that many investors were forced to sell. By March 6, 2009, the DJIA had dropped 54.4% from the October 12, 2007, high, while the S&P 500 fell 57.69%. The Canadian S&P/TSX fell 52.65% from the June 6, 2008, high to the March 6, 2009, low. (All figures are based on intraday figures.) At that point, the desire to sell had finally been exhausted. After that, U.S. equity markets began a four-year uptrend.

While the 50% declines during the 1973/1974 bear market for stocks and the 2008/2009 bear market were severe, they paled in comparison to the 89.19% loss in the value of the DJIA from the peak of 381.17 on September 3, 1929, to the low of 41.22 in July, 1932.

During the spring of 2008, oil prices were rising more and more as businesses sought to protect themselves from higher prices through buying crude oil commodity futures. Prices sometimes rose more than $10 a barrel in a day! I recall hearing a news story about legendary Texas oil and gas executive T. Boone Pickens. He is a billionaire who dines with presidents and has access to some of the sharpest minds in the oil and investment industry. Pickens mentioned that he talked to as many as fifteen of the top investment/commodity analysts every day. Yet he still lost billions of dollars when oil prices fell from $145 a barrel in July 2008 to $32.40 in December 2008. Almost no one ever expected oil prices to rise so fast in the spring and then collapse so quickly by the end of the year.

If T. Boone Pickens, with all his experience and resources, could not move to protect himself from such a precipitous move, how can we? We can, if we use the proper tools. An indicator for oil prices is shown later on in the book.

By the summer of 2000, the large Canadian telecommunications firm Nortel Networks Corporation had grown so much that the total value of Nortel shares comprised 30% of the entire Toronto Stock Exchange Index. I remember hearing and reading about Canadian investors buying Nortel shares when the share price declined after the technology bubble burst during 2001. Many investors and analysts thought that Nortel shares were an attractive investment even after the price had been falling for a year. Nortel finally filed for bankruptcy in January 2009. Some Canadian investors and analysts repeated the same scenario with BlackBerry (formerly Research in Motion, known by the symbol RIMM in the U.S. and RIM in Canada) from 2010 to 2012.

One of the most famous examples of a trend continuing much longer than expected started with Alan Greenspan on December 5, 1996. The U.S. Federal Reserve Chairman was speaking to the American Enterprise Institute when he said, "But how do we know when irrational exuberance has unduly escalated asset values, which then become subject to unexpected and prolonged contractions as they have in Japan over the last decade?" He was referring to the long run-up in technology stocks, which had brought stock prices to overvalued levels according to historical norms. The technology-heavy NASDAQ index declined right after his speech but turned around soon after. On December 5, 1996, the NASDAQ closed at 1300.10. It continued to rise, not for one or two years but for another thirty-nine months! How much did the NASDAQ gain from its overvalued level when Mr. Greenspan made his speech on December 5, 1996? The NASDAQ rose more than 100%. It then rose more than 200%. The NASDAQ index rose almost another 300% (295% to be exact) before it finally peaked more than three years later at 5,132 on March 10, 2000. (See Figure 20.1) If someone as experienced and as well connected as Mr. Greenspan can be wrong by three years, it is definite proof that trends can continue longer than expected. It also verifies that overvalued prices can become much more overvalued and remain overvalued longer than any rational person might think possible.

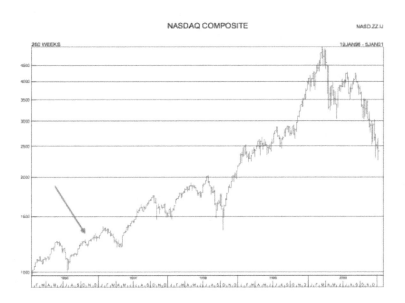

Figure 20.1: NASDAQ Composite Index 1996-2000. The arrow on the chart of the NASDAQ indicates when Chairman Greenspan became concerned about irrational exuberance in technology stocks. Source: Thomson Reuters

While the duration and magnitude of the rise in technology surprised even the most optimistic forecasters, who in 2000 ever imagined that ten years later many bellwether technology stocks would still be down more than 60% from their highs? Prices can also remain low and undervalued for much longer than expected. Markets can certainly behave in unpredictable ways.

Gold prices rose from $40 in the early 1970s to a peak of US$850 an ounce in 1980, an increase of 25 times. I became a professional in the investment industry in May of 1981. For the first decade of my career, it was conventional wisdom for investors to have 10% of their portfolio in gold. I did not follow that line of reasoning. Gold prices finally bottomed at US$252.80 an ounce on July 23, 1999, at the end of an 18-year bear market. Eighteen years is long enough to be one-half of a normal person's working life.

In early 2012, gold prices were above $1,700. Precious metal prices had risen for more than a decade for the first time since the 1970s. Oil prices rose more than fifteen times in the 1970s to peak at $38.34 on April 3, 1981. In 1980, many expected the world to run out of oil within a decade or so. You can imagine how shocked oil executives were as they watched oil prices fall from $38.34 in 1981 to the low of $10.35 on December 25, 1998. In 1980, almost no one believed there was any likelihood that oil prices would decline so much for seventeen years when there was good global economic growth. The significance of these 16- to18-year resource cycles was discussed earlier.

One of the first investments I made after finishing university in 1978 was in gold. After doing a lot of fundamental research, I purchased gold bullion futures at $400 an ounce. At the time, the only sources of information were newspaper comments, magazine articles, and reports from major research firms. When the price increased to $650 an ounce, the news showed people lining up around the block in Vancouver to buy gold. This development made me think that the price was close to its peak, so I sold all of my gold. Within two months, the price had rocketed higher to $850. The temptation to get back in was almost overwhelming, but I had purchased some real estate from a developer who had gone bankrupt when real estate prices fell as interest rates reached 15%. This was the first experience that taught me it is often a good idea to take money out of an investment that has done extremely well for a long time and to move into a different good-quality asset that has performed poorly for a long time.

Those of us who are old enough to remember the late 1970s have witnessed interest rate extremes of historical proportions. Over the last 200 years, the interest rates on U.S. Government 30-year bonds have averaged just over 5%. Of course, these long-term bond yields have fluctuated over the centuries, but not by much more than a percent or two higher or lower than the average. In the 1970s almost no one would ever have envisaged that short-term interest rates in the U.S. and Canada would rise to more than 20% in 1981. Yet, that is what happened.

In the fall of every year since 1946, the government of Canada has offered Canada Savings Bonds to its citizens. In 1981, the interest rate on the current issue was set at 19.5% for one year. The rate would be reset every fall, but the minimum interest rate on that bond was set at 10.5% for the following six years! These bonds could be cashed in at any time, and the government paid me a commission to sell them to my clients. I thought they were a wonderful investment for my clients so I worked as hard as possible to make sure that anyone who had cash could take advantage of this offer. Just weeks after setting the rate, the government realized it was a little too rich so they limited the sale of bonds to $15,000 per person. Nevertheless, these bonds provided my clients and me with a great opportunity.

When interest rates were 20% in 1981, many experts were forecasting that they would rise even more, to 25%. The Bank of Canada and the Federal Reserve started to lower interest rates in 1982. Even as interest rates were being reduced, there was a general belief that we would never again see interest rates below 10%. If anyone had said that short-term interest rates would be zero percent thirty years later, few would have believed him or her. Yet here we are in 2014, with interest rates projected to remain at historically low levels for at least another two years.

National real estate prices across the United States had a long trend to the upside. After the bear market in stocks from 2000 to 2003, investors were looking elsewhere to invest their hard-earned savings. When the Federal Reserve added liquidity (cash) to the financial system to give a boost to the economy after the recession and the 2001 terrorist attacks, this excess cash gravitated to real estate. Many thought that real estate prices would never really decline very much so the risk was low. When we look in the rearview mirror back to 2006, we can see that real estate prices increased very quickly and rose more than expected. However, since their collapse, U.S. real estate prices have stayed very low. Even though they peaked in early 2006, a glut of unsold homes is still having an impact on the American real estate market.

These are just a few recent examples of trends which have lasted much longer than envisioned and moved prices to levels no reasonable person had ever expected. The largest hedge fund failure to date resulted when Amaranth Advisors LLC invested more and more money as natural gas prices continued to fall more than anticipated. Investopedia reports, "After attracting $9 billion worth of assets under management, the hedge fund's energy strategy failed as it lost over $6 billion on natural gas futures in 2006. Faced with faulty risk models and weak natural gas prices due to mild winter conditions and a meek hurricane season, natural gas prices did not rebound to the required level to generate profits for the firm, and $5 billion was lost within a single week." It is clear that the trader was buying more and more (called averaging down) as the price fell.

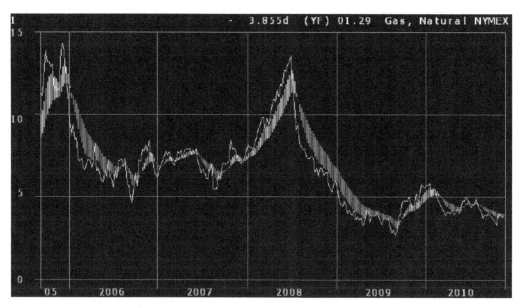

Figure 20.2: Long-Term Moving Average Crossover for Natural Gas. Data for chart compiled by Thomson Reuters

Figure 20.2 shows the steep decline in NYMEX Natural Gas prices from the end of 2005 to the low in the fall of 2006. Amaranth Advisors kept adding long positions as the price of natural gas fell, and ended up being forced to sell at a huge loss right near the lows in late 2006.

Some of the most powerful and influential people have made the mistake of believing that prices should follow a normal, rational path. Trading disasters usually occur because traders average down while prices fall much more than planned. Rogue trader Nick Leeson brought down the oldest merchant bank in England (233-year-old Barings Bank) with losses from speculative trading, as a result of holding positions which continued to work against him.

The most recent high-profile trading disaster occurred at the end of October 2011, when derivatives firm MF Global declared bankruptcy. On March 23, 2010, former CEO of Goldman Sachs and former governor of New Jersey, Jon Corzine, joined the firm. MF Global made big bets that distressed European government bonds would not default. It was as if MF Global was driving the wrong way down the Autobahn hoping that European leaders would intervene to reverse the flow of traffic to avoid an accident. They were wrong. The losses were in the billions, making this bankruptcy the eighth largest ever in the U.S. Even worse, it appears that MF Global mingled customer accounts with its own accounts, leaving a confusing paper trail that took years to sort out. This disaster happened because MF Global ignored falling bond prices and risk management practices, and "bet the farm" that governments would intervene to halt the slide. It was a very risky strategy made by very experienced traders. The trend prevailed and MF Global failed.

Sometimes prices do act in a rational manner. However, when they do not, the level of irrational prices seems to be unlimited. Those who are too proud or self-confident to accept that they might be wrong are most likely to be "decapitated" financially by long, pervasive trends. Investors and investment managers who do not understand these ramifications are likely to learn a very painful lesson at some point.

21. What if You Are Right but Your Timing Is Wrong?

In early 2012, I was introduced to a sophisticated investor who was convinced that stock prices were going to collapse. In late 2011, he went through a rigorous process to find companies he thought were soon going to run into difficulty. In December 2011, he entered into several short positions with U.S. companies that seemed to be poised for a decline. The only problem was that stock markets went up instead of down. In fact, for some U.S. market averages, the first quarter of 2012 was the best first quarter of a year since 1998. Was this investor wrong? At the time of this writing, the answer is not clear. Was his timing wrong? Most would agree that it was. This kind of investor is in a dilemma. Is it best to cover the short positions and take a major loss, or stand one's ground because markets are even more likely to decline in the future?

Earlier, I mentioned that I invested in gold (using commodity futures) at $400 and sold it in 1980 at US$650 an ounce. Right after, I purchased three acres of land from a developer who had just declared bankruptcy due to the unusually high interest rates of March 1980. By December 1980, interest rates had declined, and property prices soared for their last hurrah of the bull market in resources and commodities. (Of course no one knew this would happen until after the fact.) I was young (25) and inexperienced, so I asked the wise father of a friend of mine with a long career in the financial industry what I should do. He suggested that I double the price I had paid for the land just eight months before and advertise it in the Vancouver newspapers. To my total surprise, I sold it the next day at my asking price! The purchaser agreed to pay me half of the sale amount within days and the other half in three months, during which he would pay me 15% interest (on an annual basis). My friend's father was an exceptionally wise man, because real estate prices collapsed in January 1981 and lost half of their value within a year.

As a young man with little business or investment experience, I was off to a very good start. When markets started falling in late 1981, I thought it might be a good time to take advantage of low stock prices. I started to purchase three-month call options (a call option gives the purchaser the right to purchase an asset at a certain price within a certain time) on a U.S. stock called Tandy Corporation.

I knew this company inside and out. In the late 1970s, my brother-in-law worked as a senior manager for a company called Radio Shack (now known in Canada as The Source.) The parent company that owned Radio Shack was Tandy Corporation, which traded on the New York Stock Exchange. The company was growing fast and at that time was getting into some of the first personal computers. I thought this development would make the company even more successful. My brother-in-law was doing very well, so in late 1980 I decided to work in a Radio Shack store to get some firsthand experience with the company. I left my job at Radio Shack to begin my career as an Investment Advisor in May 1981.

According to my knowledge and the fundamental analysis I conducted, Tandy seemed like a good investment. I used the same analytical thought process to speculate in Tandy that I did to buy gold in 1979 and to buy real estate in 1980. However, North America was entering into one of the most severe recessions in decades due to the 20% interest rates. By early 1982, high-quality U.S. and Canadian stocks were trading at very reasonable valuations and paying dividends of as much as 13%. The three-month options I purchased in fall 1981 expired with no value, so I lost my entire investment. The Federal Reserve had started to lower interest rates, so I purchased some more three-month call options on Tandy Corporation. However, the recession just got worse and stocks kept declining. If the share price had risen, I would have made a lot of money. After repeating this process until summer, I lost all the money I had saved as a 50% down payment for our first home. After a severe fifteen-month bear market, U.S. and Canadian equity markets bottomed on August 13, 1982. Then they rose almost 100% during the following year.

If I had waited another nine months or so I would have made many times my money. I would have more than doubled my money if I had purchased shares of the company instead of call options, which expired every three months. I was devastated and flabbergasted that I could be so wrong when I was confident that I had done everything right. I was right, but my timing was wrong. I had to pay the price for that mistake. Sometimes there is no forgiveness or a second chance in the markets. This experience makes me think of the words of English novelist Jane Austen, who wrote, "Where so many hours have been spent in convincing myself that I have been right, is there not some reason to fear I may be wrong?"

But I was still fortunate compared to some others. On the day of the 1982 stock market bottom, a colleague in a Vancouver firm hanged himself at his family's cabin. He had only been in the profession a few years and came from a successful family. Business was so bad for so long that he had resorted to stealing money from clients' accounts to make ends meet. When he learned that his superiors had discovered his thefts, he decided to end his life instead of facing the consequences and dealing with the shame. If he had only waited a week or so, perhaps the rocketing markets might have given him just a bit more hope in the midst of what was one of the most depressing times to be in the investment industry.

Dr. Dorn and I are not just concerned about investors' portfolios. Depressing markets like 1974, 1982, 1987, 2002, and early 2009 can push investors to the limits of their mental endurance. Losses caused by errors in judgment only compound the pressure. One of the main reasons Dr. Dorn and I have written this book is to enable readers to avoid mistakes and to have a reliable method for making prudent decisions. Our purpose is not just to reduce financial losses, but also the mental anguish, breakdown in relationships, and perhaps even the loss of life that results from markets not behaving the way we think they should. This applies to stock markets, real estate, commodities, options, currencies, and derivatives. It was these kinds of situations that drove Dr. Dorn and me to spend a combined fifty years analyzing every piece of information we came across to find a reliable method for market analysis. We have shared personal stories to let readers know that we too have made mistakes. We hope you can benefit from our experience.

There are other excellent examples of investors being right, but their timing wrong. In 1980, value investor Julian Robertson raised $8 million to start Tiger Management Group. By 1997, he had earned the respect of investors to the point where he was managing the second-largest hedge fund in the world (worth $10.5 billion). In 1998, the value of the holdings increased to $22 billion. We are not talking about the kind of situation where people talk to their friends and neighbors to raise some money to manage. Professional investors do not earn the trust to manage billions of dollars without a reason. Portfolio managers like Julian Robertson are wise, astute, experienced investors with superb track records.

As a value investor, Mr. Robertson's strategy was to purchase stocks trading at low valuations and to sell overvalued companies short. (Short selling enables an investor to profit when share prices decline.) In 1998 and 1999, the shares of many technology and Internet companies were trading at high prices even when they had absolutely no earnings. Therefore, Robertson shorted many of these stocks. The problem was that the value of technology and Internet companies with no earnings, or even prospects of earnings in the near future, went from high to astronomically high during the technology bubble. In addition, Robertson's biggest long position (buying a stock and profiting from it when the share price increases in value) was U.S. Airways. Even though U.S. Airways seemed to represent good value in Mr. Robertson's analysis, its share price fell. As a result of these losing trades, Mr. Robertson closed his fund in March 2000, right at the peak of the technology bubble. Shareholders in U.S. Airways lost their entire investment when the airline declared bankruptcy in 2002.

Take a moment to ponder this example. Mr. Robertson was in the position of being one of the top money managers in the world. He was at the top of his game. He did not swing for home runs. He had a defined method which he followed in a disciplined way. He was confident in this strategy and it had served him well. Imagine everything going wrong to the point where losses are so severe and you are so demoralized that you close the fund.

These examples involve real people and actual money. Julian Robertson made a mistake with U.S. Airways, but his view of the Internet and technology stocks could not have been more accurate. The only problem was that his timing was wrong. Had he waited a year or two to short them, his fund would have made billions in profits. The previous chapter explained that Fed Chairman Alan Greenspan also thought technology stocks were overpriced in December 1996. He was correct. However, prices continued to rise for another three years. Prices did not just creep higher for three years—they exploded! The question is, can a person still be right if his or her timing is so wrong? If so, for how long?

History makes it very clear that no individual or corporation is immune from suffering an insurmountable loss, no matter how large, wealthy, connected, or powerful they are.

22. An Unexpected Event Could Still Cause a Big Loss

History shows that a 5% to 7% correction occurs approximately every seven months, while a correction in the 10% range usually happens every 26 months. After a long rise of three years or more, the chance of a bear market (a decline of 20% or more) increases. In most cases, significant stock market declines do not occur just because of an unexpected event. They occur when prices are already due for a correction.

Here are some examples of unexpected events or surprises. Stock prices had risen considerably by the summer of 1987. Valuations were high and markets had risen from the fall of 1984. There were no signs of severe stress in the marketplace. Individual and professional investors had positions in stocks, sectors, and commodities that looked promising. Stocks began to decline in September 1987. By mid-October, stock prices were in a free fall. The collapse into the stock market crash of 1987 crushed financial assets and investor confidence, but the economy kept chugging along. The demise of Long-Term Capital, the Russian Default Crisis, and the Clinton impeachment process also threw a monkey wrench into the trend of almost every asset. However, as mentioned in previous chapters, this only lasted for two months.

Due to widespread concern about Y2K (the potential failure of computer systems at the start of the new millennium), in 1999 the U.S. Federal Reserve added liquidity to the financial system. Much of this money moved into technology stocks, pushing prices much higher. Markets had already been falling for almost a year when the World Trade Center Towers in New York collapsed in September 2001. The fear and worry right after September 11, 2001, actually exhausted the selling instead of starting another leg to the downside. As a result, U.S. stock prices experienced a short-term rally from the end of September 2001 until March 2002.

By March 2003, equity markets had been in a longer-term bear market for over two years. Stock prices started rising in spite of the SARS virus and the U.S. invasion of Iraq. There had been many failed rallies since 2000, but this one turned out to be the real McCoy. During the seventeen-month period from March 2007 to July 2008, crude oil prices skyrocketed from $60 per barrel to $147, an increase of 145%. This rapid price increase had a major impact on every business that used a lot of fuel.

The market reaction to the 2008 Financial Crisis had an immediate, major impact on every asset and on global economies. Investors in commodities, bonds, and stocks were blindsided by this crisis. Every trend and strategy for every investment everywhere in the world was affected by the fear and uncertainty generated by this one unexpected development. When doom and gloom were pervasive in March 2009, Citigroup surprised markets by announcing that it was going to report a profit at the end of the current quarter. Global trends for stocks, commodities, and currencies reversed in an instant on March 10, 2009, and continued to rise for years. At the time, most institutional investors had large short positions. Conditions had seemed so hopeless that many investors waited for a very long time to react to that positive event. In August 2011, Standard and Poor's lowered its rating on U.S. government bonds from AAA to AA+. A chorus of experts, including Bill Gross of PIMCO, warned that this move would result in higher bond yields and mortgage rates. Instead, bond yields dropped down close to historic lows.

Investors and portfolio managers must have a strategy that can react to unexpected events. An investor can make the correct assumption, get the trend right, and be accurate in the timing, but still be upended by an unexpected event coming out of left field. Most momentum-based indicators and moving averages can help to guide investors, even during the most unusual situations.

Many seem to think that instantaneous, similar responses by markets all over the world are something new. While the speed of the reactions has increased a little (an hour now instead of a day or two a century ago), equity markets around the world have been acting in unity for at least one hundred years. The magnitude of the reaction may vary from region to region. However, global markets have generally been following the same trends for a very long time. The situation may have been different in 2008, but the reaction by global markets was really no different than it has been for more than a generation.

In March 2013, Richard Russell of the *Dow Theory Letters* wrote a letter telling his clients that stock markets had risen for four years because the Federal Reserve had manipulated the markets. He had been bearish for years. In his letter he said, "I have never seen anything like this." By having missed the significance of unusual or surprising action by monetary authorities, this seasoned market expert had been wrong for four years since the 2009 lows.

The information and examples presented in this and earlier chapters teach us some lessons. First, they show us that a person can do a thorough investigation of an investment and still be totally wrong. An intelligent, wise, rational man or woman can diligently look at an investment using fundamental analysis, a value approach, growth parameters, quantitative analysis, and mathematical models. Using any or all of these analytical approaches, one can still come to the wrong conclusion. Market trends can go against investors, no matter how confident they are in their well-informed opinions. History shows that price trends can continue for much longer than expected and that prices can fall or rise much more than anyone could imagine.

Second, one can be the smartest investor in the world, who has done all the analysis and arrived at the right conclusion. However, even if an investor's opinion is totally correct, acting on that opinion can be disastrous if the timing is not right. Consequently, to make profitable investment decisions and avoid serious mistakes, one must get the trend and the timing right. Even if an investor arrives at the correct conclusion and gets the trend and the timing right, an unexpected event can wash over the markets and change the situation in an instant.

Unexpected events in a business or sector can have an impact on certain commodities, bonds, or stocks. However, it usually takes a political, military, financial, or large scale economic crisis to affect global markets. Even then, unexpected events rarely cause recessions or longer-term setbacks for financial markets.

However, if an unexpected event occurs when global economies and markets are already under extreme stress due to an 80% rise in oil prices over 12 months, or an inverted yield curve in the U.S., a negative surprise can become the catalyst for turning a bull market into a bear market. That is when economic growth can stall and decline to cause a recession or even a depression.

Consequently, it is counter-productive to act as though a crisis or unexpected event could derail a bull market or strong economy at any time without warning. There are times to be worried about potential problems and there are times not to be concerned. History shows many models and strategies seem to fail when markets and economies are under extreme pressure. Professional and individual investors need an airbag that works all the time, especially in an accident. The chapter "It Is Time for a Revolutionary Change in Portfolio Management" will show investors how to use indicators that are helpful all the time.

Dow Jones Industrial Average Returns Following Crisis Events			
Events When DJIA Was **UP** 12 Months After a Crisis			
		3 Months	12 Months
Japanese bomb Pearl Harbor (Almost a gain for such a major event)	Dec 8, 1941	-9.8%	-0.8%
Hiroshima bomb	Aug 6, 1945	15.7%	24.4%
U-2 shot down - U.S. admits spying	May 9, 1960	1.1%	21.1%
Cuban Missile Crisis starts	Oct 23, 1962	18.8%	31.4%

Kennedy assassinated	Nov 22, 1963	8.8%	21.6%
Nixon imposes price controls	Aug 16, 1971	-5.0%	12.6%
Chernobyl nuclear meltdown	Apr 29, 1986	-3.8%	21.1%
1987 Stock Market Crash	Oct 19, 1987	10.2%	22.9%
Coalition bombing of Iraq	Jan 17, 1991	19.1%	29.5%
British Sterling Crisis	Sep 16, 1992	-1.3%	9.2%
U.S. Marines killed in Somalia	Oct 4, 1993	4.8%	7.3%
Fall of Mexican peso	Dec 20, 1994	7.5%	34.8%
Oklahoma City bombing	Apr 19, 1995	21.1%	32.8%
Asian Crisis begins	Jul 2, 1997	3.8%	17.2%
Clinton/Lewinsky made public	Jan 21, 1998	16.1%	18.6%
Long Term Capital bailout	Sep 23, 1998	14.5%	33.3%
Clinton impeached	Dec 19, 1998	11.2%	25.2%
Space shuttle Columbia explodes	Feb 1, 2003	4.2%	29.5%
U.S. invades Iraq	Mar 20, 2003	11.0%	21.4%
SARS virus health scare	Mar 2003	12.8%	35.3%
Hurricane Katrina floods	Aug 29, 2005	4.1%	8.8%
Fukushima nuclear meltdown	Mar 11, 2011	-0.7%	9.5%
U.S. debt ceiling dispute	Jul 25, 2011	-7.0%	3.8%
Eurozone Debt Crisis	Aug 2011	3.9%	6.9%
U.S. Fiscal Cliff Crisis	Nov 2012	5.9%	18.0%
U.S. Gov't shutdown	Oct 1, 2013	8.2%	??

Events When DJIA Was **DOWN** 12 Months After a Crisis

Watergate news reaches Senate	Jun 25, 1973	5.5%	-7.3%
U.S. V.P. Spiro Agnew resigns	Oct 10, 1973	-14.3%	-35.2%
Reagan shot	Mar 30, 1981	-0.2%	-17.8%
U.S. Marines killed in Lebanon	Oct 24, 1983	0.8%	-1.8%

U.S. invades Grenada	Oct 25, 1983	-0.5%	-2.6%
Fall of Berlin Wall	Nov 9, 1989	0.8%	-6.8%
Y2K	Dec 31, 1999	-11.9%	-6.2%
Bombing of USS Cole	Oct 12, 2000	4.9%	-6.8%
World Trade Towers destroyed	Sep 11, 2001	2.9%	-10.7%
Bear Stearns fails	Mar 14, 2008	3.0%	-39.6%
Lehman Brothers fails	Sep 15, 2008	-21.5%	-11.3%

Figure 22.1: This table on pages 274-276 shows how the DJIA performed after various crises and unexpected events from 1941 to 2013. History shows that serious economic, financial, military, or political crises do not impact equity markets as much as we might believe. In most cases, an unexpected event only causes a decline of 2% or so for a week or two before prices recover from their losses. However, why did markets rise after President Kennedy was assassinated and fall after President Reagan quickly recovered from an assassination attempt? Why did markets fall 50% during the Nixon impeachment but rise during the Clinton impeachment? Why did markets rise after U.S. Marines were killed in Somalia in 1993 but fall after U.S. Marines were killed in the bombing of the USS Cole? Why did the DJIA rise nicely after the 1997 Asian Crisis but fall after the Berlin Wall came down in 1989? The main reason markets declined after a crisis was due to a big spike in oil prices and/or a tighter monetary policy in the United States which resulted in an inverted yield curve. The only exception was from 1983 to 1984 when the DJIA consolidated for a year after rising 64% from the 1982 low to the early 1984 high. This table shows that investors should not move from equities to cash because of an unexpected event. Funds should be moved from equities to cash after oil prices jump by 80% in 12 months or the U.S. yield curve inverts. That is when an unexpected event has the potential to cause problems for financial markets. Chart prepared by Dave Harder

23. The Trader's Edge

"Trading with an edge is what separates the professionals from the amateurs. Ignore this and you will be eaten by those who don't."
Curtis Faith, *Way of the Turtle*

Human behavior is at the heart and soul of trading. This assertion gains credence as evidence continues to build showing that traders bring themselves and their brains into every aspect of trading. With this process come irrationality and cognitive biases. Three critical elements underlie successful trading and investing: risk control, money management, and edge.

What is an edge? In simple terms, an edge is what separates the amateurs from the professionals. An edge refers to specific brain synaptic strategies that are practiced until they are as natural as breathing. It refers to skills, talent, and resources unique to each individual. Edges are what separate successful from unsuccessful traders. Those traders who find and exploit edges are the ones who end up winning. Moreover, the ability to execute on an edge is at the heart of behavioral trading.

The harsh reality is that the majority of traders lose more than they win. Most enter the markets with ill-conceived beliefs and proceed to lose all or most of their money in a short period of time. In general, mastery of a subject takes ten years and 10,000 to 20,000 hours of deliberate practice. Some people become good traders in much less time, while others take longer. Most enter the markets ill-prepared and do not succeed. Because they are not trained, their trading behavior is somewhat akin to driving a race car blindfolded. They might as well be throwing darts at the markets or taking their money to a casino. Trading is a serious business. No businessperson would think about starting a business without a defined business plan. Traders also need a defined strategic plan. You may often hear the saying, "Plan your trade and trade your plan." This is a simple (but far from easy) part of finding an edge and executing it.

The major reason traders don't adhere to "plan your trade and trade your plan" is that they have not trained their trading brains to dampen down the hurricane of emotion that comes rushing in as soon as real money is placed in the markets. Traders who practice on simulation platforms can tell you how everything changes once real money is on the line. First, there is the element of risk. Every time you have monies in the market, you are in the realm of risk, and it is your responsibility to control that risk. If you do not have a strategy for risk control, you have no edge. If you deviate from your strategy by giving yourself a "little slack" regarding stops, you have no edge. If you enter a position without a clear stop and an approximate profit potential, you have no edge. If you turn a short-term trade into a longer-term investment, you have no edge. Trading is about probabilities, not perfection or black and white. The worst thing that can happen to a novice trader is for him or her to win immediately. This result is usually luck, not skill, and can cause the trader to overestimate his or her ability and become overconfident. The trader will think that he or she has it all figured out, and will start taking more and more risks. This process leads to careless trading and puts the trader on a path to taking a large loss.

Back to the edge. Edges are statistical and represent some aspect of recurring market activity that you can exploit for your own profit. In trading, the best edges are those that relate directly to cognitive biases. In order to develop your edge, it is critical to find points of entry in the market with the greatest probability for success. The emphasis here is on entry, which I believe is the most important part of any trade. It is your task as an edge trader to find those price points where the markets have the greatest probability to move in a direction that favors your position and to avoid those price points where the markets have the greatest probability to move against your position. Said another way, you enter with an approximate target price and a definite stop price. If the market moves in your direction, you take profits at or close to the target, and you manage the trade along the way. Some traders like to take partial profits and move stops to break even if the trade is going in their favor. Others hold on, especially if the trade is moving nicely and they have a good profit cushion. If the market moves against you, you take the stop immediately and close the position. There is no holding or hoping when you get into a losing position.

In his superb book entitled *Way of the Turtle*, Curtis Faith, one of the original "Turtles" chosen by Richard Dennis, provides illustrative descriptions of the edge. Faith writes, "Edges are found in the places that are battlegrounds between buyers and sellers. Your task as a trader is to find those places and wait and see who wins and who loses." Faith goes on to say, "Trading edges exist because of divergences in market perceptions and realities that result from cognitive biases. They exist because economists are wrong in their belief that market players are rational. Market players are not rational." Faith describes beautifully how support and resistance represent areas of price instability, and how these are viewed by trend traders and countertrend traders in terms of the cognitive biases of anchoring, recency, and disposition effect. Regarding trend traders, Faith says, "The source of the edge for trend followers is the gap in human perception at the time when support and resistance breaks down. At these times, people hold on to previous beliefs for too long and the market does not move quickly enough to reflect the new reality."

Figure 23.1: The three critical elements that underlie successful trading and investing are risk control, money management, and edge. Plan your trade and trade your plan. Produced by Janice Dorn

It is important to grasp that the term "trading edge" refers to nothing more than the ability to find and exploit recurring market inefficiencies. There are edges (structural and methodological) everywhere in the markets for those who look beyond the ordinary to seek them out. If you look diligently, you will find and profit from them. If you are able to consistently find and exploit edges, you will make money. If you do not find and exploit edges, you are trading so-called efficiently-priced assets and can only hope to profit if the information (readily and instantly available to all) coming into the markets is favorable to your position. This favorability would be expected to occur with a probability of about 50:50. That is not an edge or a probability that lends itself to risking your hard-earned assets.

> "I'd be a bum on the street with a tin cup if the markets were always efficient."
> Warren Buffett

Those who utilize behavioral trading believe that markets are neither random nor efficient. In other words, behavioral traders do not ascribe entirely to the Efficient Market Hypothesis or the Random Walk Theory. Some behavioral traders may lean more toward the Adaptive Markets

Hypothesis proposed in 2004 by the highly respected academician Andrew Lo. Dr. Lo's framework attempts to reconcile theories that imply markets are efficient with behavioral alternatives that utilize the principles of evolution (competition, selective adaptation, and natural selection). Markets are not entirely efficient because there are too many ill-conceived ideas and opinions floating around. Markets are not entirely random because the strong emotions of traders and investors create trends.

In order to find and profit from an edge in the markets, behavioral traders must search for and find what the famed behavioral strategist Michael Mauboussin, Managing Director and Head of Global Financial Strategies at *Credit Suisse*, has called "diversity breakdowns." These are points of instability in price where there are likely to be collective over-reactions or under-reactions caused by irrational traders and investors. For a market to be efficient (price is an unbiased estimate of value) there must be cognitive diversity among investors. This diversity occurs in the stock markets because there are bulls and bears, long- and short-term investors, technical traders and those who trade on fundamentals. Without diversity, everyone is thinking and believing the same thing and price gets out of sync with value. The key to trading and investing successfully is to look for the points of greatest instability. In other words, in order to profit maximally, it is necessary to understand both your own psychology and the collective psychology of other market players.

Technical analysis is nothing more than a plot of human emotions placed onto a grid. It is the task of the behavioral trader to find the places where emotions are running the highest and to exploit these for profit. The emotions of millions of traders in the markets result from brain-based (cognitive) biases that provide an edge for behavioral traders. Simply put, trading edges are the result of cognitive biases and are found at areas where perception diverges from reality.

No matter what time frames, wave structures, technical indicators, chart patterns, or thousands of different tools a trader uses to develop a trading plan, it is critical to look continually for an edge. Your trading edge is the advantage you have over other traders due to your having a trading method that puts the odds consistently in your favor.

> "Edges come from places where there are systematic misrepresentations as a result of cognitive biases. These places are the battleground between buyers and sellers. Good traders examine the evidence and place bets on what they perceive to be the winning side.
> They also learn to admit when they have made the wrong bet and quickly fix the situation by exiting the trade."
> Curtis Faith, *Way of the Turtle*

24. Market Bottoms Can Be Identified

"I absolutely believe that price movement patterns are being repeated. They are recurring patterns that appear over and over, with slight variations. This is because markets are driven by humans—and human nature never changes."
Jesse Livermore

History shows investors act in a very similar fashion when a serious decline comes to an end. The recurring movement of "impulse-reaction-impulse-reaction" leads to two unique formations that develop near a market low.

Double bottoms are reversal patterns. The sequence of lower lows ends when the price forms two distinct lows, often six to nine weeks apart. Double bottoms are like rainbows—they only appear when the storm is over.

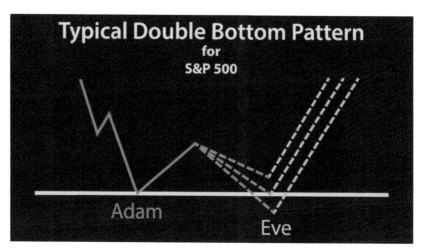

Figure 24.1: The pattern of a typical double bottom for the S&P 500 Index. Produced by Dave Harder

Ever since 1950, the S&P 500 has formed a typical double bottom to mark the end of every decline of 20% or more. The only exception was 2009. In a bear market, the S&P 500 will fall to a climactic low called the Adam low and then experience a quick rebound to recover a small portion of the losses. Then, the S&P 500 will fall sharply again to another low approximately six to nine weeks after the initial low. This second low is called the Eve low. The Eve low can either be a little higher than the Adam low, equal to the Adam low, or as much as 4% lower than the Adam low to qualify as a double bottom. A double bottom is a sign that selling has been exhausted, creating the perfect conditions for a new uptrend to begin.

As mentioned in the previous paragraph, the S&P 500 did not follow the typical pattern of forming a double bottom at the end of the financial bear market in the spring of 2009. This rare exception occurred due to the heavy weighting of major financial firms in the S&P 500. The share prices of the big banks were decimated during the Financial Crisis. However, some of the other major North American market averages such as the NASDAQ, the Russell 2000 Index, and the Canadian S&P/TSX, did form a typical double bottom. Looking at bear market bottoms from 1950 to 2003 shows that the final low of the S&P 500 held above the initial low eight times out of thirteen, or 61% of the time. The final low fell a few percentages below the initial low five times, or 39% of the time.

The process of creating a double bottom, or successfully retesting the initial low, usually takes six to eight weeks. The shortest period in a double bottom was 16 trading days in March 1980. However, it took 104 trading days in 2003, which increased the average period between lows for this period to 46 trading days, or nine weeks. During the Financial Crisis, the initial climactic low took place on November 21, 2008, while the second low occurred on March 6, 2009. This period was more than three months, which was also longer than normal. While double bottoms are not exactly the same, they have very similar characteristics.

John Bollinger (the creator of Bollinger Bands, which define investment trends) said that if you are lucky, you get to pick one exact top or bottom in your lifetime. While market tops are very difficult to determine, market bottoms are much easier to see soon after they happen if one can remain objective. Some investors/traders just cannot restrain themselves from reacting to the fear caused by the significant decline in the value of investments near a market low and the barrage of pessimistic forecasts accompanying it. As a result, asset prices can fall violently and then reverse course in an instant when the selling has finally been exhausted. The raw emotional behavior seen at market lows seems to repeat itself over and over again, creating predictable price patterns. This recurrence should not be a surprise, since human beings are creatures of habit. Thus a double bottom usually marks the end of a decline of 20% or more.

Market prices typically fall much faster than they rise, since human beings react much faster to fear than they do to the desire to make a profit. For most, fear is a stronger emotion than greed. Confidence and trust are restored slowly, but can be extinguished overnight. In a speech at the Richard Ivey School of Business in London, Ontario, on February 25, 2013, Bank of Canada Governor Mark Carney remarked,

> "It has been said that 'Trust arrives on foot, but leaves in a Ferrari.'"

This concept is something all traders and investors need to understand and respect.

Double bottoms form from the trend that precedes them. For example, downtrends are seen on a chart as a series of lower lows. The herd becomes fearful that the downtrend will continue. They sell, thinking that there is nowhere for the movement to go but down, and that they have to get out "while the getting is good." Meanwhile, something happens during the second low when prices seem to hold. It stops going down and all those who have sold are now remorseful and traumatized. They are frozen in fear and regret. Since they are looking for signs that the selling has been exhausted, traders who have been through this type of situation before see something quite different. Bottom fishers (seasoned speculators and experienced chart watchers) recognize what is really going on and slowly begin to enter long positions when they think the selling is almost completed. Then, as price begins to stabilize, increasing numbers of traders begin to recognize the pattern and jump in.

Entering near bottoms produces the highest profit for any trade. This goes without saying. However, it is important to be careful and look closely before you leap. Many losses have been incurred by trying to buy at the lowest price before there is enough evidence that selling has reached a final climax.

It is important to take an objective view of price movement and not be traumatized by the volatility that often occurs at turning points. Be safe, preserve capital, and be ready to enter if the lower low or higher low holds. When markets are experiencing a correction or bear market, it almost always pays to wait patiently for a double bottom to occur before buying. Trying to predict a market bottom based only on valuations or the extent of a decline is dangerous. Over the long term, it is much safer and more profitable to wait for prices to rise after a double bottom than to try to anticipate when the actual bottom might take place.

Famed traders and authors Alan Farley (www.hardrightedge.com) and Thomas Bulkowski (thepatternsite.com) have provided good descriptions of the various types of double bottoms. We have chosen to describe one of them—the Adam and Eve bottom—since almost every bear market for the S&P 500 since 1950 has ended with this pattern. Adam and Eve bottoms are excellent swing trades if they work this way: Adam is sharp and deep, and is a first bottom. There is, typically, a bounce from the Adam bottom for a few weeks, since investors believe that the downtrend has finally come to an end. This happened after the Adam low in early August 2011, during the most recent double bottom for the S&P 500. After the initial low, stock prices recovered for a few weeks into early September. However, when prices retreat again to form an Eve bottom, as they did on October 4, 2011, the level of fear and anxiety spikes again.

The Eve bottom usually occurs approximately six to eight weeks or, in some cases, several months from the initial Adam low. Sometimes the Eve low is softer and more rounded and rolling than the Adam low. This was the case with the Eve low in late February and early March 2009. (The Adam low of the Financial Crisis occurred three months earlier on November 21, 2008.) Be aware that a successful retest at the Eve low can still occur even if prices drop approximately 4% or so below the initial low. After the Eve low, price action sometimes begins to consolidate into a tight range. The consolidation continues until it finally breaks out strongly to the upside on volume, usually on a Tuesday (if not on a Tuesday, then on a Thursday). During the Financial Crisis, the bull market began on Tuesday, March 10, 2009. The November 21, 2008, Adam low occurred on a Thursday.

What does a real double bottom look like on a chart? As seen in Figure 24.2, a double bottom consists of two well-defined lows at approximately the same price level. Prices fall to a support level, often called Adam, then rebound from the low before declining to the support level again, often called Eve. If the Eve low was not more than 4% or so below the Adam low, a double bottom has been formed, enabling prices rise in a strong fashion. The two lows should be distinct. According to Edwards and Magee, the second bottom (Eve) can be rounded while the first bottom (Adam) should be distinct and sharp. The pattern is complete when prices rise above the highest high in the formation. The highest high is called the confirmation point.

Figure 24.2: Adam and Eve bottom shown for the Dow Jones Industrial Average 1979-1983. The red arrows on Figures 24.2 to 24.8 indicate when double bottoms were formed. Source: Thomson Reuters

The weekly chart in Figure 24.2 (each horizontal blue line is one week) of the DJIA from 1979 to 1983 shows a shorter than normal (four weeks) double bottom in the spring of 1980. The first and second lows are marked with arrows. In 1980, the lows were at a similar level.

Another major double bottom occurred during the summer of 1982, marking the beginning of the 1982 to 1998/2000 bull market that propelled the S&P 500 Index higher by more than 1400%! That double bottom occurred over a more typical eight-week time frame. You can see that the second, or Eve, low in the summer of 1982 was marginally lower than the first, or Adam, low. Markets often turn up after falling slightly (1% to 4%) below the previous low, as the last investors (or portfolio managers) who are still wondering if they should sell or not sell, sell short, thereby exhausting the selling. Remember, markets do not go up when the news is rosy; they rise when the "last investor who wants to sell has sold." A double bottom is only complete, however, when prices rise above the high end of the point that formed the second low.

The double bottom marks a downtrend in the process of becoming an uptrend. Buying right after a bear market ends produces the best returns with the least amount of risk. Therefore, detecting double bottoms and having the confidence to become fully invested without delay after a double bottom is confirmed is one of the most important skills an investor can acquire. It is also one of the easier skills to acquire, as long as one is able to keep emotions under control. Enduring a double bottom is like competing in an "emotional rodeo." A bull rider is successful if he can stay on the bull for only eight seconds. For investors, it usually takes eight weeks of mental endurance to go through a bear market bottom.

When markets are behaving normally, investors feel like they are spectators at a rodeo. When markets fall sharply, investors can feel like they have been placed on a bucking bronco. During rare moments, such as November 2008 and February 2009, investors can feel like they have been attached to a 2,000-pound bull! Market bottoms are much easier to handle if one knows what to expect in terms of market action, media comments, and one's own emotional response.

During a very severe market correction many years ago, the late Louis Rukeyser, host of the weekly PBS television program *Wall Street Week*, asked one of his panelists how he was sleeping at night. It may have been Michael Holland who replied, "I sleep like a baby. I sleep for a few hours and wake up and cry. Then I go back to sleep again." It is not uncommon for investors and traders to experience sleepless nights when market volatility is extreme near a market low.

The best way to increase the chance of detecting a double bottom when markets are declining to the second low, six to eight weeks (or sometimes months) after the first low, is to walk away from the quote screen. Turn off the television for hours at a time. This is a time when investors and traders need to follow the policies of the "go teams" (mentioned earlier in the book) who investigate aircraft accidents for the U.S. National Transportation Safety Board. Listening to media reports and expert opinions can very easily convince investors that so much is going wrong that the markets could never turn up in such an environment.

A double bottom, or retest of the low, looks benign when you look at the chart. However, that picture in no way reveals the anguish and stress that always accompany this process. Remember, it is not important to be bullish or bearish—it is most important to be right. In order to remain agnostic when every investor is focused intently on losing money, it is helpful to go to a place where the market does not matter. Take a walk to a park where mothers are playing with small children. Go to a coffee house where university students are working on their computers or visiting with friends. Visit someone in a hospital or care home. These types of activities will help to put market volatility into perspective. Fresh air is invigorating. Studies have shown that exercise is fertilizer for the brain. When market action is most intense, our minds need all the help they can get!

If one must keep up with the news, it has to be done with firm discipline. Watching the news on television and reading financial publications are only useful for one thing during a market low—to determine the level of pessimism. It is a positive indication if television channels have the market sell-off as their feature story and newspapers have it as their front-page headline. It is also a good thing if most market commentators are forecasting lower prices. The more commentators—and the lower the forecast for prices—the better. We all know that pessimism usually peaks near market lows. It can also be a positive sign if the covers of weekly magazines highlight the market decline. However, these indicators are not automatic signs to buy. If they occur after there has already been a significant market low more than a month earlier, they are signs that a double bottom could occur. They alert investors that they should not be so overcome by fear and negativity that they ignore short-term or long-term moving average crossovers that turn positive in such an environment. Moving average crossovers are particularly helpful in confirming that a downtrend is transitioning to an uptrend after a double bottom.

The Eve bottom on October 10, 2002, (shown in Figure 24.5) occurred two months after the late July 2002 low. In October, many traders had stop-loss orders in just below the July 2002 low. Other traders and investors were watching so that they could also "jump out of the way" if markets were going to fall to the next support level, which was quite a bit lower. As a result, there was a flurry of selling on October 10, 2002, when prices started falling below the July low. However, those sellers turned out to be the final sellers of the downturn. That short dip below the previous low flushed out the sellers, exhausting the desire to sell. With the bulk of the selling over, prices rebounded for months.

The same pattern occurred in early October 2011, during the European Debt Crisis. North American markets reached the initial low on August 8, 2011. Prices rebounded into early September before falling again. As prices were falling amidst extreme volatility, the International Monetary Fund (IMF) announced that the "global economy is in a dangerous new phase and the downside risks are growing." Of course, this forecast once again was not accurate, since global economies showed many positive signs of growth just a few weeks later. Nevertheless, these are the sorts of headlines investors should expect to see at market lows. Observe how many negative headlines there are, but do not let them influence your outlook.

On Monday, October 3, 2011, Dave Harder's Investment Update included examples of the 1998 and 2002 double bottoms and pointed out how declines just below the previous lows flush out the final sellers. This information was intended to help clients focus on the mechanics of what was happening, instead of the gloom and doom. The update also stated, "Pessimism is high and many market bottoms occur in October. The next few days could be very critical as markets test the lows and the resolve of investors." The closing low for a correction or bear market usually occurs on a Monday. On Tuesday, after a sharp decline in the opening hours of trading, markets usually turn around and rally sharply midway through the trading day.

Why does this process happen? After stock prices have lost a lot of value during the previous week, investors and portfolio managers take the weekend to digest the news together with current events. When the broad consensus of experts has a bleak outlook, investors tend to bail out on Monday, sending prices sharply lower once again. Therefore, when trading starts on Tuesday, investors who are barely hanging on also throw in the towel in a final act of despair. This can cause prices to fall below the previous climactic low, which happened six to eight weeks earlier. The decline triggers stop-loss orders. After all the stop-loss orders are filled and selling is basically complete, the markets usually turn on a dime, midway through Tuesday's trading day. Veteran traders have experienced this scenario so often that they are just waiting in the wings to pounce after it happens. (It becomes quite obvious after a while—like seeing a patch of blue sky after a major storm.) Consequently, the intraday low for a correction or bear market usually occurs on Turnaround Tuesday on the second low.

Market prices fell to the level of the August 8 low on Monday, October 3, 2011. The next day was Tuesday, October 4. Living on the West Coast, Dave did not even bother to check the markets for the first three hours of trading Tuesday morning, to guard his emotions. When he did look at prices at 9:30 a.m. Pacific time (12:30 Eastern time), true to form, prices had slipped another 2% below Monday's close. Dave thought, "so far, so good," since everything was progressing as expected. As mentioned earlier, markets usually turn up around 1:30 to 2:00 p.m. Eastern time on what is often called Turnaround Tuesday. Dave was quite relaxed and optimistic that a turn-around would take place. However, by 2 p.m., there was no sign of a bounce. By 2:30, nothing. Three o'clock came, and still nothing. The situation did not look good at all. What seemed to be a textbook double bottom was not materializing. Then, in the last hour of trading, markets reversed and soared. In the space of the final hour of trading on October 4, 2011, the action on the S&P 500 was transformed from a 2% decline to a 2% advance from the previous day's close. That decline indeed turned out to be the exact bear market low, completed in a classic fashion. Seventeen months later, the S&P 500 reached a new all-time high, from what turned out to be the intraday bear market low on October 4, 2011.

Even though the 2011 bear market followed a classic double bottom pattern, what happened on Tuesday, October 4, still stunned many seasoned market observers. The analysts at WJB Capital Group, the former New York institutional investment firm, were expecting the market to fall further that day. They give the best description of what happened on Tuesday, October 4: "And then in one of the great 'pulls victory from the mouth of defeat' moments in market history, the S&P embarks on a 40 handle/+4% rally in about 43 minutes to make, as one client noted yesterday afternoon, 'every clown like you and me feel like a market amateur.' How'd it happen and why did it happen? To which another client said slightly afterward, 'I looked at the market and couldn't believe I shorted the low.'"

You and I know exactly how and why it happened. After the markets fell below the previous low after eight weeks of market turmoil, the final investors who wanted to sell or sell short did so. When there was no one left to sell anymore, the preponderance of buyers caused markets to roar back. By the end of the week, U.S. markets had risen 10% from Tuesday's lows and were up for two weeks in a row for the first time in three months.

It is important to train ourselves to detect classic double bottoms. It is critical that we exercise patience to keep cash on the sidelines and to wait for the second low before buying. In this way, profits can start building immediately. Moreover, investors and clients are saved from enduring the stress of another nerve-racking selloff. Investors must do all they can do to reduce not only investment risk but also emotional stress.

When stock prices were in a free fall during February 2009, Dave noticed that some major commodity prices were not dropping below the 2008 lows. On February 20, 2009, Dave was astounded to see that the long-term moving average crossover for the Chinese Shanghai Index turned positive! The Volatility Index had also declined substantially from the highs even as the S&P 500 was dropping to lower lows. These were the first lights at the end of the tunnel. While many institutional investors were bailing, these important signposts gave Dave the confidence to discount the flood of negative opinions and buy after the double bottom on March 10, 2009. Peter Lynch said, "It isn't the head but the stomach that determines the fate of the stock picker." This is especially true at market lows. The charts in Figures 24.3 to 24.8 demonstrate how double bottoms formed after bear markets from 1982 to 2012.

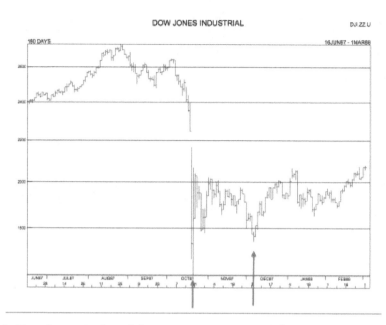

Figure 24.3: Dow Jones Industrial Average June 1987-February 1988. This is a daily chart (each bar is one day) of the double bottom after the Crash of 1987. In this case, the double bottom was close to six weeks apart, and the second low was higher than the first. Many significant lows occur in October. In any case, positive signals from moving average crossovers can be used to confirm that a successful retest has occurred. Source: Thomson Reuters

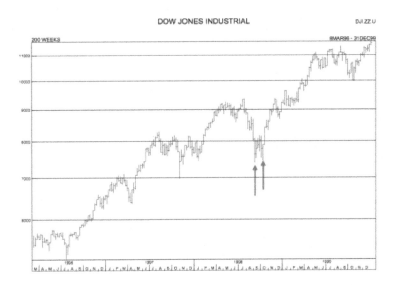

Figure 24.4: Dow Jones Industrial Average 1996-1999. This is a daily chart of the double bottom which formed during the Clinton Impeachment/Long-Term Capital Hedge Fund Collapse/Russian Default Crisis in 1998. It was a classic textbook example of a double bottom. The lows were six weeks apart and the second low was slightly higher than the first. Source: Thomson Reuters

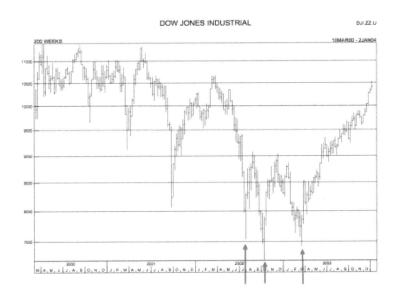

Figure 24.5: Dow Jones Industrial Average 2000-2003. This is a weekly chart of the lows which ended the longest bear market in a generation. It began when technology stocks started falling sharply in September 2000, and ended in March 2003. The

initial low occurred at the end of July 2002. The bear market was so severe, and had lasted so long, that one portfolio manager I talked to in Toronto said that he was just waiting for a storm of locusts. The second low in early October 2002, which turned out to be the ultimate bear market low, was just below the July low. The 2003-2007 bull market began when a third low was recorded in March 2003. At that time, the United States had invaded Iraq and the SARS virus was causing deaths around the world. Source: Thomson Reuters

It is very important to see how markets rallied when the U.S. Federal Reserve lowered interest rates in April 2001. However, markets fell to a lower low after September 11, 2001, and then fell to an even lower low in July 2002. Note that markets did not stop falling until after the second low (or double bottom) in October 2002. Even though there can be some spirited rallies, a bear market does not end until there is a double bottom. A single bottom is evidence that markets are still in a longer-term downtrend. Traders who are short should beware of these powerful spikes (called bear market rallies) that happen in a bear market. Short-term investors can take advantage of these moves on the long side as well. However, we cannot emphasize strongly enough how important it is to be patient and wait for a double bottom before committing capital to long-term positions!

Generally, volume in a double bottom is higher on the first bottom than the final bottom. Volume tends to be downward as the pattern forms. Volume does, however, pick up as the pattern hits its lows. Volume increases again when the pattern completes, breaking through the confirmation point.

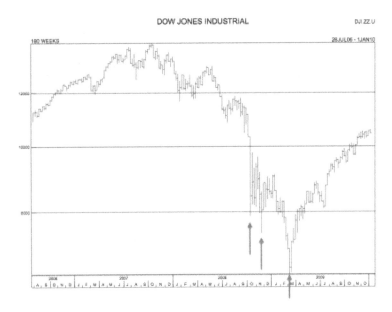

Figure 24.6: Dow Jones Industrial Average 2007-2009. Source: Thomson Reuters

The 2008 Financial Crisis bear market ended in a unique way. The DJIA and S&P 500 had climactic lows and reversals on October 8 and November 21, 2008. However, financial stocks fell even more in February 2009. Due to the heavy weighting of financial stocks in the DJIA and S&P 500, those market averages fell to lows much more than 3% below the November 2008 lows.

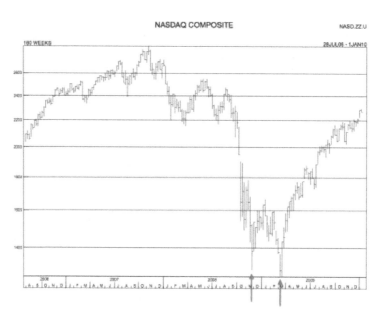

Figure 24.7: NASDAQ Composite Index 2007-2009. Source: Thomson Reuters

However, if one looked at market averages such as the NASDAQ, the Russell 2000 Index, and S&P/TSX Index in Canada, one saw a much different picture. These indexes had very normal double bottom patterns even though they were just over three months apart. Oil and copper prices, two reliable indicators of global economic growth, were stabilizing or in an uptrend in early 2009. Remember, investing is both an art and a science. A mathematical formula cannot be used to verify a double bottom. At times one has to look for divergences and accept some inconsistencies.

According to John Murphy, the technical odds usually favor the continuation of the present trend. This means that it is perfectly normal market action for prices in a downtrend to fall to a support level a couple of times, rise back up, and then resume that downtrend. It is a challenge for the analyst to determine whether the rise from the bottom is indicating the development of a valid double bottom or simply a temporary setback in the progression of a continuing downtrend. Traders call a temporary rise in downtrend a "dead cat bounce," since even a dead cat will bounce if it falls from a great height.

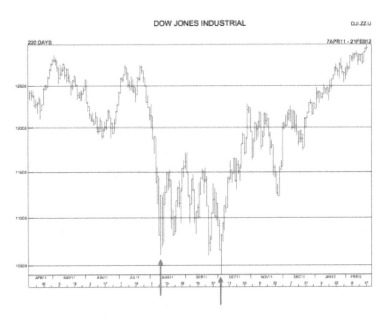

Figure 24.8: Dow Jones Industrial Average April 2011-February 2012. This is a daily chart of the 2011 European Debt Crisis bear market. The 2011 double bottom was almost exactly two months apart. The second low in October 2011 was just slightly below the August low. Even though it seemed as though Europe was still in an economic and financial quagmire throughout this period, many U.S. market averages reached record highs 18 months later in the spring of 2013. Source: Thomson Reuters

The S&P 500 Index has formed a double bottom after every bear market since 1950, except for 2009. The S&P 500 and Dow Jones Industrial Average did not form a normal double bottom pattern in 2009 because the value of shares in the financial sector collapsed. Nevertheless, many other North American market averages, such as the NASDAQ, the Russell 2000 Index, and the Canadian S&P/TSX, did form a typical double bottom.

Deep Survival: Who Lives, Who Dies, and Why by Laurence Gonzales has many lessons for traders, and one of them is illustrated through a Korean martial art called *Kumdo*. This is a brutal game that in the past involved a fight to the death with very sharp swords. Today bamboo sticks are used, but the moves are the same. *Kumdo* teaches student warriors to avoid what are called "The Four Poisons of the Mind." These are fear, confusion, hesitation, and surprise. In *Kumdo*, the student must be constantly on guard never to anticipate the next move of the opponent. Likewise, the student of markets must never allow his or her natural tendencies for prediction to get the upper hand. Having a preconceived bias of what the opponents—or what the markets—will do can lead to momentary confusion and, in the case of *Kumdo*, to death. A single blow in *Kumdo* can be lethal and is the final cut, since the object is to kill the opponent. One blow leads to death, which leads to "game over."

Instead of predicting, anticipating, and being full of fear and confusion, we must do exactly the opposite if we are to survive a death blow from the market's movements. We must watch with a calm, clear, and collected attitude, and then strike just at the right time. A few seconds of anticipation, hesitation, or confusion can mean the difference between life and death in *Kumdo*—and wins or losses in the financial markets. If we are not in tune with the four poisons of fear, confusion, hesitation, or surprise in the markets, we are at risk of loss or ruin. Ruin means that money is gone and the game is over for the investor and all of those counting on him or her to provide for them.

What can investors do about this?

- Avoid preconceived notions about what the markets or your position will do.
- Learn to execute ruthlessly and to fight for every point of execution.
- Sell and cut losses immediately when stops are hit.
- Manage risk with position sizing.
- Always ask yourself how much you can lose on a trade, rather than how much you can win.
- Never expect someone to rescue you from a bad position.
- Don't waste time looking around for confirmation that you are right; rather, stay focused on what is in front of you.
- Avoid the four poisons of the trading mind: fear, confusion, hesitation, and surprise.
- Replace fear with faith in your model and trading plan.
- Replace confusion with the attitude of being comfortable with uncertainty.

- Replace hesitation with decisive action.
- Replace surprise with taking nothing for granted and preparing yourself for anything.

The many examples of double bottoms and the information provided in previous pages should encourage all investors not to add money to investments during a severe sell-off or a long-term decline unless a double bottom has occurred. Long, devastating declines in U.S. equity markets after 1929, in gold after 1980, in Japanese stocks after 1989, and in the NASDAQ after 2000 remind us of the carnage that can happen even after asset prices have experienced major losses. The best time to be aggressive and "jump in with both feet" is not when prices have been rising for months or years, but when prices advance and moving average crossovers turn positive after a double bottom has been completed.

Shorter-term moving average crossovers, oscillators, relative strength data, and divergences can be helpful for those who are intent on trying to react to market bottoms as soon as possible. Shorter-term moving average crossovers can then be used to limit risk if the timing is off.

In this kind of situation the news will be bleak. Market experts will be warning that problems have not been solved and that another sharp sell-off is just around the corner. Large, well-respected institutions such as the IMF and the World Bank could well be issuing dire forecasts. It does not matter, however, because the selling has been exhausted and the decline is over. Then, months later, all of a sudden the outlook will start to improve. By then, prices will likely be more than 20% or 30% higher. With practice and discipline, investors can recognize and profit from double bottoms. The discipline of waiting for double bottoms also reduces mental stress for investors, who can and should use double bottoms to their advantage. See Figure 24.9 showing the front page of the business section of Canada's *Globe and Mail,* the equivalent to the *Wall Street Journal,* just after the 2008 Financial Crisis bear market ended on March 9, 2009. North American economies started to improve soon after this information was published.

Figure 24.9: The cover page of the Toronto *Globe and Mail* Report on Business section, March 18, 2009. Reprinted by permission of the *Globe and Mail*

What is the mood like at a bear market bottom? Below are some excerpts from an article entitled "Wall Street Merry-Go-Round," published in the August 16, 1982, issue of *Time* magazine. This article was published on the exact day that U.S. stock markets turned up after the 1981-1982 bear market, during one of the most severe recessions since the Great Depression. (August 16, 1982, also marked the day U.S. equity markets started a new 18-year growth phase when North American prime interest rates were at 15%.)

> … The Government will have to borrow at least $100 billion in fresh cash during the rest of 1982, and must raise $35 billion by the end of September.

> … Says Irwin Kellner, chief economist of Manufacturers Hanover Trust Co. in New York City: "If you want higher interest rates, just wait a few days. They'll come along very soon."

... Says Raymond Dalio, Economist of Bridgewater Associates, a Westport, Conn., economic forecasting firm: "I think we'll see a repeat of the Crash of 1929."

"... I believe we are already in the early stages of a depression."

... In spite of the tentative signs that the recession is beginning to bottom out, the climate for business continues to deteriorate.

... Nearly 500 enterprises shut their doors every week, the heaviest corporate failure toll since the early '30s.

... Even the most conservative forecasters are clearly rattled by the grim climate for investors. They are particularly worried by the stubborn refusal of borrowing costs to drop more than a few percentage points.

... Says Economist Paul Wexler of the Bank of New York: "The financial underpinnings of American industry have weakened to the point where a major unexpected bankruptcy is now a real risk."

Towering interest rates also worry Robert Farrell, the highly regarded chief strategist at Merrill Lynch.

In contrast, here are excerpts from a *Time* magazine article entitled "Happy Birthday, Bull Market," published one year later, on August 22, 1983:

... Even so, nothing can change the fact that it has been quite a ride—and, despite the inevitable "corrections," it might have a lot more mileage in it.

... A year ago the Dow stood at 779.92. In June it reached a record 1248.30, up 61%.

> … Many Wall Street watchers remain bullish. Says Treasury Secretary Donald Regan, former chairman of Merrill Lynch, "The market was due for a pause. But it isn't overdone." Indeed, in the view of Regan and almost everyone else, the bull market still has a lot of life left in it. Says Arthur Zeikel, president of Merrill Lynch Asset Management: "We are in the fourth or fifth inning of a nine-inning ball game."

While U.S. equity markets corrected by approximately 10% during the twelve months after August 1983, markets continued to race ahead to what seemed like continuous new all-time highs from the end of 1984 until the peak in August 1987. Those who did not feel comfortable buying at record highs in 1985 and 1986 missed out on some of the best gains in decades.

Market participants should be aware that huge one-day price gains (bear market rallies) can occur in a sharp sell-off. For example, the DJIA had the biggest one-day point gains ever during the 1987 and 2008 declines. These spectacular one-day spikes actually turned out to be a signal that a bigger decline was in the offing. Investors should be on the lookout for these kinds of gains so they are not seduced into thinking that the decline is over. Here are the details: after prices fell for a month, the DJIA had the biggest point gain ever when it rose 75 points or 3% from 2,493 to 2,568 on September 22, 1987. After that, the DJIA rose another 3.3% until October 2 and then plunged until October 20 when it touched an intraday low of 1,616. From the day of the biggest point to the low just a month later, the DJIA fell 37.1%!

After prices had already collapsed for more than a month in October 2008, the DJIA broke the record for the biggest one-day point gain in history when it soared 937 points from 8,451 to 9,388 on October 13, 2008. Prices moved up another 4.3% for three weeks after this 11.1% spike and then turned into an elevator shaft. From the October 13, 2008 close to the November 21, 2008 low, the DJIA fell 20.6%. From the October 13, 2008 close to the bear market low on March 6, 2009, the DJIA fell a total of 31.1%. These rare examples teach us that exceptional one-day gains during a decline are harbingers of greater losses to come in the very, very near future. When the biggest one-day point rise in history occurs during a sharp sell-off, it is a sign to reduce exposure to equities.

In conclusion, major market bottoms have very similar characteristics. Information about them has been included so that investors and traders can be familiar with what to expect at a market bottom, and be prepared to act when moving average crossovers turn positive at a time when the outlook seems absolutely dreadful. Often the biggest gains are made during the shortest period of time right after a severe bear market ends. Although it is unrealistic to expect that all of the gains from a market bottom can be captured, it is important for investors and traders to use the information in this section so that they can benefit from most of those gains.

25. It Is Very Challenging to Determine a Market Top

As mentioned in an earlier chapter, the typical double bottom pattern can enable experienced, disciplined investors to determine market bottoms. In our opinion it is three times more difficult to call a market top than a market bottom. Market tops do not have classic similar patterns like bottoms do. Sometimes markets hover around the highs for months (the DJIA in 1981, 2000 and 2007). Sometimes prices go straight up to a peak, turn around on a dime, and then go straight down (crude oil in 1981, crude oil in 2008). If there is a common pattern at a major long-term market top, it is characterized by a peak, followed by a sharp decline of 15% to 40%, and then a strong rebound six weeks to six months later that takes prices within approximately 20% of the previous high before prices fall some more (gold in 1980, the DJIA in 1987, the NASDAQ in 2000, the S&P/TSX in 2008). See examples of major market tops in Figures 25.1 to 25.12.

Although we have not experienced "wailing and gnashing of teeth," our brains have been branded with the painful memory of bear markets. Experience has taught us that one of the best ways to forecast a market high is simply to monitor the passage of time. If prices have been in a steady rise for close to three consecutive years without a correction of 20% or more, a bear market is due. The longer prices continue to rise after three years without a 20% correction, the worse the decline will be when it finally starts. For example, North American equity markets rocketed higher after the bear market bottomed in August 1982. Prices corrected by 10% or less in 1984, 1985, 1986, and May 1987. By August 1987, stock prices had risen five years without a 20% correction. Then, from Labor Day 1987 to October 19, 1987, stock prices fell close to 40% across the board.

North American equity markets were strong in 1995, 1996, and 1997. In the summer of 1998 they fell 20% in two months. That decline enabled markets to rise again in 1999 and 2000. Then, from September 2000 to March 2003, equity markets experienced one of the longest bear markets in a generation, lasting for thirty months. A thirty-month downtrend taxes the patience of investors. It also strains the sanity of those who have a career in the investment industry.

North American equity markets started a new bull market in March 2003. By the spring of 2008, markets had risen for five years without a correction of much more than 10%. As in 1987, markets went into a 50% free fall after Labor Day 2008.

When we think back on the worst bear markets in recent decades, we realize that they seem to begin in earnest after Labor Day. The gut-wrenching 1981-1982, 1987, 2000, and 2008 bear markets all started right after, or very shortly after, everyone returned to work after summer vacation. The 20% decline in 1998 was reversed in short order as markets rose to new highs, so it was not nearly as devastating as the other declines.

High levels of optimism and overvaluation are common characteristics at a market peak. That was the case in 1981, 1987, and 2000. However, while there were high levels of valuation and optimism for real estate in 2006, there was very little optimism or overvaluation of stocks before the bear market in 2008.

One sign of over-optimism is people quitting their jobs to invest in an asset. There were many reports of Americans quitting their jobs to day trade in 2000. Then tech stocks collapsed. In 2006, news stories and television programs profiled Americans who were quitting their jobs to buy a house, renovate it, and then flip it. Shortly thereafter, real estate prices collapsed, resulting in the Financial Crisis. As mentioned before, there were stories of shortages of hotel maids in Shanghai, China, during 2007. They said they could make more money investing than working. Chinese stocks started a vicious bear market after 2007. It is easy to make money when markets are strong, but a bull market does not last forever. That is why those who have learned the hard way say, "Never confuse genius with a bull market." Line-ups to buy investments such as gold or condominiums are also a sign of over-optimism. When new television shows or magazines crop up about a new investment fad, they are a sign that it could be near its end as well. A sign that an investment trend may end in the near future occurs when it is featured on a prominent magazine cover. Publicity about plans to build the world's tallest building can also provide signs of an approximate peak in an asset or economy.

Taking profits by selling too soon can work well in this type of market, as long as one can withstand the temptation not to buy back if prices continue to advance. Do not underestimate the power of this temptation!

The story of SemGroup's trading disaster illustrates how important it is not to short an investment that is still in a strong uptrend just because it seems like it should peak. As mentioned earlier, we believe that moving average crossovers are the best tools to use to stick with a trend until it ends. They are also the best tools for discerning when a trend reverses so that an investor can determine when to change from long to short positions, short to long positions, or go into cash.

In summary, it is very challenging to determine when prices are peaking. Sometimes prices will rise very quickly and then fall just as quickly. An asset may only trade at the peak price for minutes before falling. Many times a peak can only be recognized well after it happens. Looking for signs of over-confidence and overvaluation can be helpful. It would seem that the best way to ensure that one avoids a severe bear market is to sell on the first day after Labor Day every year if asset prices have been rising for approximately thirty-six months and moving average crossovers are negative. This did not work in 2007, so it is not perfect either. However, when it is right, it works very well.

Simply relying on moving average crossovers to turn negative to confirm a peak can work well, too. Unfortunately, moving average crossovers will usually give a signal that the trend has peaked after prices have already declined from their highest point. We must accept the fact that investing is not an exact science. Therefore, investors have to discipline themselves to be content with being approximately right instead of precisely wrong. Baseball heroes still strike out many times. It is not necessary to sell right at the peak or buy right at the precise low to be successful investors. To sell at a price 10% below the peak can be disappointing. However, a year later it can seem like the best move one ever made. As mentioned before, the primary goal is to be right more than one is wrong. Following moving average crossovers should help investors to be more right than wrong over the longer term.

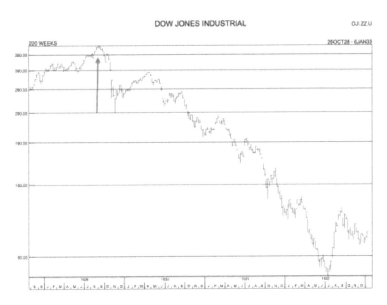

Figure 25.1: Dow Jones Industrial Average 1929-1932. This chart shows the famous stock market peak in 1929 before the October crash. Prices fell close to 90% from the high before this most devastating bear market finally came to an end more than 30 months after the record high. Source: Thomson Reuters

Figure 25.2: S&P 500 1972-1975. Source: Thomson Reuters

Stock prices fell close to 50% during the 1973-1974 bear market. Charts like these do not in any way convey the mental agony and stress investors feel, just like pictures cannot show heat and oppressive humidity. Investment Advisors in Vancouver, B.C., took to driving taxicabs in the evenings to try to support their families during this period.

Figure 25.3: Gold Bullion London PM Fix 1979-1982. Source: Thomson Reuters

Gold skyrocketed to a magnificent peak in 1980 and then fell very quickly. Years later, one would have been very happy to have sold at $600 or $700.

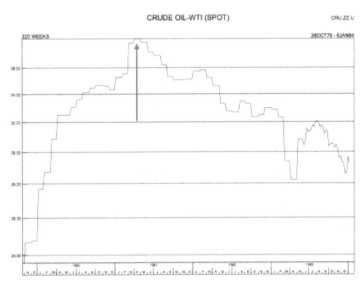

Figure 25.4: Crude Oil - WTI (Spot) 1980-1983. Source: Thomson Reuters

Crude oil prices peaked in the spring of 1981 and had perhaps one of the most orderly declines. The peak of gold and oil prices marked the end of the 1966-1982 consolidation phase of the 16-year cycle.

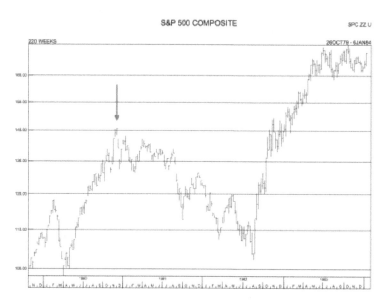

Figure 25.5: S&P 500 1980-1983. Source: Thomson Reuters

Figure 25.5 shows the peak of the S&P 500 before the final bear market in the 16-year consolidation cycle.

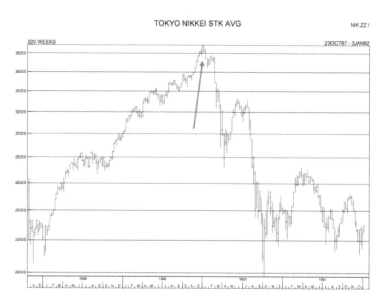

Figure 25.6: Tokyo Nikkei Index 1988-1991. Source: Thomson Reuters

Japanese stocks and real estate were very overvalued in 1989. More than twenty years later, the Tokyo Nikkei 225 Index is still down close to 50% from this peak!

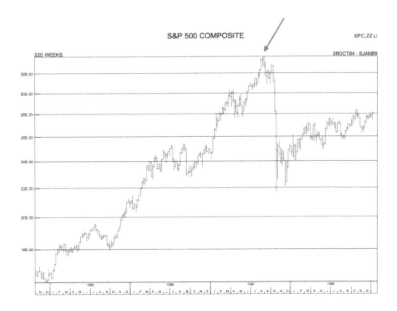

Figure 25.7: S&P 500 1985-1988. Source: Thomson Reuters

U.S. market averages had steady gains from 1985 to August 1987. According to some measures, stock prices were overvalued by as much as 40% in August 1987. While prices fell 40% in September and October, the S&P 500 Index ended 1987 near the same level as it started the year.

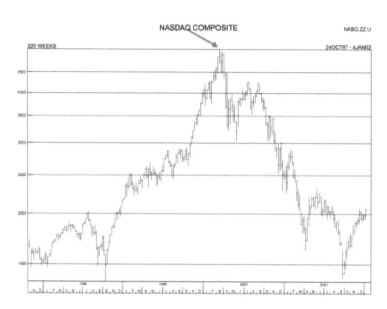

Figure 25.8: NASDAQ Composite Index 1998-2001. Source: Thomson Reuters

Figure 25.8 shows the peak of the bubble in technology stocks. This is another case where selling six months after the peak may have been disappointing at the time, but would have been viewed as a brilliant decision many years thereafter.

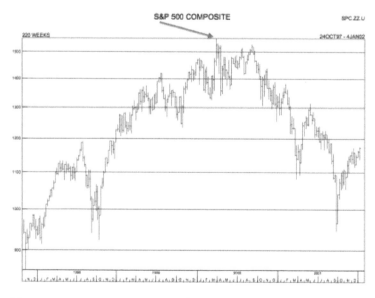

Figure 25.9: S&P 500 1998-2001. Source: Thomson Reuters

Figure 25.9 is a chart of the S&P 500 Index showing the 2000 peak, marking the end of a powerful 18-year uptrend which began in 1982. To those employed in the investment industry, the long bear market from 2000 to 2003 felt like a plague of biblical proportions. The only thing missing was the swarm of locusts.

Figure 25.10: Crude Oil - WTI (Spot) 2006-2009. Source: Thomson Reuters

Crude oil prices experienced a stellar rise to new record highs in 2008 before collapsing. This peak was of the "straight up and down" variety.

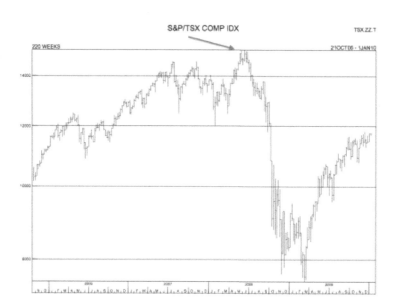

Figure 25.11: S&P/TSX Composite Index 2006-2009. Source: Thomson Reuters

Figure 25.11 is a chart of the Canadian S&P/TSX Index during the Financial Crisis. Prices started to really fall right after Labor Day 2008. By February 2009, 50% of investment advisors in Canada were either clinically depressed or very close to it. The toll that a bear market like this takes on the emotions, physical health, and relationships of those employed in the financial industry cannot be described in words. It also has a significant impact on investors, especially those who are counting on investment returns for retirement income. It is worth using moving average crossovers to try to reduce the financial and emotional damage that goes along with bear markets.

Figure 25.12: S&P 500 2006-2009. Source: Thomson Reuters

The U.S. S&P 500 Index peaked many months before the S&P/TSX in October 2007. As you can see, there is not a common pattern for a market peak. There are often opportunities to sell at respectable prices six months or so after a peak when the long-term moving average crossovers turn negative. In cases where there are sharp, quick declines as there were in 1987, a stop-loss limit of 15% from the peak of the S&P 500 will provide protection to minimize losses.

There are many corrections during a bull market. Figure 25.13 provides an idea of what investors can expect to experience, even when equity markets are in an uptrend.

Corrections During a Bull Market
S&P 500

Bull Markets	Duration (years)	Number of 5%+ Corrections	Number of 10%+ Corrections
06/01/1932 – 07/18/1933	1.2	4	3
03/14/1935 – 03/06/1937	2.0	8	1
03/31/1938 – 11/09/1938	0.6	3	2
04/28/1942 – 05/29/1946	4.1	6	2
05/17/1947 – 06/15/1948	1.1	1	1
06/13/1949 – 08/02/1956	7.2	12	3
10/22/1957 – 12/12/1961	4.2	2	1
06/26/1962 – 02/09/1966	3.7	3	1
10/07/1966 – 11/29/1968	2.2	3	1
05/26/1970 – 01/11/1973	2.7	4	1
10/03/1974 – 11/28/1980	6.2	8	5
08/12/1982 – 08/25/1987	5.0	8	1
12/04/1987 – 07/16/1990	2.6	6	1
10/11/1990 – 03/24/2000	9.4	19	3
10/09/2002 – 10/09/2007	5.0	8	1
03/09/2009 – Current	4.2	10	2

Frequency of Corrections
Over the past 80 years of bull markets:
- There have been 105 corrections of greater than 5%
  ... or one every 7.0 months on average.
- There have been 29 corrections of greater than 10%
  ... or one every 25.3 months on average.

InvesTech Research

Figure 25.13: Chart of corrections in the S&P 500 during bull markets from 1932 to May 13, 2013. Produced by InvesTech Research

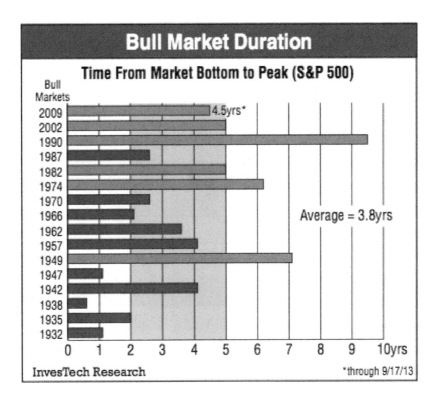

Figure 25.14: Chart showing the duration of bull markets from 1932 to September 2013. Produced by InvesTech Research

Figures 25.15and 25.16 show the duration and magnitude of bull and bear markets in the S&P 500 and the S&P/TSX from 1956 to June 2013.

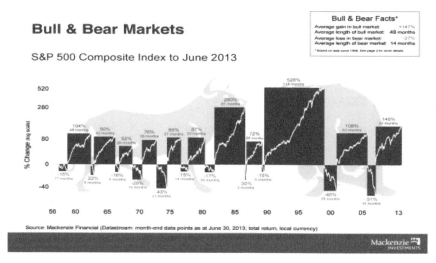

Figure 25.15: Duration and length of bull and bear markets for the S&P 500 from 1956 to June 2013. Included with permission from Mackenzie Financial

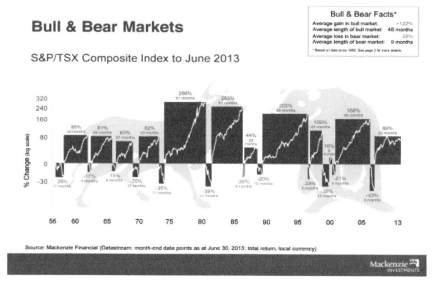

Figure 25.16: Duration and length of bull and bear markets for the S&P/TSX from 1956 to June 2013. Included with permission from Mackenzie Financial

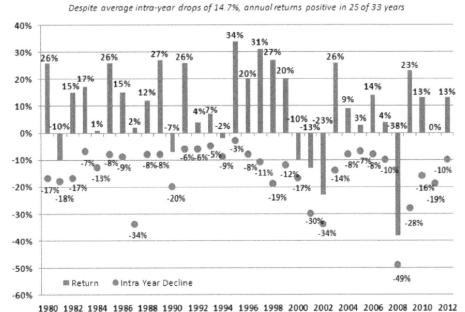

S&P 500 Intra-Year Declines vs. Calendar Year Returns
Despite average intra-year drops of 14.7%, annual returns positive in 25 of 33 years

Figure 25.17: Even though the S&P 500 may have produced an attractive return for a year, this does not mean it was easy for investors to earn it. The gold bars in Figure 25.17 illustrate the returns for each calendar year from 1980 to 2012. The red dots show the intra-year declines for every year. Corrections of 6% to 10% are common. However, there were 13 declines greater than 15%, with an average decline of 27.1%. Therefore, investors who want to limit losses or volatility can reduce equity exposure when the S&P 500 falls by 15%. The chapter "It is Time for a Revolutionary Change in Portfolio Management" will discuss a stop-loss strategy in greater detail. Included with permission from FactSet

26. Reading Tomorrow's Newspaper Today: 2 to 1 Advance/Decline Buy Signals

Market bottoms do not occur when the economic outlook improves, earnings rise, and unemployment declines. Bear market lows happen in the midst of doom, gloom, and fear. Most importantly, they begin when the selling of stocks is exhausted and strong buying comes in to take advantage of it. One of the best ways to measure the strength of a turnaround like this is to examine how many issues (an issue is a company trading on the stock exchange) are advancing, compared to the numbers which are declining. It is a very simple tool. Data for the NYSE Advance/Decline ratio are easy to find and easy to calculate. One does not need a computer, a CFA certificate or a degree in accounting to use this. Simple addition and subtraction skills are all that is required. When there are twice as many issues advancing as declining on average for ten consecutive trading days, a buy signal is issued.

In his book *Winning on Wall Street*, Marty Zweig pointed out that this is one of the best signals that a strong, long-term uptrend has started. There have only been eleven signals or clusters of buy signals since 1953. The most recent cluster of buy signals from the 2-1 Advance/Decline indicator was seen first on March 23, 2009. This was only two weeks after the Financial Crisis Bear Market ended on March 9, 2009. (The March 23, 2009, buy signal was the first of three buy signals triggered in 2009.) The 2-1 Advance/ Decline indicator also issued buy signals at the start of the two major long-term market advances in the last forty years. It triggered a buy signal several weeks after the 1973-1974 bear market ended (which has many similarities to the Financial Crisis bear market) and two weeks after the bottom in the 1982 bear market. The 1973-1974 and 1982 recessions were the worst in the last fifty years. The S&P 500 Index and the DJIA both lost almost 50% of their value by the end of the 1973-1974 bear market. The powerful rally off the August 1982 bear market low ushered in the start of a new long-term uptrend that lasted eighteen years and raised the value of the S&P 500 and DJIA close to 1,400% from the lows in 1982. More recently, three 2-1 Advance/Decline buy signals were issued in 2009 after the Financial Crisis bear market ended.

Why is it so important to monitor this very basic indicator? As mentioned above, the 2-1 Advance/Decline indicator is like a siren on the rooftops indicating that a tsunami of cash is washing over U.S. equity markets. When U.S. market averages rise, most global equity markets follow along as well, so this has major implications for all equity markets all over the world. A 2-1 Advance/Decline buy signal is so helpful because it usually occurs at the embryonic stages of a new long-term bull market. Since this indicator is more reliable than most, it gives investors the confidence to become fully invested within days or weeks of a major market bottom, when most other investors are still shell-shocked by the big losses, anxiety, and the dire state of the global economy.

Previous chapters have explained that the current 16- to 18-year cycle, during which financial assets are in a downtrend, is scheduled to end sometime around 2016 to 2018. This means that a brand new 16- to 18-year uptrend for financial assets should begin in that time frame. That new uptrend should provide huge returns for investors, just like the 1982 to 2000 bull market did. Those who are able to get themselves in a position to profit from that new cycle as soon as possible after it starts will be able to benefit the most. Since there are such high returns in the early stage of a new bull market, professional money managers who can move from a conservative posture to an aggressive posture at the earliest opportunity can have an edge in performance over their competitors for years to come.

I distributed a Special Investment Update to my clients on March 23, 2009, just days after the Financial Crisis bear market ended. That was the first time since 1982 that there were twice as many issues advancing on the New York Stock Exchange (NYSE) than declining, on average, for ten consecutive days. That Special Update informed readers of the buy signal, the historical record, and what it implied. Six months later, on September 9, 2009, I received an email from John Thiessen, CEO of Vertex One Asset Management Inc., one of the top hedge funds (with assets totaling more than $1 billion) in western Canada. It read, "Thanks for all your help. We are up 57% this year because I read Harder." That was the ultimate compliment for the information he received which enabled him to invest heavily in the very early stages of the bull market when many were still concerned about selling.

The Special Update on March 23, 2009, and an April 20, 2009, Investment Update showed how U.S. stocks reacted after advancing issues outnumbered declining issues by a ratio of more than 2 to 1, on average, for a ten-day period. The Updates illustrated that markets continued to rise for many months after such a strong, rare burst of buying. This rare display of buying power emerged when there was still a lot of apprehension and little data to support an economic recovery or a more positive outlook for stocks.

The second 2-1 Advance/Decline buy signal in the 2009 cluster happened after a mild, brief correction ended on July 10, 2009. As of July 23, 2009, 20,704 stocks advanced while only 9,474 declined over the previous ten-day period. This produced the second of two Advance/Decline buy signals within four months. This had only happened three other times since 1950. It happened in July and November 1962, when the world was on the verge of nuclear war over the Cuban Missile Crisis. It occurred again in January and February 1975 after a severe recession, a 50% drop in the DJIA, Nixon's impeachment, and a big rise in oil prices. The next occurrence was in August and October 1982 as interest rates were declining from all-time record highs during a severe recession.

A four-year rise, which began in 1962, was the final stage of a sixteen-year rise. The 1975 rise marked the end of the recession and bear market as well as the beginning of a commodity boom. The rise in 1982 marked the end of the recession, the end of the bear market, and the beginning of a sixteen-year bull market, which rose 300% in the first three years! Of all the previous examples, conditions in 2009 seemed most similar to 1975. Having two buy signals only months apart showed that, for whatever reason, investors and money managers seemed as eager to buy stocks in 2009 as they were to sell them during the Financial Crisis.

On September 17, 2009, yet another 2-1 Advance/Decline buy signal was triggered. To the best of our knowledge, this is the only time in history that there has been a cluster of three 2-1 Advance/Decline buy signals in such short order. It does not matter who you are or how much money you have; going against momentum like this is like standing in front of a freight train. History shows that this is one of the most reliable indicators that a strong rise has started. Ignoring it, or not being aware of it, could result in your missing out on a major advance. The following pages contain charts showing how equity markets acted when this has happened.

Market bottoms do not occur when earnings rise, the economy springs to life, and the outlook improves. Bear markets end when everyone who wants to sell has sold. When the selling is exhausted, stock prices rise even if the negative news continues. There is a well-known saying that markets "climb a wall of worry." Do not expect much good news for a while after a bear market ends. Markets usually bottom many months before the economy improves, and peak many months before the economy slows down. Although the 2-1 Advance/Decline signals are rare, there is no other indicator we are aware of that provides such a reliable buy signal so close (usually within ten trading days) to a major market low.

Most traders and investors wish they could have tomorrow's newspaper today just one time. This indicator may be as close as we will ever come to realizing that fantasy.

Many say that it is impossible to time the markets. We would agree that it is impossible to time the markets all of the time. However, the 2-1 Advance/Decline indicator and the long-term moving average crossovers show that one can indeed accurately time the markets on many occasions. Take advantage of these opportunities when they occur. The 2-1 Advance/ Decline indicator does not tell us what analysts or economists think should happen. It does not tell us why prices are rising all of a sudden either. It only tells us that cash is flowing into equities like water flowing over Niagara Falls. Figures 26.1 to 26.4 show when 2-1 Advance/Decline buys signals have occurred. Listen to the message of the markets when they are shouting from the rooftops!

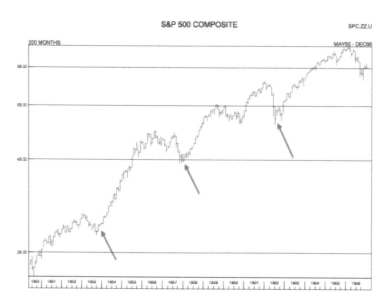

Figure 26.1: S&P 500 1950-1966. Source: Thomson Reuters

The arrows in Figure 26.1 show when the 2-1 Advance/Decline indicator triggered buy signals in 1953, 1958, and 1962.

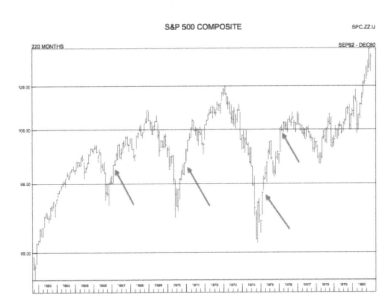

Figure 26.2: S&P 500 1963-1980. Source: Thomson Reuters

2-1 Advance/Decline buy signals also occurred in 1967, 1971, 1975, and 1976.

Figure 26.3: S&P 500 1974-1990. Source: Thomson Reuters

It took seven years for the next 2-1 Advance/Decline buy signal to occur after 1976. A buy signal was triggered on August 26, 1982, ten trading days after the 1981-1982 bear market low, marking the beginning of a new 16-year cycle. Additional signals were given in January 1985 and January 1987.

Figure 26.4: S&P 500 2002-2011. Source: Thomson Reuters

There was a gap of twenty-two years between the most recent 2-1 Advance/Decline buy signal in 1987 and the next buy signal on March 23, 2009. The Financial Crisis bear market reached the low on March 6, 2009. North American equity markets began to surge on March 10. The buy signal on March 23, 2009, occurred only ten trading days after a new bull market was born. At that time there was still very little confidence that the bear market was over. I distributed a Special Update to my readers on the day of the buy signal to inform investors about the significance and reliability of this indicator.

It turned out that the March 23, 2009, buy signal was just the first of three buy signals in short order. Another 2-1 buy signal was issued on July 23, 2009, and the third was triggered on September 17, 2009. Consequently, there could be no doubt that the bear market was over.

Three months after the first 2-1 Advance/Decline Buy Signal on March 23, 2009, the S&P 500 had risen 8.5%. Six months after, the S&P 500 was up 29%. One year later, it had gained 42.6%. Two years later it had rallied 57.6%, and four years later the increase was 89.2%. After observing the historical record provided in these pages, readers can see how accurate and reliable this simple indicator has been in the past. See the headline of Dave Harder's Special Update distributed on March 23, 2009, which was as forceful as I was permitted to make it. It states, "2-1 ADVANCE/DECLINE INDICATOR GIVES RARE BUY SIGNAL. THIS INDICATES THAT THE DECLINE, WHICH BEGAN LAST SUMMER, IS LIKELY OVER. (DONE, FINISHED, HISTORY?) THE DEBATE IS OVER. THE LOWS SHOULD BE IN PLACE AND A NEW LONGER TERM ADVANCE HAS STARTED."

Giving You The Confidence To Outperform
SPECIAL UPDATE FOR MARCH 23, 2009

2-1 ADVANCE/DECLINE INDICATOR GIVES RARE BUY SIGNAL. THIS INDICATES THAT THE DECLINE, WHICH BEGAN LAST SUMMER, IS LIKELY OVER. (DONE, FINISHED, HISTORY?) THE DEBATE IS OVER. THE LOWS SHOULD BE IN PLACE AND A NEW LONGER TERM ADVANCE HAS STARTED.

Almost two weeks ago, on March 10, 2009, global equity markets experienced a strong rise after reaching new lows for the bear market. Equity markets have continued to move higher since March 10th but the markets have had strong moves before, only to turn back down and decline to previous lows or even new lows. This time it is different.

Market bottoms do not occur when the economic outlook improves, earnings rise and unemployment improves. They happen when there is doom and gloom. Most importantly, they begin when the selling of stocks is exhausted and strong buying comes in. One of the best ways to measure the strength of an uptrend is to examine how many issues (an issue is a company trading on the stock exchange) are advancing compared to the number that are declining. I have examined all the US stock market advances since 1970 and have discovered that market bottoms have been reached and strong uptrends have followed when there are more than twice as many advancing issues compared to the number of declining issues on average, for ten

Figure 26.5: Dave Harder's March 23, 2009, Special Update pointing out the significance of the 2-1 Advance/Decline buy signal which occurred on that day.

27. History of Tallest Structures Provides Warning Signals

"Pride goes before destruction, a haughty spirit before a fall."
Proverbs 18:12

From the time of the Tower of Babel and Egyptian pyramids to the Burj Khalifa in Dubai, people have desired to showcase their achievements by building a major physical structure as a permanent symbol. For most of history, the physical footprint was the measure of size. It wasn't until Elisha Otis invented a safety brake for the elevator that skyscrapers became the ultimate trophy for businessmen who became very successful and thought they had the world by the tail. However, history shows that the desire to build the tallest building on earth usually occurs at the end of a business cycle when people become overconfident. Buildings are usually built as an investment in order to make a reasonable return on one's capital. It is a sign of overconfidence and pride when that goal is replaced with the primary objective of having the bragging rights that go along with constructing and owning the tallest building in the world. As a result, news of the proposed construction of the tallest building in the world has been like a siren on the rooftops, signaling that a boom is about to end and that an economic collapse could be forthcoming.

As an example, construction for the Empire State Building began on March 17, 1930, four months after the stock market crash of 1929. This means that the plans were already in place before the crash. Walter Chrysler and the creator of General Motors were competing to see who could build the world's tallest building. After a long economic boom, the Great Depression was just getting started.

Building activity for the Sears Tower in Chicago (now renamed the Willis Tower) and the CN Tower in Toronto began in 1973, just as the ribbon was being cut to open the World Trade Center Towers in New York. This marked the peak in the North American auto industry. Shortly after this, there was a severe recession and bear market during 1973 and 1974 in the midst of a 16-year consolidation phase for U.S. stock prices.

Perhaps putting a man on the moon in July 1969 could be included in this category as well. The decision to devote money and resources to show Russia and the world that the U.S. was the leader in space was made in good economic times. These events occurred just after the 16- to18-year uptrend in stock prices was making the transition to the consolidation phase in 1966. The decade of the 1970s was a very difficult period for the United States.

The Petronas Towers were completed in 1998 in Kuala Lumpur, Malaysia, rising just thirty-three feet higher than the Sears Tower. This occurred just as the foundation was being prepared for the Taipei 101 in Taiwan, which would eclipse the Petronas Towers. After a seemingly endless economic expansion, the Asian currencies collapsed at the end of October 1997. Asian stock markets also fell sharply and stayed depressed for a long time. I gave a presentation to a group of Thai businessmen in Bangkok during June 1998 and remember them lamenting the fact that their companies' stocks had lost 90% of their value during the previous twelve months.

President John F. Kennedy presented a very ambitious and challenging goal in the 1960s when he informed Americans that they were going to put a man on the moon. However, that was not as challenging as what President Bill Clinton tried to do near the end of the 16- to18-year uptrend in stock prices during his final term. He tried to change human nature and behavior.

In the mid-1990s, the U.S. Department of Housing and Urban Development directed Freddie Mac and Fannie Mae (U.S. government-sponsored enterprises that purchase mortgages) to buy mortgages made to low-income borrowers. Since America was so prosperous, Bill Clinton and the Democrats wanted more people to be able to live the American dream and own their own home.

Centuries of lending experience led banks and mortgage companies to develop lending standards. These lending standards enabled as many people as possible to receive financing for a home and still allow the lender to stay in business. Government leaders had good intentions and thought financial firms were being stingy and greedy. They reasoned that if financial firms would only lower their standards and give up some profits, more families could live in their own home instead of renting. As time went on more institutions lowered their lending standards to the point that some had adopted the lending practices of a drunken sailor.

No one wanted to rain on the parade of a very strong housing market, including President George W. Bush. It is the responsibility of the Federal Reserve to "take the punch bowl away from the party" when the economy gets too strong. Mr. Greenspan talked about irrational exuberance in 1996, but he had little to say as the housing bubble developed. He trusted the directors and executives of financial firms to act in their own best interests, since they would in turn protect the companies they worked for, the financial system, and the economy as a whole.

Consequently, instead of taking the punch bowl away, Greenspan allowed it to overflow. As lending practices deteriorated and housing prices rose, it was equivalent to adding more alcohol to the punch bowl. Greenspan expected all those at the party to leave and go home in a responsible manner. Instead, there was such a major accident on the global financial highway that it almost brought traffic everywhere to a standstill.

Not everyone has the means, discipline, or stability to own a home. Bill Clinton and the Democrats did not understand that. Lending standards were developed for good reason. The result of this experiment proved to be a disaster for many U.S. individuals, families, and financial firms. It is taking years to repair the damage to the economy and the U.S. real estate market. Over-optimism in the midst of a long period of economic growth led to this unfortunate situation. The boom and bust in the U.S. housing market after

2000 shows that the human nature of politicians and individuals has not changed. Bill Clinton tried to "build the tallest building" by enabling many more people to buy a home. The experiment failed.

Which was the tallest building to be built after the U.S. housing bubble burst? The height of the world's tallest building had slowly expanded from 381 meters for the Empire State Building in the 1930s to 509 meters for the Taipei 101. The owners of Dubai World Corporation were so overconfident that they went all out to make sure they would have the distinction of possessing the highest building for a long time. Construction began in 2004 and the Burj Khalifa in Dubai opened in January 2010 at a height of 818 meters! Oil prices may have reached a high for this cycle with the peak price of $147 in July 2008. Then oil and global real estate prices plummeted in 2008. Oil prices rebounded to the $100 level in 2012, but it remains to be seen if prices can rise above the 2008 high before the uptrend for resource prices is scheduled to peak in a few years.

Instead of feeling proud of their accomplishment, Dubai World (the corporate flagship of Dubai) declared in November 2009 that they could not make payments on over $50 billion of loans. Dubai relied heavily on oil prices. Once again, the tallest building was built in a region where prices where high and were about to fall.

The Empire State Building, World Trade Center, CN Tower, Sears Tower, Petronas Towers, Taipei 101, and the Burj Khalifa show that the goal of building the world's tallest building is a sign that economic trouble may be approaching. It is a signal that the region of the world where the building is being built could be heading for, or already be in, a significant downturn. The timing is not specific. However, it is a very easy sign to look for that can warn investors that an economic reversal may occur in the region where the structure is being built. Major developments that make a statement, such as planning to put a man on the moon or lowering lending standards, are also a sign that an economy has been strong for so long that a major downturn could be in store.

As of 2014, there are plans for the Azerbaijan Tower to become the tallest building in the world after the Kingdom Tower, which is to be built in Saudi

Arabia. Azerbaijan and Saudi Arabia are oil-rich countries. The history of 16- to 18-year cycles suggests that crude oil prices could start a 16-year down-trend sometime in the next few years. These building plans seem to confirm this prediction.

In 2012, plans were announced for the world's tallest building to be built in China. In 2013, there was another announcement that a businessman was planning to build the tallest building in China from start to finish in only six months!

The Book of the Wisdom of Solomon, written thousands of years ago, describes what happens to those who ignore history and become overly enamored with their success: "Pride goes before destruction." In 2013 there seemed to be so many people planning to build the world's tallest building that this may have broader, longer-term implications for the global economy. It will be interesting to see who will be the next global contender to succumb to temptation and fall into this trap. There might be a good bargain on a modern hotel in Azerbaijan, Saudi Arabia, or China by 2020!

28. It Is Time for a Revolutionary Change in Portfolio Management

"Mr. Buffett put it to me recently, 'You couldn't advance in a finance department in this country unless you taught that the world was flat.'"
Joseph Nocera, "The Heresy That Made Them Rich,"
The *New York Times*, October 29, 2005

In the quote above, Warren Buffett is pointing out that much of the teaching about investing is out of touch with reality. The teachings and philosophies do not take into account how markets actually function.

For example, in the past, investment decisions were based on the Efficient Market Hypothesis, the Capital Asset Pricing Model, and the Black-Scholes Model. It took far too long, but the flaws in these concepts finally became so obvious that they had to be addressed. What was once accepted as gospel truth was debunked. I believe the thinking behind the many ways portfolios are managed is also flawed and needs to change. Just because there is consensus among experts who believe something and the masses follow it, does not mean it is right. Just because intellectuals at prestigious universities develop sophisticated models and theories of how they believe markets function, does not mean they are correct either. The comments by Mr. Buffett confirm that it is time individual and professional investors take a fresh look at what they are employing to make decisions. This is what Tony Kettle did when he took a fresh look at an engineering challenge.

The area near Falkirk, Scotland, had a series of eleven locks that had fallen into disrepair after the 1930s. An initiative was undertaken to rejuvenate the locks in the late 1990s, and Tony Kettle's design won over all other entries.

Tony Kettle used his daughter's Lego set to develop a concept that used a wheel instead of eleven locks to accommodate the 79-foot or 24-meter change in elevation. The weight in each caisson (or gondola) can be balanced perfectly by adjusting the volume of water in it. Instead of taking more than an hour to go through eleven locks and using all sorts of energy to pump water back and forth, this wheel takes only five-and-a-half minutes to move 180 degrees. It only requires a 22.5 kilowatt or 30.2 horsepower electric motor to power the wheel. It uses as much energy to move the wheel 180 degrees as it does to boil eight kettles of water! The Falkirk Wheel is the only kind of boatlift like this in the world. See pictures of the Falkirk Wheel in Figures 28.1 and 28.2.

Figure 28.1: Picture used with permission from thefalkirkwheel.co.uk.

Figure 28.2: Picture used with permission from thefalkirkwheel.co.uk.

The writers have analyzed investing with the same approach Mr. Kettle used to design a much simpler, faster, more efficient way to raise or lower vessels so they can travel along the waterway.

An investment strategy should be simple. When it comes to investments, complexity can be dangerous. Legendary stock picker during the 1980s and 1990s, Peter Lynch, warned,

"Never invest in an idea you can't illustrate with a crayon."

When the fourth president of the United States, James Madison, was drafting the Constitution, he did not want to create laws "so voluminous that they cannot be read, or so incoherent that they cannot be understood." In the same way, an investment strategy should be simple and understandable.

In the long run, history shows that equities outperform bonds and bonds outperform cash. (Even so, interest rates were so high in 1981 that U.S. Government bonds actually outperformed U.S. stocks for the thirty-year period from 1982 to 2012—the first time in recent history.) However, the volatility of equities is also higher than that of either bonds or cash. This is why there is broad agreement that an asset mix of 60% to 65% invested in equities and 35% to 40% invested in fixed income investments will provide attractive returns that should keep up with inflation and reduce volatility to a level that most people can handle. Hence, even though equities provide the highest returns in the long run, it is deemed acceptable to sacrifice one-third of the returns of a 100% equity portfolio in order to reduce portfolio volatility and investor stress.

Since experts say that no one can time the markets, the most common investment strategy is to try to maintain equity exposure close to the 65% level, bond exposure in the 25% range, and cash in the 10% range, regardless of what happens to prices and market conditions. Some portfolio strategists suggest that investors should always hold 10% of their portfolio in gold bullion as well. This makes as much sense as placing a driver in a car that is driving down a major cross-country highway on cruise control at 60 miles per hour (or 100 kilometers per hour) that cannot be adjusted for blizzards, downpours, fog, construction, traffic jams, or accidents. It is similar to asking someone to wear the same type of clothing all year round in an area where there are distinct seasons.

Moreover, this breaks the cardinal rule of investing, which is to invest with the trend. When the trend changes, one should seriously consider altering the asset mix of a portfolio. Longer-term moving average crossover indicators provide a simple method that investors can use to make asset mix adjustments in a disciplined manner as market trends evolve. They also remove emotions from the decision making process. The study by strategist Myles Zyblock shows that momentum-based investing should be an integral part of the investment process because it produces good results. Yet, it appears that investors are persuaded to ignore momentum and embrace the buy-and-hold strategy regardless of what happens.

Experts are quick to point out how well the traditional 65/35 mix has worked over the years. However, the last thirty years included a period when bonds produced exceptionally high returns as yields declined from the mid-teens to less than 2%. However, bonds don't always offset losses in equities as they have since 2000. During the severe 1973-1974 bear market, U.S. ten-year government bond yields rose from 6.41% to 7.40%. (Bond prices decline as yields increase and vice versa.) As inflation rates increased in the 1970s, interest rates on U.S. ten-year government bonds soared from a low of 5.38% in March 1971 to a high of 15.84% in September 1981! Those who were investing or managing money during that time will never forget the excruciating losses in government bonds during that ten-year period which seemed to last forever. Conversely, since 1981, North American government bonds have been stellar performers as rates fell from all-time highs to historic lows. While it is possible for stock prices to keep advancing without limit, it is absolutely impossible for bonds to repeat the performance of the last thirty years unless interest rates rise to 15% and start to decline again. At some point, interest rates should rise a few percentage points just to return to the average interest rate of slightly over 5% for U.S. Government 30-year bonds over the last 200 years. When that happens, bonds will drag down the return of a portfolio instead of boosting it. If yields rise above the average long-term average rate of return, the losses will be even greater. It is important to invest with the trend with bonds, too. Those who started to invest after 1981 may not realize this; however, they will likely learn to appreciate how much bond prices can decline at some point in the future. Hopefully they will under-stand and take action on this before it is too late. Few wanted to invest in bonds in 1981 and 1982 because yields were expected to move even higher. It is interesting that bond funds have often been the most popular funds for new purchases in recent years when yields on ten-year bonds are close to 2%. Bonds may have been in a bubble during 2013.

Some say that one should automatically rebalance a portfolio by investing more in equities as they decline and reducing equity exposure as prices rise. This also breaks the cardinal rule of investing. Nevertheless, buying more equities worked well when markets fell in 2008 and 2009, because it was a relatively short bear market that really lasted only six months. However, adding cash to a declining asset like equities was dangerous during the devas-tating 1928-1932 bear market, the long, severe 1973-1974 bear market, the Nikkei "lost decade" after 1989, and the 2000-2003 bear market. Investors who automatically rebalanced by moving more cash to equities every quarter during these long declines would have ended up in a very uncomfortable position for a long time.

John Kenneth Galbraith described what happened to investors who rebalanced or averaged down after the 1929 Crash in his book *The Great Crash 1929*. He writes:

> The singular feature of the great crash of 1929 was that the worst continued to worsen. What looked one day like the end proved on the next day to have been only the beginning. Nothing could have been more ingeniously designed to maximize the suffering, and also insure that as few as possible escaped the common misfortune. The fortunate speculator who had funds to answer the first margin call presently got another and equally urgent one, and if he met that there would still be another. In the end all the money he had was extracted from him and lost. The man with the smart money, who was safely out of the market when the first crash came, naturally went back in to pick up bargains. (Not only were a recorded 12,894,650 shares sold on October 24; precisely the same number were bought.) The bargains then suffered a ruinous fall. Even the man who waited out all of October and all of November, who saw the volume of trading return to normal and saw Wall Street become as placid as a produce market, and who then bought common stocks would see their value drop to a third or fourth of the purchase price in the next twenty-four months. The Coolidge bull market was a remarkable phenomenon. The ruthlessness of its liquidation was, in its own way, equally remarkable.

Just because the share prices of most big U.S. blue chip companies have not lost 90% of their value in the last eighty years does not mean it cannot happen again. Those who are tempted to add capital to an investment only because it has lost value, without waiting for confirmation of a trend change, should heed the paragraphs above as a warning.

Selling equities in 1978, 1979, and 1980 in order to add capital to bonds was not prudent either. It is often safer, more comfortable, and more profitable to wait for trend changes before buying equities or bonds in a long-term downtrend, rather than adding capital to them just because the price is falling. Recall John Maynard Keynes's comment: "Markets can stay irrational longer than you can remain solvent."

Since markets usually have a classic double bottom when a downtrend ends, it is possible to determine bear market lows shortly after they occur. After a decline of 20% or more, money should be added to an asset after a classic double bottom has appeared and moving average crossovers have confirmed that the trend has changed. A rise of 80% or more in oil prices has occurred in the past, before or in the early stages of every long-term bear market since 1973. (Although this rise may not always happen in the future, it is still a reliable indicator.) Since 1968, a bear market in U.S. equities has eventually followed every time there has been an inverted yield curve except for the 1987 crash and the 2011 bear market. Advance/Decline buy signals often occur within ten trading days of significant bear market lows as well. This happened during sharp rallies right after the historic 1974, 1982, and 2008 market bottoms. While a 2-1 Advance/Decline buy signal did not occur after the 1987 crash or the 2003 market bottom, prices slowly recovered so that moving average crossovers were able to provide buy signals very soon after the lows. Prevailing wisdom states that we cannot time the markets, yet almost every portfolio manager mentions that they are raising cash or increasing equity or fixed income exposure from time to time. Many individual investors also trade their accounts actively. Analysis by Ned Davis Research Inc. in 2013 showed that the average holding period for stocks declined from 7.4 years in 1975 to 1.2 years in 1988, and less than 3 months in 2009. In 2013, the average holding period increased to 6 months. However, a number of studies suggest short-term traders generally have very poor results. One of the more recent studies was highlighted by Mark Hulbert of *Barron's* in "The Dark Side of ETFs," April 11, 2013. (ETFs are Exchange Traded Funds. ETFs typically invest in a basket of securities that match a market index or include a diversified mix of securities in a certain sector. There is typically a prescribed formula for how the securities in the ETF are chosen, so there is no portfolio manager involved as there is in a mutual fund. Therefore, the annual fees on ETFs are usually much lower than those for a mutual fund. ETFs trade on the stock exchange like a stock does. There are pros and cons for investing in ETFs instead of mutual funds.)

Mark Hulbert writes, "New research shows that the very features of ETFs that make them so attractive are actually leading many investors to earn lower returns. The problem with ETFs is not that they are inherently flawed; it's just that they tempt investors into money-losing behavior." Mr. Hulbert examined a study conducted by Indiana University finance professor Utpal Bhattacharya and four colleagues from Goethe University in Germany. He commented, "The study, 'The Dark Side of ETFs and Index Funds,' found that 'easy-to-trade index-linked securities' such as ETFs encourage users to 'make bets on market phases, and they bet wrong.'"

Brad Barber, a finance professor at the University of California at Davis, led a study examining fifteen years of transaction history from the stock exchange in Taiwan. (Day trading is very common in Taiwan.) He discovered that 80% of traders lose money in a given year and only 1% followed a strategy that could reasonably be expected to earn a profit in the long term.

If one is going to make asset allocation or investing and trading decisions, he or she must employ a disciplined strategy instead of emotional reactions. William Bernstein, a former neurologist who is now a financial theorist, wrote,

> "Investment success accrues not so much to the brilliant,
> but to the disciplined."

> Legendary UCLA basketball coach John Wooden said,
> "Don't mistake activity for achievement."

Not every move will turn out to be correct, even if one is disciplined. However, one should be able to be right more often than wrong. Investing is not about being exact. In the words of former mutual fund manager Peter Lynch, "In this business, if you are good, you are right six times out of ten."

It is important for every investment discipline to include indicators which are based on momentum. In order to use a discipline like this, investors need to prepare their minds for taking action when it is called for.

In 2012 my Search and Rescue team had an incident where a rescue turned out very well because the subjects were prepared and disciplined (as investors should also be). In October 2012, three men left Vancouver and drove 100 kilometers (62 miles) east to the Chehalis area to fish for salmon. One of the men, chef Josh Wolfe, owned a mobile restaurant in Vancouver, B.C., called Fresh Local Wild. There were torrential rains for hours before they arrived at an area near the bottom of a mountain range. They hiked through the bush and crossed some small gentle streams where the water was below their knees to reach the area they were looking for. They did not realize that the water levels in that area can rise very quickly after heavy rains. When it was time to return near dusk, they went back to the stream and realized the cold water was now over their heads! They assessed the situation and wisely decided to stay put and call 911 from a cell phone. It was dark by the time the Search and Rescue team members arrived and proceeded into the dense bush wearing drysuits. As searchers made their way through the chest-high water, they could feel thirty-pound salmon bumping into them in the dark of evening.

The fishermen said they always prepared for emergencies so they had a fire going, had some food along with them, and were in good condition. Unfortunately, searchers were not able to locate them by late evening. Since the fishermen were healthy, strong, well dressed, and in good condition, the search was called off until first light. The Chilliwack Search and Rescue team was called in to assist the next morning. A helicopter was used to guide a jet boat up one of the many river channels to the campfire so that the fishermen could be evacuated. They were returned to their vehicle early in the morning. It was one of the few rescues in which our team has been involved where the subjects had prepared themselves mentally and physically for an emergency or unexpected event. The rescue went very smoothly, but that does not mean it was effortless.

After the fishermen were rescued they drove to the closest Denny's restaurant and sat down to order breakfast, something they had talked about doing during the night. When the waitress, whom they had never met before, arrived at their table, she asked, "Where have you been?" They responded, "Why do you ask?" She said, "You look like you have just seen a ghost!" Even though they were prepared and everything went smoothly, the experience had still taken an obvious toll on them.

Chef Josh Wolfe was so grateful for the effort of the Search and Rescue volunteers that he brought his mobile restaurant to our Search and Rescue base in Agassiz, B.C., in November and served us all a delicious lunch. (See the pictures in Figures 28.3 and 28.4.)

Figure 28.3: Two Search and Rescue members walking/swimming across a channel, where the water is up to their necks, in Chehalis, B.C. (One member has a red helmet and the other is carrying a blue dry bag on his shoulders near the brush.) The morning before, this was only a small narrow stream that fishermen waded through with water less than a meter deep! Photo by Dan McAuliffe, Chilliwack Search and Rescue

Figure 28.4: Chef Josh Wolfe of Fresh Local Wild talking about the rescue with Kent Harrison Search and Rescue Search Manager Neil Brewer after serving lunch to those who participated in bringing him and his friends to safety. A television crewman is filming the event at the Kent Harrison Search and Rescue base in Agassiz, B.C. Photo by Dave Harder

Whether one is going out into the backwoods or investing, the outcome is always better if one is physically and emotionally prepared for unexpected events, because they do happen! One evening I was visiting a friend and colleague at his home in Hollywood Beach, Florida. As we were walking home in the dark after a dinner out, I did not notice that I was about to step off a six-inch curb. Even though it was only a very small step down, I almost lost my balance, since I was not expecting it. If I had known it was there, I would have easily kept walking without missing a beat. Knowing what to expect definitely makes it easier to react appropriately.

It is important for readers to know that neither Dr. Janice Dorn nor I are perfect traders or investors. Even National Football League quarterbacks throw interceptions. National Hockey League goalies and FIFA World Cup soccer goalies have games where they let in too many goals. Major League Baseball players are heroes if they strike out six out of ten times at bat. We are still striving to learn and become more disciplined. We are merely passing on what we have learned so far along this journey. Some lessons were learned decades ago. Others have been learned very recently. It is important that readers keep this in mind as they peruse this book.

Here are some examples of how investors with different personalities and objectives can use the tools described in the previous chapters. Over the long term, these personalized strategies will enable investors to participate in market gains and minimize losses. They will help readers to use well-diversified investments to create a portfolio tailored to their personal objectives. The simple, specific but sound strategies will help readers to be more comfortable since they will be able to navigate the ever-changing economic and market environment. They will also assist in making wise business decisions, especially the most vexing question faced by most investors and business owners: when to sell.

Personalized Investment Strategies

Investors should consult a professional financial advisor and accountant before using any of the strategies mentioned below. They may want to start off by following the strategies with just a portion of their investment portfolio. It is always prudent to remember that past performance does not guarantee future results.

The first strategy is for investor Scared Stiff Stefan. Peter Lynch said, "Everyone has the power to make money in stocks. Not everyone has the stomach." Scared Stiff Stefan does not "have the stomach" for investing in equities, and that is fine. Everyone is different. Each investor must be comfortable with the way his or her hard-earned savings are invested. Scared Stiff Stefan does not care if he matches the returns of a benchmark like a market index. If he could, he would just invest his money in guaranteed investments. However, he also realizes he cannot meet his needs and goals by investing entirely in interest-bearing instruments when interest rates are close to 0%. He would like to participate in some of the dividends and capital gains equity investments can provide, but the stress of long or steep market declines is simply too much for him to handle. He wants to minimize his losses.

Strategy for Scared Stiff Stefan: When long-term moving average cross-overs (LTMACs) for the S&P 500 and the Canadian S&P/TSX turn positive (the LTMAC for the S&P 500 and S&P/TSX are used in all of these examples), Scared Stiff Stefan can invest 50% of his portfolio in a good quality ETF that matches a broad market index. An investment that includes or tracks stocks in the S&P MidCap 400 Index, or S&P 400 Index, as it is often referred to, is preferable. (More information about why the S&P MidCap 400 Index is preferable is provided in the following pages.)

Another option is to invest in a conservative equity or balanced mutual fund with a manager who has a good track record of consistent attractive returns, especially during downturns. (ETFs that match market averages can have concentration issues at times. That is why a mutual fund can sometimes be a better choice than an ETF. A balanced mutual fund invests in a mix of equities and bonds. A balanced mutual fund should only be considered if bond prices are not in a long-term downtrend.) If oil prices have risen more than 80% in the previous twelve months and/or the U.S. yield curve has inverted, Scared Stiff Stefan should consider moving to 100% cash. History shows that the worst market declines eventually occur within eighteen months or so after one or both of these happen. Scared Stiff Stefan should only invest again if the LTMACs for the S&P 500 and the S&P/TSX turn positive after there has been a double bottom in North American market averages after a decline of 20% or more in the S&P 500. (The S&P 500 has formed a double bottom after every bear market since 1950, except for 2009. In 2009, the NASDAQ, the Russell 2000 Index, the S&P 400 MidCap Index, and the Canadian S&P/TSX did form double bottoms.)

History indicates that there are times for investors to worry about severe declines and times not to worry. One should not think of building an ark every time it rains. When oil price increases have been moderate and long-term interest rates are higher than short-term rates, the odds that a severe bear market will occur is very low. Since 1973, the only time there has been a bear market without an 80% increase in oil prices was in 1998. In the summer of 1998, the S&P 500 Index fell 20% as Russia defaulted on its debt, President Clinton faced possible impeachment, and the Long-Term Capital

Hedge Fund collapsed. However, U.S. markets began to recover in early October 1998 and the S&P 500 still ended the year at all-time highs.

If oil prices have been stable and the U.S. yield curve is normal, probabilities of a decline of more than 13% or so are low. However, investors must always respect the trend. Therefore, if the S&P 500 declines 15% or more from the previous closing high, without an inverted yield curve or an 80% advance in oil prices, Scared Stiff Stefan should sell his equity positions and move to 100% cash. When the LTMACs for the S&P 500 and S&P/TSX turn positive, he can move to 50% equities again. Most corrections are less than 15%. There might be the odd time that equities will fall exactly 15% and then rise again, forcing Scared Stiff Stefan to buy back at a higher price than he sold for. On the other hand, if the S&P 500 declines 20% or more and it takes many months for markets to recover, Scared Stiff Stefan will be relieved that he has a strategy in place to limit his losses. In a scenario like this, he may be able to buy back at a lower price than he sold for.

Winston Churchill said, "However beautiful the strategy, you should occasionally look at the results." Backtesting this list of factors over several decades can help readers to see how an investment strategy might be expected to perform in the future. So, how would this strategy have performed for Scared Stiff Stefan since January 1, 2000? Oil prices rose more than 80% in a twelve-month time frame in July 1999, so he would have been in cash as of that date. Moreover, the U.S. yield curve inverted in July 2000, providing another warning signal that risk had increased. The first time a double bottom occurred after the bear market began in the fall of 2000 was October 2002. The LTMACs turned positive for the S&P 500 and S&P/TSX in November 2002, creating a buy signal for Scared Stiff Stefan. If Stefan had invested in the S&P 400 MidCap Index at the highest close in November and sold at the lowest day in July 2006 when the U.S. yield curve inverted again, he would have gained 57.6% in forty-three months. Three years later, he would have bought the S&P 400 on April 29, 2009, and sold at the lowest close in December 2009 for a gain of 23.4% in eight months. He would have bought again on January 23, 2012. By the end of 2012, he would have gained another 9.7% in twelve months. For the twelve-year period from January

1, 2000 to the end of 2012, Scared Stiff Stefan would have been invested in equities for 63 out of 156 months, or 40.3% of the time. He would have significantly outperformed the major benchmarks by gaining a total of 90.7% without including dividends or portfolio management costs. This is 17.3% per year in simple returns when invested in equities. Just as important for someone with Scared Stiff Stefan's personality, he would also have avoided most of the periods of gut-wrenching volatility over this thirteen-year period when the S&P 500 and the S&P/TSX made little progress. (More information about the S&P MidCap 400 Index is provided in the following pages.)

Going back even further, Scared Stiff Stefan would have owned equities for almost the entire period from February 28, 1991, to July 30, 1999. July 1999 was the first time since 1990 that oil prices rose more than 80% in the previous twelve months. During these 100 months, the S&P 400 rose 248%, or 29.8% per year. Stefan would have been stopped out in August 1998 when the S&P 500 fell more than 20% due to the Clinton impeachment, the Long-Term Capital Hedge Fund collapse, and the Russian Default Crisis. He would have been forced to sell when the S&P 500 fell 15% from the high on a closing basis. He would have bought back in early November 1998. By the end of 1998, the S&P 500 was right back to a new all-time high, so this decline was not that notable. Nevertheless, it is always good to have a "runaway lane." Even if Stefan had to buy back at a slightly higher price, he protected his capital from a more serious loss. The following table (Figure 28.5) shows how the equity portion of Scared Stiff Stefan's portfolio would have performed from December 31, 1980, to December 31, 2012, compared to a buy-and-hold strategy for the S&P 500, the Canadian S&P/TSX, and the U.S. S&P 400 MidCap Index.

Harder Asset Allocation Strategy
Results for
Scared Stiff Stefan

	S&P 500	S&P/TSX	S&P400 Mid Cap
Compound Rates of Return on $100,000 invested on December 31, 1980 and held until December 31, 2012 (not including dividends)	$1,050,523.98	$548,045.13	$2,867,987.63
	7.63%	5.46%	11.06%
Compound Annual Return on $100,000 invested in Harder Asset Allocation System for Scared Stiff from December 31, 1980 and held until December 31, 2012 (not including dividends)	$1,746,204.82	$1,005,968.00	$2,211,395.37
	9.35%	7.48%	10.16%

Scared Stiff Stefan
Returns
December 31, 2000 to December 31, 2012
With $1,000,000*

	S&P 500	S&P/TSX	S&P 400 Mid Cap
Buy and Hold	$1,080,000	$1,392,000	$1,975,000
Compound Annual Returns	0.64%	2.79%	5.84%
Harder Strategy	$1,951,447.61	$2,305,167.60	$2,481,016.68
Compound Annual Returns	5.73%	7.21%	7.87%

*In currency of Index
Not including dividends or interest

The equity portion of Scared Stiff Stefan's portfolio was securely in cash for 80 months out of this 144 month period. See the dates of the buys and sells for the equity portion of Scared Stiff Stefan's equity portfolio that was invested in the Harder Asset Allocation Strategy below.

Harder Asset Allocation Strategy
Results for
Scared Stiff Stefan
December 31, 1980 to December 31, 2012

	S&P 500	S&P/TSX	S&P400 Mid Cap
December 31, 1980 value	135.76	2,268.70	35.58
Buy August 26, 1982 2-1 Advance/Decline Buy Signal	118.55	1,588.67	35.76* (Aug 31, 1982)
Sell January 9, 1987 Oil prices rise more than 80% in past 12 months	258.73	3,208.76	80.42
Gain	**118.25%**	**101.98%**	**124.89%**
Buy March 18, 1988	271.12	3,322.56	80.58
Sell June 30, 1989 Yield curve inverts	317.98	3,761.0	98.15
Gain	**17.28%**	**13.20%**	**21.80%**
Buy February 1, 1991	343.05	3,293.50	108.55
Sell August 27, 1998 15% - stop loss limit S&P500	1,042.60	5,799.46	304.95
Gain	**203.92%**	**76.09%**	**180.93%**
Buy November 27, 1998	1,192.29	6,468.32	359.74
Sell June 30, 1999 Oil prices rise 80% in previous 12 months	1,372.71	7,010.07	416.70
Gain	**15.13%**	**8.38%**	**15.83%**
Buy November 29, 2002	936.31	6,570.42	448.63
Sell August 9, 2006 Yield curve inverts	1,265.95	12,008.2	726.77
Gain	**35.21%**	**82.76%**	**62.00%**
Buy March 23, 2009 2-1 Advance/Decline Buy Signal	822.92	8,958.50	498.60
Sell December 9, 2009 Oil prices rise 80% in 12 months	1,095.95	11,379.2	696.14
Gain	**33.18%**	**27.02%**	**39.62%**

Buy January 23, 2012	1,316.00	12,521.70	930.29
Value December 31, 2012	1,426.19	12,433.50	1,020.43
Change in Value for 2012 (no sell signals issued)	8.37%	-0.70%	9.69%

Figure 28.5: Performance for Scared Stiff Stefan's strategy. These results have been backtested on a hypothetical portfolio.

The next example is for Cautious Cathy. Cautious Cathy feels comfortable with her investments most of the time. However, she does not know if she can handle another market decline of more than 20% that lasts a long time. She can't help watching the news when markets are volatile, and then it just makes her worry too much.

Strategy for Cautious Cathy: When the LTMACs turn positive, Cautious Cathy can invest 65% of her portfolio in ETFs that match the least volatile major market average (such as the DJIA, S&P 500, or S&P 400 in the U.S. or the S&P/TSX in Canada). Cautious Cathy can also purchase a good quality equity or balanced mutual fund. (She should only consider a balanced fund if bond prices are not in a long-term downtrend.) She can hold her positions until oil prices have risen more than 80% during the previous twelve months, and/or the U.S. yield curve has inverted. If either of those two conditions exists, she should reduce her equity positions from 65% to 35%. When the LTMACs for the S&P 500 and S&P/TSX turn negative after oil prices have risen more than 80% in the previous twelve months and/or the U.S. yield curve has inverted, Cautious Cathy should sell the positions she still holds to reduce her equity exposure to 0%. When the major U.S. market averages have declined 20% or more, when there has been a double bottom, and when the LTMACs for the S&P 500 and S&P/TSX turn positive, the strategy can return to normal. Cautious Cathy should be very alert after Labor Day if oil prices have been up more than 80% in the previous twelve months. If the S&P 500 falls more than 15%, Cautious Cathy should reduce her equity exposure to 0% and buy back again once the LTMACs for the S&P 500 and S&P/TSX have turned positive. If the decline was more than 20%, she should wait for the LTMACs for the S&P 500 and the S&P/TSX to turn positive after a double bottom has occurred before buying back.

Normal Norman is the average investor who is comfortable with the normal mix of 65% in equities and 35% in fixed income securities. He may have sold his business for a large sum of money and wants to continue to earn a reasonable return on his holdings. He can invest in ETFs, good quality equity mutual funds, or a diversified portfolio of individual equities. He does not like going through severe market downturns, but neither does anyone else. He has experienced bear markets and recessions while owning his business. He is very familiar with the emotional roller coaster that accompanies them.

Strategy for Normal Norman: Normal Norman can increase his equity weighting to 85% when the LTMACs for the S&P 500 and S&P/TSX turn positive. In a normal market environment it is appropriate to buy on the dips.

However, when the LTMACs turn negative after oil prices have rallied more than 80% in the previous twelve months, Normal Norman should reduce his equity exposure from 85% to 35% until there has been a decline of 20% or more in the S&P 500 or Dow Jones Industrial Average. Normal Norman may even want to reduce his holdings to 0% if this happens after a bull market that has lasted five years or more. After there has been a double bottom and the LTMACs for the S&P 500 and S&P/TSX turn green again, Normal Norman can increase his equity exposure to 85%. Normal Norman should be very alert after Labor Day if oil prices have been up more than 80% in the previous twelve months and/or the U.S. yield curve has inverted. If the S&P 500 falls more than 15%, Normal Norman should reduce his equity exposure to 45% even though oil prices and interest rates may not have changed much. (From 1981 to September 30, 2013, there were only two corrections greater than 15% during a bull market. Declines close to 20% occurred in August 1998 and October 2011. The 20% decline in 1998 was the only decline greater than 15% when the U.S. yield curve had not inverted and oil prices had not increased by 80% or more.)

When the LTMACs for the S&P 500 and S&P/TSX turn positive again, he can increase his equity position to 85% once more. This strategy will enable Normal Norman to benefit from the many years when equity returns are attractive, yet still provide a way to reduce volatility when markets are turbulent. The following table (Figure 28.6) shows how the equity portion of Normal Norman's equity portfolio invested in the asset allocation strategy would have performed for the S&P 500, S&P/TSX, and the S&P 400 MidCap Index compared to a buy-and-hold approach.

Harder Asset Allocation Strategy
Results for
Normal Norman

	S&P 500	S&P/TSX	S&P400 Mid Cap
Compound Rates of Return on $100,000 invested on December 31, 1980 and held until December 31, 2012 (not including dividends)	$1,050,523.98	$548,045.13	$2,867,987.63
	7.63%	5.46%	11.06%
Compound Annual Return on $100,000 invested in Harder Asset Allocation System for Normal Norman from December 31, 1980 and held until December 31, 2012 (not including dividends)	$1,717,272.48	$1,535,015.44	$2,876,280.96
	9.29%	8.91%	11.07%

Normal Norman
Returns
December 31, 2000 to December 31, 2012
With $1,000,000*

	S&P 500	S&P/TSX	S&P400 Mid Cap
Buy and Hold	$1,080,000	$1,392,000	$1,975,000
Compound Annual Returns	0.64%	2.79%	5.84%
Harder Strategy	$1,814,807.75	$2,666,767.77	$2,758,799.97
Compound Annual Returns	5.09%	8.52%	8.82%

*In currency of Index
Not including dividends or interest

The strategy portion of Normal Norman's portfolio was securely in cash for 50 months out of this 144 month period. See the buys and sells for the equity portion of Normal Norman's portfolio that was invested in the Harder Asset Allocation Strategy below.

Harder Asset Allocation Strategy
Results for
Normal Norman
December 31, 1980 to December 31, 2012

	S&P 500	S&P/TSX	S&P400 Mid Cap
December 31, 1980 value	135.76	2,268.70	35.58
Buy August 26, 1982 2-1 Advance/Decline Buy Signal	118.55	1,588.67	35.76* (Aug 31, 1982)
Sell October 16, 1987 S&P 500 down 15% - stop loss	282.70	3,598.60	82.95
Gain	**138.46%**	**126.52%**	**131.96%**
Buy March 18, 1988	271.12	3,322.56	80.58
Sell August 16, 1990 Oil up 80% in 12 months LTMAC turn negative	332.39	3,510.00	100.00
Gain	**22.60%**	**5.64%**	**24.10%**
Buy February 1, 1991	343.05	3,293.50	108.55
Sell August 31, 1998 S&P500 down 15% - stop loss	957.28	5,530.71	281.10
Gain	**179.05%**	**67.93%**	**158.96%**
Buy November 27, 1998	1,192.29	6,468.32	359.74
Sell November 14, 2000 Oil prices rise 80% in 12 months LTMAC turn negative	1,382.95	9,265.30	503.14
Gain	**15.99%**	**43.24%**	**39.86%**
Buy November 29, 2002	936.31	6,570.42	448.63
Sell July 14, 2008 Oil prices rise 80% LTMAC turn negative	1,228.3	13,741.3	779.96
Gain	**31.19%**	**109.14%**	**73.85%**
Buy March 23, 2009 2-1 Advance/Decline Buy	822.92	8,959.50	498.60

Signal			
Sell June 7, 2010 Oil prices rise 80% LTMAC turn negative	1,050.47	11,504.70	721.31
Gain	**27.65%**	**28.41%**	**44.67%**
Buy January 23, 2012	1,316.00	12,521.70	930.29
Value December 31, 2012	1,426.19	12,433.50	1,020.43
Change in Value for 2012 (no sell signals issued)	**8.37%**	**-0.7%**	**9.69%**

Figure 28.6: Performance for Normal Norman's strategy. These results have been backtested on a hypothetical portfolio.

Another investor, Up-and-Coming Carli, can use the same strategy as Normal Norman. Up-and-Coming Carli represents young women and men in their twenties and early thirties who have been focused on studying, starting a business, becoming a professional athlete, professional musician, making it to the big screen or developing another skill. All that dedication and hard work has finally paid off, and now Up-and-Coming Carli is in a position that offers substantial financial benefits. In some cases, Up-and-Coming Carli may not know how long these very high earnings will continue. Carli has been so busy focusing on her goal that she knows next to nothing about investing or how markets function. I can relate.

When I graduated from university in 1978, I celebrated by driving to California with a friend for a two-week vacation. I recall sitting by the pool at the Gene Autry Hotel in Palm Springs observing a distinguished gentleman reading the *Wall Street Journal*. I remember thinking to myself, one day I would like to understand what all the numbers on those business pages mean.

This book was written for people like Up-and-Coming Carli. She will likely have to rely entirely on other people to guide her and invest her savings. If the person who invests her savings can follow the strategy of Normal Norman, she should earn a very acceptable return and still protect much of her capital from loss. Once Carli has experienced her first bear market, she will be in a better position to decide how conservative or aggressive she wants to be. Then she can adjust her asset mix and strategy accordingly.

The next example is Aggressive Agnes. It bothers Aggressive Agnes more when she misses out on gains than when she experiences losses. She is often tempted to "swing for the fence." Agnes is busy, successful, and has a high income. She has a large concentration in the shares of the company she works for. Aggressive Agnes is still working on making her fortune so she is interested in buying investments that have greater potential for gain, such as investments that concentrate in Japan, the beaten-down solar sector, and 3D printing companies. However, in the past she has sometimes been too busy, overconfident, and aggressive at the wrong time.

Strategy for Aggressive Agnes: Agnes can move to 100% invested when the LTMACs turn positive. Investing in ETFs or equity mutual funds that concentrate on small to mid-sized companies can be appropriate for her if relative strength information supports that. I am not recommending that she use leverage to invest. However, if she is going to borrow funds to invest, or buy leveraged ETFs, the time to do that is when the LTMACs have turned positive after a correction or bear market. If she uses leverage, she should reduce or eliminate leverage if the yield curve inverts and/or oil prices rise 80% or more in the previous twelve months. Any leverage must be totally eliminated when the LTMACs for the S&P 500 and S&P/TSX turn negative if either of these two conditions has been met. If oil prices have risen by 80% or more in the previous twelve months, Aggressive Agnes should also consider moving from 100% equities to 50% when the LTMACs for the S&P 500 and S&P/TSX turn negative, in order to protect the gains she has made. This should give her the opportunity to reinvest her cash at lower prices or at least preserve much of the profit she has earned.

Aggressive Agnes should move from small-cap or mid-cap investments to big, blue chip companies if relative strength data supports this. (In most cases, blue chip companies will fall less than small-cap companies when markets are experiencing a severe decline.) When the LTMACs turn negative after oil prices have risen by 80% or more in a twelve-month period, Agnes should consider taking measures to protect the value of the concentrated equity position she has in the company she works for. When markets have declined more than 20%, when there has been a double bottom, and when the LTMACs for the S&P 500 and S&P/TSX turn positive, the strategy can return to normal. She can then remove any hedges or protection against her concentrated position. Aggressive Agnes has to slow down to take five minutes a week to evaluate her portfolio after oil prices have leaped higher, especially after Labor Day. Agnes should be on a higher stage of alert when equity markets have been in an uptrend for five years or more. That is when longer, severe bear markets often occur. It may feel like the best time to increase leverage, but it may not be.

If the U.S. yield curve is normal and oil price volatility is normal, Aggressive Agnes can remain fully invested because the LTMACs may cause her to buy back at a higher price than she sells for when there are only minor 10% corrections. Corrections of 10% typically happen once a year. However, if the S&P 500 drops 15% or more, Aggressive Agnes should eliminate leverage and reduce equity exposure to 50% until the LTMACs turn positive.

Sometimes people find themselves in a position like Charla the Chairperson. Charla is a busy, gifted woman who wants to give back to her community. As the chairperson of an investment committee for an institution, she has a fiduciary responsibility to ensure that the assets entrusted to the organization are managed in a responsible way. As long as Charla and her committee members follow what most other organizations and professionals deem is acceptable, it would be hard to find fault with them. Consequently, there is reluctance to explore other investment processes that may involve more asset allocation.

This means that Charla and her committee members have to resign themselves to the fact that the value of the portfolio they oversee could fall significantly during the next bear market or crisis. If Charla and her colleagues believe there has to a better way of protecting capital, they can add a stop-loss limit of 15% to at least a portion of the equity portfolio. Equity positions should be reduced when long-term moving average crossovers for the S&P 500 and the S&P/TSX turn negative after oil prices increase more than 80% in a twelve-month period. When the long-term moving average crossover for the S&P 500 and the S&P/TSX turns positive after there has been a double bottom in U.S. market averages, equity positions can be increased to the maximum.

The maximum portion of the portfolio invested in equities could be greater than the standard 60% to 65% when the U.S. yield curve is not inverted and oil prices have not risen by 80% or more. Charla should also ensure that at least 30% of the equity portfolio is invested in U.S. mid-sized companies. By doing this, Charla can have confidence that the portfolio has measures in place to preserve capital for the next time markets unravel or collapse as they did from 1929 to 1932.

Then there is Benchmark Ben. Benchmark Ben is a professional portfolio manager for: a major pension fund, insurance company, endowment fund, investment firm, or hedge fund. His mandate is to outperform the market benchmarks stated in the Investment Policy Statements (IPS) of the accounts he manages. If equity markets fall 15% and the portfolio he manages declines only 12%, he is doing well.

Strategy for Benchmark Ben: It is unlikely that LTMACs will help Benchmark Ben to outperform the markets when there are only quick 4%, 7%, or 10% declines. He should use relative strength information to determine when he should invest in midsized companies that track the S&P MidCap 400 Index, or smaller companies which track the Russell 2000 Index, or smaller companies on the S&P/TSX Index. Using relative strength data to overweight the strongest global markets and underweight the weakest can help him. He can do the same with market sectors. Watching the LTMACs to see which equity markets or sectors turn positive first can help Benchmark Ben to determine which areas of investing might have the best upside potential and capture less of the downside in the market trend which follows.

If the U.S. yield curve has been inverted recently, Benchmark Ben needs to accept the fact that the risk has increased. When oil prices have increased more than 80% in a twelve-month time frame and the LTMACs turn negative, Benchmark Ben should reduce equity exposure by 20% or more. Doing so in small increments as the markets move lower might be easier than making a large reduction at one time. In a long bear market such as 2000-2003, equity positions can be increased and reduced when the LTMACs turn positive or negative. However, until there has been a double bottom, he must remember that the long-term downtrend is likely to continue. One must have the patience to wait for a double bottom to happen before positioning the portfolio as if the coast is clear. Trying to be a hero by adding positions during a bear market before the LTMACs turn positive, just because valuations are cheap, can be a dangerous, career-ending game. That is not the time to buy the dips. Averaging down can cause underperformance. It can also turn a bad situation into a disaster! Benchmark Ben should inform his clients of the strategy he has in place, which can act as a circuit breaker before periods of higher volatility. Benchmark Ben should also consider reducing equity exposure if the S&P 500 declines 15% from the most recent closing high.

If there is a 2-1 Advance/Decline buy signal, Benchmark Ben should make sure he is 100% invested so that he does not miss out on the high returns that often follow a development like this. Scared Stiff Stefan, Cautious Cathy, Normal Norman, Up-and-Coming Carli, Aggressive Agnes and Charla, the Chairperson, should also move to their maximum equity exposure if there is a 2-1 Advance/Decline buy signal. After a 2-1 Advance/Decline buy signal, investors and traders should watch the LTMAC for the S&P 500 and the S&P/TSX to confirm that an uptrend has started.

All of the investors mentioned above can invest in medium- to longer-term government bonds instead of cash when equity positions are reduced to increase returns. However, this should only be done as long as the long-term moving average crossovers are positive for fixed income investments.

The examples above have been provided for equity investors. There are also other assets to consider. Bonny the Bond Trader can use the long-term moving average crossovers to reduce or increase the duration of her portfolio or to change the overall exposure to bonds. Bonny should expect that interest rates will fall at some point after the U.S. yield curve has inverted and a recession has started.

Curtis, the Currency and Commodity Trader, can use long-term and shorter-term moving average crossovers to add confirmation that his trades are in line with the trends. Understanding the impact of the 16-year cycle on the very long-term trends of commodity prices should help Curtis to realize why resource-based commodities are acting the way they are.

Tracy the Trader is making short-term trading decisions all the time. Tracy can use very short-term, short-term, and long-term moving average cross-overs as a guide to make sure her positions are in line with the trend. She should realize that an inverted yield curve and an 80% increase in oil prices have the potential to cause major havoc in markets at some point. Tracy must be aware that risk and volatility are likely to increase significantly when the LTMACs turn negative.

Gloria the Gold Bug believes the money printing experiment in Europe, Japan, and the United States is going to end very badly. She has much of her investable assets invested in gold bullion, which pays no dividends or interest. Gloria can use the long-term moving average crossovers for gold bullion to increase or reduce her holdings in gold if she wants to. However, there have been extended periods of approximately 16 to 18 years where gold bullion has outperformed and then underperformed financial assets. Therefore, Gloria the Gold Bug must consider reducing her position in gold bullion in a material way when the very long-term moving average crossover turns negative for gold bullion as it did in April 2013. If faith in paper currencies wanes, and gold prices rise again, the very long-term moving average crossover will turn positive and Gloria can buy gold bullion again. It is simply not prudent money management for Gloria to hold a large position in gold bullion when it has the potential to lose value for more than a decade at a time. Continuing to hold more than 10% of one's portfolio in gold when the very long-term moving average crossovers have turned negative is like refusing to put on a jacket before going outside during a freezing cold day because you don't want summer to end.

Last but not least, Buck the Business Owner started his own company, worked very hard, and has taken risks to build it up over the years. When his business is doing really well and there is a need to expand, Buck should be careful if the U.S. yield curve is inverted and/or oil prices have risen more than 80% in the past twelve months. If those conditions exist, Buck the Business Owner might be better off saving his earnings and waiting for a recession to end, instead of extending himself too much just before the profits from his company might decline. If he has enough cash on hand and his business is on a strong footing, Buck might be able to buy out another business or a competitor that was not as prudent as he was.

If Buck the Business Owner decides to sell his business for shares of another company, he should take measures to protect the value of the shares if the U.S. yield curve is inverted and/or oil prices have risen more than 80% in the previous twelve months, and the LTMACs for the S&P 500 and S&P/TSX have turned negative. Buck should use the LTMACs for a concentrated position and take action if the relative strength of the position deteriorates and the LTMACs turn negative. These are examples of how the indicators in this book can be used to make wise decisions.

The strategies above include the U.S. S&P 400 MidCap Index because mid-sized companies offer exceptional growth without a significant increase in volatility. Mid-sized companies, which have a market capitalization between $750 million and $3 billion in the Unites States, are still large businesses by global standards. Some examples of mid-sized companies are: Alaska Air Group Inc., Barnes and Noble Inc., The Cheesecake Factory Inc., Crane Co., Dick's Sporting Goods Inc., Office Depot Inc., Raymond James Financial Inc., Saks Inc., Tupperware Corp., Under Armour Inc., United Rentals Inc., and Wendy's Co.

Mid-sized companies often have more growth potential than big blue chip firms. Compared to very large companies, mid-sized corporations have less potential to produce pride and overconfidence, which can sow the seeds of their own demise. Many analysts think it is more profitable to focus their efforts on the more popular companies in the S&P 500, so mid-sized companies are sometimes overlooked. In the longer term, mid-sized companies have produced much higher returns than DJIA or S&P 500 companies with similar volatility. Consequently, out of all the major North American market averages, U.S. mid-sized companies tend to provide the best balance between returns and risk. In fact, the losses of mid-sized companies during the 2000-2003 bear market were significantly lower than for most other market averages.

Investing in mid-sized companies using the strategies described earlier can make it easier to outperform the S&P 500, which is used as a benchmark for many portfolios. (See information in Figure 28.7 comparing the simple returns of the S&P 500, the S&P MidCap 400, and the Canadian S&P/TSX during the long-term growth cycle from December 31, 1980, to December 31, 2000, and the long-term consolidation phase from December 31, 2000, to December 31, 2012.)

Various Market Returns from 1980 to 2012 (Not Including Dividends)

Index	Dec. 31, 1980 – Dec. 31, 2000 In Currency of Index	Dec. 31, 2000 – Dec. 31, 2012 In Canadian Dollars	Dec. 31, 2000 – Dec. 31, 2012 In US Dollars
S&P 500	872.5%	–43.1%	8.0%
S&P Mid Cap 400	1,352.4%	46.4%	97.5%
Russell 2000	546.43%	24.5%	75.6%
S&P/TSX	293.78%	39.2%	90.3%

Figure 28.7: The returns above do not include dividends. Returns for the S&P 500 and S&P MidCap 400 Index are in U.S. dollars. Foreign investors should be aware that the U.S. dollar was weak after 2000. For example, the Canadian dollar rose close to 50% from the 2002 lows. Therefore, the returns for Canadians who invested in the S&P 500 or the S&P MidCap 400 at the end of 2000 would have been reduced by as much as 50%. Since the Canadian dollar was close to par with the U.S. dollar in 2013, currency losses like this for Canadian investors should be much less likely in future years.

The returns for the strategies above assumed funds were invested in short-term guaranteed investments or cash when equity positions were at 0%. If one invested in U.S. government bonds instead of cash, using the iShares Barclays 20+ Year Treasury Bond ETF (AMEX symbol TLT), if the LTMAC was positive, the returns for each strategy would have been increased. The strategies described earlier provide much better returns compared to earning interest, or investing in equities with a buy-and-hold approach. The results also outperformed the common benchmarks of the S&P 500 in the U.S. and the S&P/TSX in Canada. However, no matter how attractive returns have been in the past, we must always remember that past performance cannot guarantee future results.

It is very easy to look back and think, "I can do that." However, it is not that simple to follow indicators that may at the time seem to make no sense. It will not seem urgent to sell when the outlook seems so promising. It usually seems utterly foolish to buy when the indicators turn positive during a severe economic recession and bear market. People prefer to have an explanation for what they should be doing. Often an explanation arrives only after it is too late. It is much easier for an aircraft pilot to fly when he can see visual references on the ground. It takes training and discipline to fly only by instruments. Often the instruments on an aircraft will provide information that seems totally opposite to what the pilot is feeling and thinking. If a pilot chooses to react to his or her feelings instead of the instruments, he or she is usually doomed in less than a minute. For many people, the challenges are very similar when using indicators to make investment or business decisions. That's the difficult aspect of using any market indicators.

The upside to using these indicators is that it takes very little time to understand, watch, and follow them. One does not have to read any market reports or listen to a whole host of market opinions in the hope of trying to make the right choice. Only a few minutes a week, or in most cases only five minutes a month, is required to update the checklist of long-term moving average crossovers, the change in oil prices, and the status of the U.S. yield curve. In fact, the less time one spends listening to all sorts of other opinions, the easier it is to stick to the discipline. For those who want to focus on their profession, sport, art, craft, business, charity, young children, elderly parents, etc., and still give their investments all the attention they deserve, this is the ideal way to manage investments. In fact, someone working at the research center in Antarctica might be the best at putting this strategy into action since he or she will not have the same exposure to the sentiment and opinions of people around them.

See charts of the LTMAC for the S&P 500, S&P/TSX, and TLT illustrated again in Figures 28.8 to 28.10.

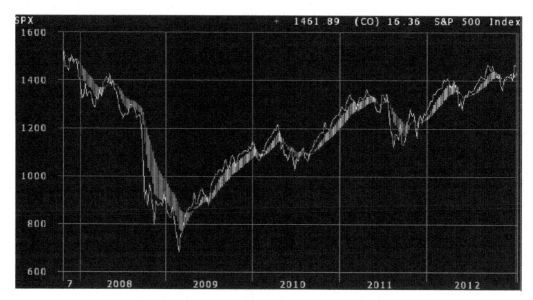

Figure 28.8: Long-term moving average crossover for S&P 500 Index 2007-2012. Data for charts compiled by Thomson Reuters

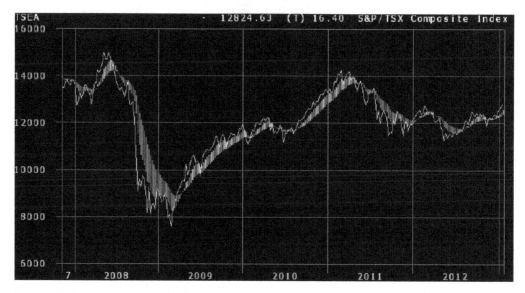

Figure 28.9: Long-term moving average crossover chart of S&P/TSX Index 2007-2012. Data for chart compiled by Thomson Reuters

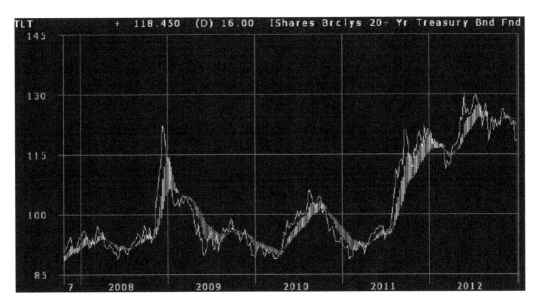

Figure 28.10: Long-term moving average crossover for iShares Barclays 20+ Year Treasury Bond Fund 2007-2012. Data for chart compiled by Thomson Reuters

Many investors and clients would be much more comfortable if they had confidence that at least some adjustments would be made to reduce and increase equity exposure as market conditions change. When investors see that adjustments have been made to their portfolios in a disciplined manner, they have more confidence in their portfolio managers, too. If a money manager is always positive, and there is a severe decline, clients cannot gain any comfort from an optimistic outlook. If a portfolio manager can at least change his or her outlook and warn investors to expect some volatility at certain times, it makes clients more comfortable. It also helps clients to maintain confidence and trust in those who are managing their money. Taking the additional step to make portfolio adjustments may well relieve stress and anxiety for both investors and advisors. Taking steps to reduce equity exposure when markets are down 15% from the peak can be better than selling out the entire portfolio when fear takes hold 30% below the high. Corrie ten Boom said, "Worry does not empty tomorrow of its sorrow; it empties today of its strength." Following the investment guidelines in this chapter can help to reduce worry and negative effects that go along with it. As highlighted earlier, highways in the mountainous areas of British Columbia have runaway lanes for heavy trucks and trailers to stop themselves if their brakes fail on a long downhill. Investors also need this kind of safety valve. Individual and institutional investors already endured a stomach-churning crisis in 2008. No one knows if the European nations with high debt levels will be able to survive without massive defaults. No one is certain that the massive money printing experiment in Japan will be successful either. Can the global financial system handle current levels of sovereign indebtedness? No one, not even central bankers, can predict what will happen in the future.

John (Jack) Bogle is the founder of the Vanguard Group (Vanguard is the largest mutual fund group in the world) and the President of Vanguard's Bogle Financial Markets Research Center. Mr. Bogle has been working in the investment industry since 1951, so he has more market experience than most. In an April 1, 2013, interview, CNBC anchor Scott Wapner asked Jack Bogle, "You say, 'prepare for at least two declines of 25-30 percent, maybe even 50%, in the coming decade.' For the buy-and-hold guy, that's a little concerning, don't you think?"

Declines of 25%, 30%, or 50% are concerning to everyone, especially after the Financial Crisis and the poor returns since 2000. Consequently, individual investors, institutional investors, and those responsible for pension funds want to know that the portfolio managers in whom they have based their trust have the option of a "runaway lane" for their portfolio when the next bear market occurs, because it will happen. If there is another financial crisis, investors may react in a different fashion than they did in 2009. We must use portfolio management methods that follow the cardinal rule of investing, not concepts that ignore it.

During the 1990s I twice competed in the Cheakamus Challenge Mountain Bike Race in Whistler, B.C. It is ranked as the most challenging point-to-point mountain bike race in North America with a 6,000-foot (1,800-meter) vertical climb. A rider has to get off his or her bike more than 100 times to cross logs and boulders along the route. To prepare for this race I purchased a Specialized Stumpjumper mountain bike a year earlier. It has a good quality frame and sturdy components. I trained hard by climbing steep hills for hours at a time to get into good shape. I am not a natural athlete so

I have to work hard just to get to the point where I can complete a race like that in the average time. Two weeks before the race, I took my bike to a local bike shop to make sure everything was in good working order. A new chain was installed and some rear sprockets were replaced since the teeth were curled forward from the stress of doing so much hill climbing. After all the adjustments were made, I did a few more training rides to make sure everything still worked well before the event. I had worked hard for some time to train for this event so I did not want to see that effort sabotaged by a simple mechanical problem.

When I arrived at the starting line of my first race at 6:30 a.m., the rain had just stopped after pouring all night long. As the race began, the trails turned into mud very quickly. After an hour or two of riding the muddy trails, some were having problems shifting gears. I distinctly recall one young man walking up and down a trail asking, "Has anybody seen a chain?" That poor man! There was no way someone could find a chain in all that mud. His race probably ended right there. Fortunately, my Stumpjumper worked very well even though it jumped stumps in name only with me riding it. When I crossed the finish line in the Whistler Village four-and-a-half hours later, I was covered in mud except for my sunglasses. I had to yell to my family as I crossed the finish line so they would realize it was me. All of my preparation and training had paid off.

Investors, traders, and business owners are dealing with challenging markets all the time. People have worked very hard to earn and save funds to invest. These individuals and institutions need to rely on an investment discipline that is built on a strong foundation in order to achieve the desired results. The strategies provided above offer promising opportunities.

Self-preservation and career advancement preclude many who are employed in the investment community from thinking outside the box or taking bold action. It is nice to be right when everyone is wrong, but that involves taking a big risk. It is much safer for analysts and portfolio managers to be wrong when everyone else is wrong than to take the risk of being wrong alone. Like economics, the existing philosophy of portfolio investment must be re-thought. It's difficult to replace old, accepted ways of behavior with concepts that fly in the face of the beliefs behind current methods of making asset allocation decisions. Carl Jung said that "change is perceived by the ego as death." We maintain that change is not only good, but necessary. We also propose that such change will do the following: mitigate anxiety or stress, both for the investor and the portfolio manager, and produce better returns over the long term when there are long severe bear markets.

History teaches us valuable lessons. When I look back over the last forty years, the most devastating bear markets for equities (1973-1974, 1981-1982, 1987, 2000-2003, 2008-2009) have had several things in common. First, they all started in earnest after the DJIA had been up almost every calendar year for four or five consecutive years by Labor Day of a given year (1982-1987, 1995-2000, 2003-2007). Second, they all started within eighteen months after oil prices had increased more than 80% in a twelve-month period (Leeb's Law for oil). An inverted yield curve also preceded most bear markets.

Prominent Scottish hedge fund manager Hugh Hendry recently stated, "It is my assertion that what makes a great fund manager first and foremost is the ability to establish a contentious premise outside of the existing belief system and have it go on to become adopted by the broader financial community." His statement can also apply to individual investors. The strategies described in this chapter typically reduce equity exposure when an uptrend has existed for 48 months or longer, when the consensus opinion has produced too much confidence that prices are going to rise even more. Conversely, it enables investors to buy early in a new uptrend when the prevailing thought still remains focused on deteriorating market conditions. There are a myriad of factors impacting global markets every day. However, there are some that are much more important and reliable than others. It is as Winston Churchill said: "Out of intense complexities intense simplicities emerge." Dr. Dorn and I have examined many of the complexities of investing in order to provide readers with "intense simplicities."

It sounds as if it should be very easy to follow this strategy. However, that could not be farther from the truth. Decades of experience have taught us that it is very difficult to sell when prices are down from their high and conditions do not seem that negative. If investors cannot bring themselves to follow this approach, they should follow it with at least a small portion of their portfolio at the next opportunity. This will allow them to build confidence in this discipline.

I enjoy cliff jumping. I did not start by jumping off a ten-meter or thirty-foot cliff. I started by jumping off three-meter, five-meter, and then ten-meter diving boards when I was twelve years old. Feeling pain when I hit the water taught me to keep my legs together, point my toes downward and keep my arms either up or down, but not in a horizontal position. The photograph in Figure 28.11 was taken when I jumped off a cliff at Shipwreck Beach in Kauai, Hawaii. This is the same cliff from which Anne Heche and Harrison Ford jumped in the early minutes of the 1998 movie *Six Days, Seven Nights*.

One has to prepare a little before jumping. Preparations are not made standing at a precarious spot on the cliff. I want to jump off the cliff in control, not fall off out of control! I think of the things I want to do when I hit the water and I get myself emotionally prepared to step off into thin air where there is no turning back. This way, when I walk to the edge to jump, I will not linger and put myself in danger of slipping accidentally.

It helps for investors to prepare in advance of using the indicators described in the previous chapters. It is always challenging to make a serious investment decision and follow a discipline that is new. I have found that it is important to prepare for the action that may be necessary. One should realize there will be all sorts of doubts and reasons to delay making a change to one's investment portfolio. Emotions and comments in the media can be a significant distraction. Nevertheless, preparing to make a transaction when it seems like a change in trend may be about to occur can make it easier to have the discipline to actually carry it out if it is necessary.

Figure 28.11: Photo of Dave Harder cliff-jumping at Shipwreck Beach in Poipu, Kauai. Photo by my son-in-law, Luke DeJong, who also took the leap.

All the buy and sell signals for the portfolio management strategies are based on the action of the S&P 500 Index and the Canadian S&P/TSX Index. Since the value of U.S. equity markets comprise close to half of the value for all the equity markets in the world, most markets in the world follow the trend of the S&P 500 and DJIA very closely. For the most part, global markets have been moving together for at least a century—this synchronization is not a new phenomenon caused by globalization. While the magnitude of the moves might well vary from one market to the next, it is very unusual for one or more major equity markets in the world to rise while others fall. When it does happen, it is unlikely to last very long. (Japan has been the exception for decades.) Anyone who thinks that diversifying among global markets will reduce volatility, because some will fall while others rise, is almost certain to be disappointed.

We have all learned a lot as a result of the Financial Crisis. The saying "We get too soon old and too late smart" comes to mind. Nevertheless, getting smart is better late than never. There are simple, sound indicators and tools that investors and portfolio managers can use to adjust the mix of a portfolio to reduce risk and anxiety without sacrificing returns. We hope and trust that individual and professional investors will scrutinize portfolio management concepts to ensure that they are in line with how markets really operate. The investment community needs people with discipline, wisdom, and a sound simple strategy, more than it needs individuals with more complicated systems that try to predict the future.

29. What Really Matters

"We tend to forget that happiness doesn't come as a result of getting something we don't have, but rather of recognizing and appreciating what we do have."
Frederick Koenig

There is a great story about little Johnny who told his teacher, "When I grow up I want to live in a big mansion with no bathtubs." The teacher asked, "Johnny, why don't you want any bathtubs in your house?" Johnny replied, "I want to be filthy rich."

We all know that money cannot buy happiness. Robert Charles Forbes started *Forbes* magazine, known for features such as "The World's Billionaires" and "The 400 Richest Americans." Having met many rich and famous people around the world, he concluded, "Those who have earned the greatest wealth have not always earned the greatest happiness." On November 28, 1940, at the age of 63, trading legend Jesse Livermore walked into the cloakroom of the Sherry Netherland Hotel in New York, sat down calmly, and shot himself in the head with a .32 Colt automatic. The suicide note to his wife said he was "a failure" and "tired of fighting." He left $5 million in irrevocable trusts.

An anonymous writer said, "Life does not have to be easy to be wonderful." Surveys show that the citizens of the tiny country of Bhutan are amongst the happiest people in the world even though their average annual income is very low. The goal of this book was to pass on what we have learned from our experiences over decades of being involved in the markets every day. Most of the lessons we learned resulted from painful consequences. We hope to spare you some of that anguish if you have the discipline to follow the advice in this book so you can make prudent and wise decisions, instead of learning on your own, the hard way.

There is always a "tuition" to be paid in order to become a successful investor or trader. Think of this book as a discount on that tuition.

Another goal of this book is to provide investors, money managers, business executives, and government leaders with tools that are reliable and easy to understand. They are also very efficient tools that take much less time to use than reading volumes of research material.

We can use up tremendous amounts of time reading and studying current information in order to determine the proper investment strategy. Even after all of this, we can still end up being dead wrong. On the other hand, it only takes a few minutes a week to observe if there are any changes in moving average crossover indicators. It takes just a few minutes a month to check changes in the U.S. yield curve or crude oil prices. Taking a few moments to monitor these variables on a regular basis will set you on the right track and give you the confidence to make changes when they need to be made. Using these tools will give investors time to do other things that are more important, such as building relationships with family, friends, and coworkers, helping others, maintaining a healthy lifestyle, excelling in a career, etc.

We believe that money is important, but has much less value if one has a physical or mental illness. It is a very sobering and thought-provoking experience to be on a search and rescue call where I have to bring the lifeless body of a young man out from the bush to the logging road where his father is waiting. Accidents happen when you least expect them. The late Walter Peyton, likely the most prolific running back in NFL history, is quoted as saying, "Remember, tomorrow is promised to no one."

It is important that investors and professionals in the finance industry try to maintain a healthy balance in their lives. Our priorities tend to shift as we age. No one wants to look back later in life and realize, as Mr. Livermore did, that he or she has failed.

Canadian-American chemist and author Dr. O. A. Battista wrote, "You have reached the pinnacle of success as soon as you become uninterested in money, compliments, or publicity." Steve Jobs said, "Remembering that I'll be dead soon is the most important tool I've ever encountered to help me make the big choices in life."

When Dave was four years old, his mother had a brain aneurysm that ruptured (subarachnoid hemorrhage) and she was not expected to survive. After being in severe pain but conscious for five days, she underwent surgery. Medical technology was not very advanced in the 1950s, so the chances of her surviving without brain damage were very remote. Many prayers were answered when she made a complete recovery, as only one in a hundred did at the time. Today she lives a full and vibrant life, thoroughly enjoying her children, grandchildren and great-grandchildren. She and Dave's father were a major help in editing this book.

Nevertheless, his mother's illness had an impact on Dave. "I have always had mild headaches on a regular basis. With my mother's history; I have lived with the thought that my life could end at any moment ever since I can remember. This has helped me to foster a healthy balance in life. I can look back at my life and say that I really would not have done things much differently."

Dr. Janice Dorn's mother and father both died of cancer when she was a teenager. Amid the trauma of early parental loss, Janice had to make some very difficult decisions about her future. She came to the conclusion that life is not about what happens—it is about what we do with what happens. As a result, she devoted herself to education, earning two doctorate degrees and multiple board certifications. To this day she remains acutely aware of the fragility of life and sets her priorities according to what really matters most to her: living with purpose, listening intently, practicing wellness, laughing with abandon, appreciating friends and family, showing and telling those she loves that she loves them, and living each moment as if it truly is all that exists.

Figure 29.1: Photo of Peter and Katherine Harder celebrating their sixtieth wedding anniversary in 2013. Photo by Dave Harder

Figure 29.2: Photo of Dr. Janice Dorn hiking in the mountains of New Mexico. Photo credit: Janice Dorn

People can become so busy that they do not take the time to assess where they are really going in life. In his book *This Book Is Not for Sale,* humorist Jarod Kintz writes, "If I told you I worked hard to get where I'm at, I'd be lying, because I have no idea where I am at right now." Albert Einstein said, "Any man who can drive safely while kissing a pretty girl is simply not giving the kiss the attention it deserves." It is very easy for us to get so involved in things that we miss taking in the most important experiences in life, experiences that really are special and provide true fulfillment.

Often it takes a crisis for people to discover what ultimately brings happiness. On January 3, 2012, the Toronto *Globe and Mail* included a story about a very competitive, prominent Ontario lawyer named Harvey Strosberg who suffered a stroke, which left him without the ability to speak. He could not write anything other than his name. Mr. Strosberg was a senior partner at Sutts, Strosberg LLP and in the 1990s was the head of the Law Society of Upper Canada. He was known as a "tenacious bulldog of a lawyer." By working very hard to regain his ability to speak and write, he "rediscovered the pleasure of speaking to his five grandchildren, all of whom are under the age of six." The article goes on to quote Strosberg: "'They were perfectly content to speak slowly to me because they spoke slowly themselves,' he said, adding with a laugh, '…they were the only people who were patient with me.'"

After a year of therapy and very hard work, Strosberg made a remarkable recovery and was ready to enter the courtroom again. However, the article points out, "He has lost 40 pounds, meditates and naps every day, does yoga, and says that he has changed his outlook on life. 'I was so grateful for being alive. I forgave anyone that was being mean to me, or did bad things to me,' Mr. Strosberg said. '…And I asked forgiveness for everyone that I did badly to. Then I was free. …I'm the happiest man in the world.'" I wonder how many of us, especially those who are involved in the investment profession, have set our priorities to the point that we can say we are the happiest man or woman in the world?

It is our natural inclination to pursue goals that will benefit us. It would seem to make sense that the more wealth, goods, or power we possess, the better our life will be. When we are taught that we are alive now because of the principle of the survival of the fittest, it should not be a surprise that some will take that to an extreme. Movies such as *Wall Street* and *The Wolf of Wall Street*, together with the U.S. television program *American Greed*, display the evil of despicable criminals who will lie, cheat, and steal to hurt people financially in order to feed their own selfish desires. In fact, insider trading, fraud, and sociopathic behavior have become such a concern that colleges and universities are adding ethics courses to their business programs.

Like investing, life in some ways is also counterintuitive. Harvey Strosberg discovered that forgiveness is better than revenge, and that greater fulfillment and happiness is attained when one treats fellow human beings with respect as opposed to mowing over whomever or whatever is in our way. Success, fame, power, or wealth, on their own, can leave one feeling empty inside. It is as though we each have an internal vacuum that only God can fill.

The authors have found that treating our fellow human beings the way we like to be treated, forgiving others, and using some of our resources to help those who are less fortunate are very satisfying and rewarding pursuits. We have made a commitment to serve others. If we give 10% of our income and time to those in need, it seems as though God can do more with the 90% that is left. Donating a portion of our income can help us not to become obsessed with accumulating more possessions and amassing more wealth.

If more people in their twenties and thirties could comprehend what actually produces true happiness when they begin their careers, there might be a little less greed and a little more integrity displayed throughout the financial institutions around the world. Integrity not only benefits us and society as a whole—in the long run, it is also good for business. The only problem is that we seem to focus more and more on the short term. This distracts us from contemplating the fact that, in the long term, we cannot take anything with us when our time on this earth is over.

Money is a very important part of our life. We need to provide for our physical needs, but it is also important to meet our emotional and spiritual needs through a healthy relationship with people and a right relationship with God. It is our hope that the information we have been able to pass on to you in this book will enable you to have peace of mind, a balance in your life, and an awareness of what really matters.

Conclusion

In the summer of 2012, I accompanied my daughter and infant grand-daughter to Whistler to watch my son-in-law complete the Tough Mudder Challenge. The Tough Mudder event is a 10-to-12 mile (or 15-kilometer) obstacle course designed by British Special Forces. See pictures of two of the obstacles in Figures 30.1 and 30.2.

Figure 30.1: In this obstacle called the Funky Monkey, participants try to go from rung to rung with their hands. Some of the rungs have grease on them so even

the best athletes can end up in the cold muddy water. As long as you attempt the obstacle, you can proceed. This event is meant to be fun. Photo by Dave Harder

Figure 30.2: This obstacle is called Trench Warfare. Participants have to crawl through a tunnel of dirty snow. Photo by Dave Harder

When I talked to participants after the event, most of them said they did not expect to be so exhausted. They did a lot of strength training for the obstacles, the most exciting part of the event. However, most neglected to train for the less glamorous 10-mile or 15-kilometer run or walk over hilly terrain.

As investors, traders, or business people, we also can get caught up in following the factors which attract the most attention and lose sight of what is really important.

As mentioned earlier, without our human nature and emotions we would be robots. The same characteristics, qualities, and emotions that help us in so many ways work against us when it comes to dealing with investments and markets. Markets function in a way that is totally different than most other things we deal with in life. Booms, bubbles, panics, and busts are part of history—that is a fact no one can ignore. In economics and markets, human nature manifests itself in similar patterns, but not in precisely the same way. Experienced investors and market experts have tried to devise methods and systems to forecast how prices for various assets will perform in the future. History shows that all of these forecasting tools and systems either have serious shortcomings or fail to function adequately when market prices experience extreme volatility. If sophisticated investment strategies were airplanes, no one would fly in them because they would be so prone to crashing.

History also shows us that even the brightest, most successful, and most experienced money managers can end up in disastrous situations with the funds investors have entrusted to them.

When I began my career, I believed central bank officials, analysts, and economists were so wise and knowledgeable that they could foresee how the economy and markets would react in the future. After three decades of experience and numerous studies, I now know that not even the most talented or most connected experts in the world can predict the future. All they can reasonably do is make projections based on the premise that current trends will continue. After that, they make adjustments as the facts change. Since there is so much human sentiment affecting market prices, analyzing markets is more like forecasting election results.

No one makes the right investment decisions all the time. Consequently, even the most astute investors have made purchases or short sales that do not work out. Sometimes investors can make the right investment decision, but the timing turns out to be wrong. On other occasions, investors can come to the right conclusion, be right on the timing, but have their strategies disrupted by an outlying or surprise event. When investment decisions go wrong, emotions such as pride, denial, overconfidence, fear, and desperation can result in severe losses and trauma.

In the opinion of the authors, individual and professional money managers should use momentum-based tools such as moving crossovers as one of the major factors in the decision-making process. These tools are not new or complicated, so they always function as they are supposed to. What makes them so reliable is that they do not provide forecasts or projections for the future—they only show an investor what the trend is at the current time.

Since human nature is not entirely predictable, and these indicators are not designed to predict the future, they are free to adapt to how markets respond at any time, in any circumstance. They can also adapt to structural changes in markets such as the growth of High Frequency Trading as well as the development of other financially engineered products. This is why moving average crossovers worked well even during the Financial Crisis when most other systems were rendered useless.

They also provide a clear signal when a trend changes. This is significant, for the most important rule of investing is to follow the trend and change one's strategy as the trend changes. It is easier to follow a discipline that is clear and unequivocal, than one that is subject to varying opinions. It still requires patience and discipline to use moving average crossovers, but they do help investors take emotions out of the decision-making process. Taking these emotions out of the decision-making process is still a challenge, regardless of how good market indicators are. At market highs and lows, the news and expert opinion are usually one-sided in assuring investors that the trend which has been in place will continue for some time, well after it has reversed. It takes a strong constitution for even the most seasoned investors to act in a way that is contrary to the expert consensus.

The magnitude of change in oil prices is also a simple, very reliable indicator. History has verified that an increase in oil prices of 80% or more over a 12-month period is a good warning signal that a market decline of 20% or more is likely within 18 months. An inverted U.S. yield curve is also a very simple reliable warning that an economic recession and a bear market in equities could happen at any time. Double bottoms at the end of bear markets are very common, even though they are always slightly different. Following a strategy of using these indicators, together with simple 200-day moving averages or moving average crossovers, can enable investors to avoid a good portion of the losses and most of the anxiety associated with severe bear markets that long-term investors will invariably encounter.

Even though human beings are very intelligent, we still need to create visual reminders for ourselves when the risk has increased or decreased to ensure that we do not get distracted by other things as time passes.

History also shows that various markets and economies have distinct long-term cycles that last 16 to 18 years. Real assets, such as commodities, resources and precious metals, are usually strong while financial assets like stocks are weak. Then, after 16 to 18 years, the trends reverse. According to these cycles, we are now 14 years or so into the consolidation phase where real assets are in a strong uptrend and financial assets are in a consolidation phase. Assets tend to have the best performance in the final years of these long-term cycles. This implies that commodities, resources, and precious metals could perform very well for a few more years before they enter another long-term consolidation phase. If this is going to happen, the long-term moving average crossovers have to turn positive for these sectors. If that does not occur, perhaps commodities and real assets peaked in 2011.

Even though financial assets are in a consolidation phase, previous cycles have demonstrated that stocks usually perform very well in the final few years of this phase as well. The record of cycles suggests that there could be one more serious decline and recession that should begin around 2015 before the next 16-year to 18-year cycle begins. That cycle should result once again in high returns for financial assets like stocks. This should also be the time when strong political leaders will emerge in the U.S. and Europe. These leaders will likely get their financial house in order and enable these economies to embark on a prudent path to prosperity again. This is when the buy, hold, and prosper strategy will replace the buy, hold, and suffer strategy. On the other hand, some believe that a new long-term growth phase already started in 2012. They may be correct. However, it is more important to follow the trend than to try to predict how cycles will manifest themselves. Long-term cycles have many implications, so investors must be aware of their pervasive influence.

Pride and overconfidence are easy to spot when there is a plan to build the world's tallest building or accomplish something that has never been done before. These types of developments can be good warning signs. They can also help investors not to get too carried away with a long-term trend. These plans can alert investors to potential trouble spots for investments around the world.

There are few indicators that are as simple, as relevant, and as reliable as 2-1 Advance/Decline buy signals. The only problem with this indicator is that the signals are rare. Even so, it is a very simple indicator to calculate and use. This can be one of the best tools to use for investing heavily just after a severe bear market, near the beginning of a new powerful uptrend such as in 1975, 1982, 1987, and 2009.

When we invest, we seem to follow what we have been instructed to believe, rather than analyzing what we are doing to see if it is really practical. There are long periods of time when buying and holding makes sense. However, there can also be a decade or more where little or no progress is made. Investment strategies must change with the investment climate, not just one's age or financial status. There is a disciplined way to do this by using just a few of the most relevant indicators along with a stop-loss mechanism in case there is an unexpected event. It is easy to use stop-losses. The hard part is knowing when and having the courage to buy back after one has been stopped out. Moving average crossovers together with double bottoms are very useful for helping us to deal with our emotions and providing good re-entry points.

While most of the attention in North America is devoted to the S&P 500, DJIA, NASDAQ, and S&P/TSX, mid-sized and smaller companies are often ignored. They should not be. History shows mid-sized companies have significantly outperformed larger companies over the longer term without increasing volatility. By using a disciplined investment strategy together with a portfolio of mid-sized companies that is well diversified, individual and institutional investors have the potential to produce attractive returns that significantly outperform a buy-and-hold approach as well as major benchmarks. Just as important, a disciplined strategy, based on the best indicators, can help to minimize losses and enable investors to be more comfortable, since they have a strategy to navigate markets as global economies evolve.

Figure 30.3: Calm waters are serene—similar to low volatility markets trending higher. This book offers strategies that make it possible to portage the whitewater and waterfalls that damage portfolios. Photo taken in Moose Factory, Ontario, by Marianne Harder

Investors are able to make more rational decisions when losses are limited. By focusing on the information in this book, we believe investors, traders, and business owners can be much more efficient with their time and energy so they can focus more on what is really important in life, without sacrificing long-term returns.

Finally, life is about more than making money. Most of us know that, but with human nature being what it is, it can be hard to live our lives in a way that reflects long-term priorities when it seems as though there are more urgent short-term issues to deal with. As children leave the home and we see more acquaintances deal with illness or death, we have a clearer view of what is really important in this short life.

It is our sincere desire that the information within these pages will help you to be successful in all of your endeavors and that you will be fulfilled and at peace with the way you have lived your life. May God bless you!

Dave Harder and Dr. Janice Dorn

THE END

Works Cited

"2010 Survey Results." Gross National Happiness. The Centre for Bhutan Studies and GNH Research, 2010. <http://www.grossnationalhap piness.com/survey-results/index/>.

Argo. Dir. Ben Affleck. Warner Bros. Entertainment, 2013.

Banff Mountain Film Festival Magazine. 2012-2013 World Tour, Cottage Life Media. <http://www.banffcentre.ca/mountainfestival/worldtour>.

Barber, Brad M., et al. "Just How Much Do Individual Investors Lose By Trading?" *Review of Financial Studies* 22.2 (2009): 609-632. <http:// dx.doi.org/10.2139/ssrn.529062>.

Barber, Brad M., and Terrance Odean. "The Behavior of Individual Investors." *Handbook of Economics of Finance* 2.B (2013): 1533-1570. <http://dx.doi.org/10.2139/ssrn.1872211>.

Barber, Brad M., and Terrance Odean. "Trading Is Hazardous to Your Wealth: The Common Stock Investment Performance of Individual Investors." *Journal of Finance* 55.2 (Apr. 2000): 773-806. <http:// onlinelibrary.wiley.com/doi/10.1111/0022-1082.00226/abstract>.

Batra, Ravi. *The Great Depression of 1990: Why It's Got to Happen—How to Protect Yourself.* New York: Simon & Schuster, 1987.

Beebe, William. *Edge of the Jungle.* New York: Henry Holt, 1921.

Bharucha, Jamshed. "What Will Change Everything? The Synchronization of Brains." *Edge*. Edge.org, 2009. <http://edge.org/response-detail/11802>.

Bhattacharya , Utpal, et al. "The Dark Side of ETFs." *Social Science Research Network*. Social Science Electronic Publishing, 19 Dec. 2013. <http://dx.doi.org/10.2139/ssrn.2022442>.

Blodget, Henry. "The Complete Guide to Wall Street Self-Defense." *Slate*. Slate, 19 Oct. 2004. <http://www.slate.com/articles/arts/wall_street_selfdefense/2004/08/the_complete_guide_to_wall_street_selfdefense.html>.

Brightman, Chris. "The Trouble with Quants." *Fundamentals*. Research Affiliates, Aug. 2011. <https://www.researchaffiliates.com/Our%20Ideas/Insights/Fundamentals/Pages/F_2011_Aug_Trouble_with_Quants.aspx>. Bulkowski, Thomas N. Encyclopedia of Chart Patterns. Hoboken: John Wiley & Sons, 2005.

Cain, Susan. *Quiet: The Power of Introverts in a World That Can't Stop Talking*. New York: Crown, 2012.

"Canoes and Airplanes." *Callout: Search and Rescue*. Season 2, Episode 5. <http://www.khsar.com/>.

Carmichael, Kevin. "IMF Sees an Even Deeper Recession." *The Globe and Mail*. Globe and Mail, 18 Mar. 2009. <http://www.theglobeandmail.com/report-on-business/imf-sees-an-even-deeper-recession/article1150169>.

Carter, Jimmy. *White House Diary*. New York: Farrar, Straus and Giroux, 2010.

Cassidy, John. *How Markets Fail: The Logic of Economic Calamities*. New York: Farrar, Straus and Giroux, 2008.

Castrission, James. *Crossing the Ditch. Sydney*: Harper Collins, 2009. <http://casandjonesy.com.au/shop/crossing-the-ditch-documentary>.

Catalano, Vinny. "Bottoms No Place for Fundamentals Alone." *Minyanville*. Minyanville Media, 13 Nov. 2008. <http://www.minyanville.com/businessmarkets/articles/gm-Investment-democrats-general-motors-strategy/11/13/2008/id/19964>.

Cherniawski, Anthony, and Janice Dorn. "Where Does Hot Money Go Next?" *Minyanville*. Minyanville Media, 4 Sep. 2012. <http://www.minyanville.com/sectors/emerging-markets/articles/china-economy-chinese-economy-Shanghai-Stock/9/4/2012/id/43709>.

Conway, Brendan, and Tomi Kilgore. "Crossing a Golden Barrier." *The Wall Street Journal*. Dow Jones, 11 Feb. 2012. <http://online.wsj.com/news/articles/SB10001424052970204642604577213282197344736>.

Demott, John S. "Happy Birthday, Bull Market." *Time*, 22 Aug. 1983. Archived online <http://content.time.com/time/magazine/article/0,9171,926103,00.html>.

Dorn, Janice. *Personal Responsibility: The Power of You*. Tempe: Pat Gorman Talks, 2007.

Dorn, Janice. "So You Think You Can Trade?" *CNBC*. CNBC, 26 Dec. 2008. <http://www.cnbc.com/id/28390714>.

Dorn, Janice. "This Is Your Brain On Trading." *Stocks, Futures and Options*, July 2007. Available online <http://sharpbrains.com/blog/2008/06/05/your-brain-on-trading-101/>.

Dunbar, Nicholas. *Inventing Money: The Story of Long-Term Capital Management and the Legends Behind It*. Chichester: John Wiley & Sons, 2000.

Durden, Tyler. "Hugh Hendry Is Back—Full Eclectica Letter." *Zerohedge.* ZeroHedge.com/ABC Media, LTD, 29 Apr. 2012. <http://www. zerohedge.com/news/hugh-hendry-back-full-eclectica-letter>.

Edwards, Robert D., John Magee, and W.H.C. Bassetti. *Technical Analysis of Stock Trends.* 10th ed. Boca Raton: CRC, 2012.

Estrella, Arturo, and Frederic S. Mishkin. "The Yield Curve as a Predictor of U.S. Recessions." *Current Issues in Economics and Finance* 2.7 (June 1996): n. pag. Available online <http://newyorkfed.org/research/ current_issues/ci2-7.pdf >.

Etzel, Barbara J. *Webster's New World Finance and Investment Dictionary.* Hoboken: Wiley, 2003.

Faith, Curtis M. *Way of the Turtle: The Secret Methods that Turned Ordinary People into Legendary Traders.* New York: McGraw-Hill, 2007.

Farley, Alan S. *The Master Swing Trader: Tools and Techniques to Profit from Outstanding Short-Term Trading Opportunities.* New York: McGraw-Hill, 2001.

Feynman, Richard P. T*he Pleasure of Finding Things Out: The Best Short Works of Richard P. Feynman.* Ed. Jeffrey Robbins. Cambridge: Perseus, 1999.

Fox, Justin. *The Myth of the Rational Market: A History of Risk, Reward, and Delusion on Wall Street.* New York: Harper Collins, 2010.

Galbraith, John Kenneth. *The Great Crash 1929.* New York: Houghton Mifflin Harcourt, 1997.

Gardner, Dan. Future Babble: *Why Expert Predictions Fail—And Why We Believe Them Anyway.* Toronto: McClelland & Stewart, 2010.

Genstein, Edgar S. *Stock Market Profit without Forecasting: A Research Report on Investment by Formula.* Larchmont: American Research Council, 1956.

Gonzales, Laurence. *Deep Survival: Who Lives, Who Dies, and Why*. New York: W. W. Norton, 2004.

Graham, Benjamin. *The Intelligent Investor: A Book of Practical Counsel*. Intro. and App. Warren E. Buffet. New York: Harper Collins, 1986.

Grantham, Jeremy. "Part 2: Time to Be Serious (and Probably Too Early) Once Again." *GMO Quarterly Letter* (May 2011): 1-5. Available online <http://www.realclearmarkets.com/blog/JGLetterPart2_1Q11.pdf >.

Gray, Jeff. "A Debilitating Stroke, a Remarkable Recovery." *The Globe and Mail*. Globe and Mail, 3 Jan. 2012. <http://www.theglobeandmail.com/report-on-business/industry-news/the-law-page/a-debilitating-stroke-a-remarkable-recovery/article4085883>.

Greenspan, Alan. *The Age of Turbulence: Adventures in a New World*. New York: Penguin Press, 2007.

Greenwald, John. "Wall Street Merry-Go-Round." *Time,* 16 Aug. 1982. Archived online <http://content.time.com/time/magazine/article/0,9171,950744,00.html>.

Hallam, Andrew. "Outsmarting the Market: Don't Be a Sucker." *The Globe and Mail*. Globe and Mail, 2 Dec. 2012. <http://www.theglobeandmail.com/globe-investor/investment-ideas/strategy-lab/index-investing/outsmarting-the-market-dont-be-a-sucker/article5899962>.

Harper, Christine, and Zachary Mider. "Goldman Loses at Least 37 Partners in Weakest Year Since 2008." *Blooomberg*. Bloomberg, 14 Dec. 2011. <http://www.bloomberg.com/news/2011-12-14/goldman-loses-at-least-37-partners-in-weakest-year-since-2008.html>.

Helman, Christopher. "Inside the Semgroup Bust." *Forbes*. Forbes.com, 28 July 2008. <http://www.forbes.com/2008/07/28/semgroup-oil-kivisto-biz-energy-cz_ch_0728semgroup.html>.

Herbst-Bayliss, Svea. "After Huge Hedge Fund Failure, Amaranth Trader Woos Investors for New Fund." *USA Today*. Reuters, USA Today, 23 Mar. 2007. <http://usatoday30.usatoday.com/money/markets/2007-03-23-amaranth_N.htm?csp=34>.

Hill, Kashmir. "Beware, Tech Abandoners. People Without Facebook Accounts Are 'Suspicious.'" *Forbes*. Forbes.com, 6 Aug. 2012. <http://www.forbes.com/sites/kashmirhill/2012/08/06/beware-tech-abandoners-people-without-facebook-accounts-are-suspicious>.

Hirsch, Yale, and Jeffrey A. Hirsch. *Stock Trader's Almanac* 2005. Hoboken: John Wiley & Sons, 2004.

Hock, Dee. *Birth of the Chaordic Age*. San Francisco: Berrett-Koehler, 2000.

Hulbert, Mark. "The Dark Side of ETFs." *Barron's*. Dow Jones, 11 Apr. 2013. <http://online.barrons.com/news/articles/SB50001424052748704567604578416593357026504>.

Huprich, P. Art. "Market Truisms and Axioms." *Day Hagen Asset Management*. <http://dayhagan.com>.

"In Plato's Cave." *The Economist*. Economist Newspaper, 22 Jan. 2009. <http://www.economist.com/node/12957753>.

Jakab, Spencer. "Fed's Crystal Ball Could Use Some Shining." *The Wall Street Journal*. Dow Jones, 18 Mar. 2013. <http://online.wsj.com/news/articles/SB10001424127887323639604578368612422280712>.

Kahneman, Daniel. "The Thought Leader Interview." *Strategy+Business* 33 (Winter 2003): 1-6. Online version <http://www.strategy-business.com/article/03409?pg=all>.

Kaufman, Henry. "How the Credit Crisis Will Change the Way America Does Business." *The Wall Street Journal. Dow* Jones, 6 Dec. 2008. <http://online.wsj.com/news/articles/SB122852289752684407>.

Keynes, John Maynard. *The Collected Writings of John Maynard Keynes.* Cambridge: Cambridge U P, 2012. Online index <http://www.cambridge.org/aus/series/sSeries.asp?code=CJMK>.

Kintz, Jarod. *This Book Is Not for Sale.* Kindle ed. n.p., 2011.

Kliesen, Kevin L., and Daniel L. Thornton. "How Good Are the Government's Deficit and Debt Projections and Should We Care?" *Federal Reserve Bank of St. Louis Review* 94.1 (Jan/Feb 2012): 21-39. Available online <http://research.stlouisfed.org/publications/review/article/9081>.

Lao-tzu. *The Tao Te Ching of Lao Tzu.* Trans. Brian Browne Walker. New York: St. Martin's Griffin, 1995.

Lao-tzu. *Te-tao Ching.* A New Translation Based on the Recently Discovered Ma-wang-tui Texts (Classics of Ancient China). Trans. Robert C. Hendricks. New York: Random House, 1992.

Leeb, Stephen, and Donna Leeb. *The Oil Factor: Protect Yourself—and Profit—from the Coming Energy Crisis.* New York: Warner Business Books, 2005.

Lefèvre, Edwin. *Reminiscences of a Stock Operator.* New York: John Wiley & Sons, 1994.

Lewis, Michael. *Liar's Poker: Rising Through the Wreckage on Wall Street.* New York: Norton, 1989.

Lo, Andrew W. "The Adaptive Markets Hypothesis: Market Efficiency from an Evolutionary Standpoint." *Journal of Portfolio Management,* 30th Anniversary Issue (2004): 15-29. Available online <http://web.mit.edu/alo/www/Papers/JPM2004_Pub.pdf>.

Lo, Andrew, and A. Craig MacKinlay. *A Non-Random Walk Down Wall Street*. Princeton: Princeton U P, 1999.

Loeb, Gerald M. *The Battle for Investment Survival*. New York: Simon & Schuster, 1957.

Lynch, Peter, with John Rothchild. *One Up on Wall Street: How to Use What You Already Know to Make Money in the Market*. New York: Simon & Schuster, 2000.

Mackay, Charles. *Memoirs of Extraordinary Popular Delusions and the Madness of Crowds*. London: Office of the National Illustrated Library, 1852.

Maierhofer, Simon. "S&P Triggers 200-day MA Death Cross—What Does This Mean?" *ETFguide*. ETFguide, 12 Aug. 2011. <http://archive. etfguide.com/research/618/8/S-P-Triggers-200-day-MA-Death-Cross-What-Does-this-Mean?/>.

Marks, Howard. *The Most Important Thing: Uncommon Sense for the Thoughtful Investor*. New York: Columbia U P, 2011.

Matlack, Carol. "Soci?t? G?n?rale's Fraud: What Now?" *Bloomberg Businessweek*. Bloomberg, 24 Jan. 2008. <http://www.businessweek. com/stories/2008-01-24/soci-t-g-n-rales-fraud-what-now-business week-business-news-stock-market-and-financial-advice>.

Mauboussin, Michael J. *More Than You Know: Finding Financial Wisdom in Unconventional Places*. Updated and Expanded. New York: Columbia U P, 2007.

Mauboussin, Michael J. *Think Twice: Harnessing the Power of Counterintuition*. Boston: Harvard Business Press, 2009.

Mauldin, John. "The Yield Curve." *321gold*. 321gold, 31 Dec. 2005. <http:// www.321gold.com/editorials/mauldin/mauldin123105.html>.

Milner, Brian. "Sun Finally Sets on Notion That Markets Are Rational." *The Globe and Mail*. Globe and Mail, 3 July 2009. <http://www.theglobeandmail.com/globe-investor/investment-ideas/sun-finally-sets-on-notion-that-markets-are-rational/article4301916>.

Montier, James. *Behavioural Investing: A Practitioner's Guide to Applying Behavioural Finance*. Chichester: John Wiley & Sons, 2007.

Morgenson, G. "Behind Insurer's Crisis, Blind Eye to a Web of Risk." *The New York Times*. New York Times, 28 Sep. 2008. <http://www.nytimes.com/2008/09/28/business/28melt.html?pagewanted=all&_r=0>.

Munger, Charles. "On the Psychology of Human Misjudgment." Harvard University, Cambridge MA. Circa June 1995. Speech. Transcription online <http://buffettmungerwisdom.files.wordpress.com/2013/01/mungerspeech_june_95.pdf>.

Murphy, Austin. "An Analysis of the Financial Crisis of 2008: Causes and Solutions." *Oakland Journal* 17 (Fall 2009): 61-82. <http://dx.doi.org/10.2139/ssrn.1295344>.

Murphy, John J. *Technical Analysis of the Futures Markets: A Comprehensive Guide to Trading Methods and Applications*. New York: New York Institute of Finance, 1999.

Neill, Humphrey B. *The Art of Contrary Thinking*. Caldwell: Caxton, 1954.

Nocera, Joseph. "The Heresy That Made Them Rich." *The New York Times*. New York Times, 29 Oct. 2005. <http://query.nytimes.com/gst/fullpage.html?res=9B00E1D71E3FF93AA15753C1A9639C8B63>.

Odean, Terrance. "Do Investors Trade Too Much?" *American Economic Review* 89.5 (1999): 1279-1298. <http://www.aeaweb.org/articles.php?doi=10.1257/aer.89.5.1279>.

Orrell, David. *Economyths: Ten Ways Economics Gets It Wrong*. Mississauga: John Wiley & Sons Canada, 2010.

Orrell, David. *The Future of Everything: The Science of Prediction*. New York: Thunder's Mouth, 2007.

O'Shaughnessy, James P. *What Works On Wall Street: A Guide to the Best-Performing Investment Strategies of All Time*. 3rd ed. New York: McGraw-Hill, 2005.

Peterson, Richard L. Inside the *Investor's Brain: The Power of Mind over Money*. Hoboken: John Wiley & Sons, 2007.

"Quantitative Analysis of Investor Behavior, 2009." *DALBAR, Inc.* Available online <http://www.grandwealth.com/files/DALBAR%20 QAIB%202009.pdf>.

"Quantitative Analysis of Investor Behavior, 2013." *DALBAR, Inc.* Available online <http://www.grandwealth.com/files/DALBAR%20QAIB% 202013.pdf.>.

Rajan, Uday, Amit Seru, and Vikrant Vig. "The Failure of Models that Predict Failure: Distance, Incentives and Defaults." *Social Science Research* Network. Social Science Electronic Publishing, 1 Aug. 2010. <http://papers.ssrn.com/sol3/papers. cfm?abstract_id=1296982>.

Schneirla, T. C. "A Unique Case of Circular Milling in Ants Considered in Relation to Trail Following and the General Problem of Orientation." *American Museum Novitates* 1253 (8 Apr. 1944): 1-26. Archived online <http://digitallibrary.amnh.org/dspace/ bitstream/handle/2246/3733//v2/dspace/ingest/pdfSource/nov/ N1253.pdf?sequence=1>.

Schultz, Harry D. *Panics & Crashes and How You Can Make Money Out of Them*. New Rochelle: Arlington House, 1980.

Schulze, Katrin. "Machen sich Facebook-Verweigerer Verdächtig?" *Der Tagesspiegel*. Der Tagesspiegel, 24 July 2012. <http://www.tagesspie gel.de/weltspiegel/nach-dem-attentat-von-denver-machen-sich-facebook-verweigerer-verdaechtig/6911648.html>.

Schwager, Jack D. *Stock Market Wizards: Interviews with America's Top Stock Traders.* New York: Harper Collins, 2003.

Sheimo, Michael D. *Stock Market Rules: 50 of the Most Widely Held Investment Axioms Explained, Examined, and Exposed.* New York: McGraw-Hill, 2012.

Six Days Seven Nights. Dir. Ivan Reitman. Touchstone, 1998.

Skousen, Mark. *The Maxims of Wall Street: A Compendium of Financial Adages, Ancient Proverbs, and Worldly Wisdom.* Skousen, 2011.

Smusiak, Cara. "Extreme Breath-Holding: How It's Possible." *Discovery.* Discovery Communications, 17 Feb. 2010. <http://news.discovery.com/human/evolution/breath-holding-human.htm>.

Statman, Meir. *What Investors Really Want: Discover What Drives Investor Behavior and Make Smarter Financial Decisions.* New York: McGraw-Hill, 2011.

Surowiecki, James. *The Wisdom of Crowds.* New York: Anchor Books, 2005.

Swedroe, Larry E. "The Behavior of Individual Investors: To Err Is Human." *CBS Moneywatch.* CBS Interactive, 5 Oct. 2011. <http://www.cbsnews.com/news/the-behavior-of-individual-investors-to-err-is-human/>.

Swedroe, Larry E. *The Only Guide to a Winning Investment Strategy You'll Ever Need: Index Funds and Beyond—The Way Smart Money Invests Today.* New York: St. Martin's, 2005.

Swedroe, Larry E. *The Successful Investor Today: 14 Simple Truths You Must Know When You Invest.* New York: St. Martin's Griffin, 2006.

Taleb, Nassim. *The Black Swan: The Impact of the Highly Improbable*. New York: Random House, 2010.

The Wolf of Wall Street. Dir. Martin Scorsese. Paramount, 2013.

Tversky, Amos, and Daniel Kahneman. "Belief in the Law of Small Numbers." *Psychological Bulletin* 76.2 (Aug. 1971): 105-110. Available online <http://psycnet.apa.org/index.cfm?fa=buy.optionToBuy&id=1972-01934-001>.

Tversky, Amos, and Daniel Kahneman. "Judgment under Uncertainty: Heuristics and Biases." *Science* 185.4157 (27 Sep. 1974): 1124-1131. Available online <http://www.sciencemag.org/content/185/4157/1124>.

Umiastowski, Chris. "The Five Biggest Mistakes of Growth Investors." *The Globe and Mail*. Globe and Mail, 12 Mar. 2013. <http://www.theglobeandmail.com/globe-investor/investment-ideas/strategy-lab/growth-investing/the-five-biggest-mistakes-of-growth-investors/article9696394>.

Wall Street. Dir. Oliver Stone. 20th Century Fox, 1987.

Warde, Ibrahim. "LTCM, a Hedge Fund above Suspicion." *Le Monde diplomatique*, English Ed. Le Monde diplomatique, Nov. 1998. <http://mondediplo.com/1998/11/05warde2>.

Warren, George F., and Frank A. Pearson. *Prices*. New York: John Wiley & Sons, 1933.

Wessel, David. *In FED We Trust: Ben Bernanke's War on the Great Panic*. New York: Crown, 2009.

Wood, Alan. *Bertrand Russell: The Passionate Sceptic*. New York: Simon & Schuster, 1958.

Wood, Cynthia. "The Dutch Tulip Bubble of 1637." *Damninteresting.* Damninteresting.com, 16 Mar. 2006. <http://www.damninteresting. com/the-dutch-tulip-bubble-of-1637>.

Zweig, Jason. "This Is Your Brain on a Hot Streak." *The Wall Street Journal.* Dow Jones, 11 Feb. 2012. <http://online.wsj.com/news/articles/ SB10001424052970204642604577215133261921346>.

Zweig, Martin E. *Martin Zweig's Winning on Wall Street.* New York: Warner Books, 1994.

Zyblock, Myles. "Momentum: Style's Third Domain or a Replacement for Growth." RBC Equity *Strategy Weekly* 11 (May 2011): 1-11. Available online <http://dorseywrightmm.com/downloads/ hrs_research/RBC%20Momentum.pdf>.

General References and Credits

http://online.barrons.com/home-page
http://www.berkshirehathaway.com/
http://www.bestmindsinc.com/
http://www.bloomberg.com/
http://www.bravotv.com/
http://www.canaaninthedesert.com/
http://www.cnbc.com/
http://www.cornerstonemacro.com/
http://coxeadvisors.net/
http://coxeadvisors.net/category/market-commentary/
http://www.dailyspeculations.com/wordpress/
http://ww1.dowtheoryletters.com/
http://www.economist.com/
http://www.elliottwave.com/
http://www.financialsense.com/
http://finviz.com/
http://www.forbes.com/
http://www.foxbusiness.com/index.html
http://www.theglobeandmail.com/
http://www.hardrightedge.com/
http://www.investopedia.com/

http://investorplace.com/ (Credit for photo of
Dr. Janice Dorn to InvestorPlaceMedia)
http://www.investorsintelligence.com/x/default.html
http://www.investtech.com/main/index.php?layout=x
http://kirkreport.com/
http://www.leggmason.com/
http://www.manyblessings.net/jimsbiog.html
https://www.marketpsych.com/
http://www.minyanville.com/
http://www.newnownext.com/
http://odb.org/
http://thepatternsite.com/
http://www.thepracticalinvestor.com/
http://www.quotationspage.com/
http://www.ritholtz.com/blog/
http://www.socionomics.net/
http://en.thinkexist.com/
http://traderdannorcini.blogspot.com/
http://traderfeed.blogspot.com/
https://www.wikipedia.org/
http://online.wsj.com/home-page
http://www.zerohedge.com/

Index

About the Authors

Dave Harder

Dave Harder, FCSI, is Vice President and Portfolio Manager with Canada's largest financial firm, which is also one of the most respected financial corporations in the world. He has written more than 300 reports about momentum indicators and active asset allocation. Dave is a marathon runner, Ironman triathlete, and a professionally trained Search and Rescue volunteer.

Janice Dorn

Janice Dorn, M.D., Ph.D., received a Ph.D. in Anatomy (Neuroanatomy) from the Albert Einstein College of Medicine in New York. She is also an M.D. Psychiatrist certified by the American Board of Psychiatry and Neurology and the American Board of Addiction Medicine. She has written over 1,000 articles on trading psychology and behavioral finance. Dr. Dorn is dedicated to providing education and training about how the brain, psychology, and emotions impact financial decision-making. Janice is an advocate for the elderly, a lifelong dancer, and a pianist.

About Mind, Money & Markets

By Dave Harder and Janice Dorn, M.D., Ph.D.

After losing much of his money when the South Sea Bubble burst in 1720, English physicist and mathematician Isaac Newton stated, "I can calculate the motion of heavenly bodies, but not the madness of people." Even though Isaac Newton was a brilliant man, he did not realize that markets function in a way that is opposite to almost everything else we do. For example, if people are lining up around the block to purchase an iPad, it is a sign that it is a good product. If people are lining up around the block to buy a condominium, it is a bad sign for real estate. Markets do not always act in a rational or logical manner. *Mind, Money & Markets* explains why they act the way they do. It is critical for every person to understand this in order to make wise decisions ranging from buying a home to operating a business.

Expert advice is much less reliable than we expect it to be because no one can accurately predict the future on a consistent basis. Gigantic losses like the $6.2 billion trading loss at JP Morgan in 2012 show that investors are not giving momentum (following the trend) the respect it deserves. *Mind, Money & Markets* offers a momentum filter—specifically, a screening tool from which every individual and professional investor should benefit. The book also provides a "circuit breaker" that enables investors to limit losses in case of an unexpected event in financial markets. Using powerful and poignant analogies from their life experiences, including Dave Harder's twelve years as a Search and Rescue volunteer, we provide readers with a simple discipline to preserve precious hard-earned capital during severe downturns and to outperform benchmarks when markets are in an uptrend.

It is easier to know what to do than to actually do it. Psychiatrist Dr. Janice Dorn specializes in helping traders and investors deal with emotions and aspects of human nature that hinder them from making astute investment decisions for stocks, bonds, real estate, currencies, or commodities. We have passed on many words of wisdom collected from market sages and great thinkers. We also highlight some major misconceptions about investing, and show the reader how to overcome them and prosper.

With a compelling mixture of fascinating stories and more than 100 colored charts and photographs, this is truly a unique work about how human beings react to markets. The book helps individual as well as professional investors to be efficient with their time and energy by teaching them to focus only on a few factors which have the most significant impact on financial markets. The personalized strategies provided in these pages will enable readers to maximize gains, minimize losses, and have more time to spend on things that matter the most in their lives.